The Bathroom
Trivia Almanac

Contributors

Compiled by: Russ "The Flush" Edwards

"Head" Editor: Ellen Fischbein

Significant Others: Angela Demers
Jack Kreismer
Geoff Scowcroft
"Go with the Flo" Ventrice

RED-LETTER PRESS, INC.
SADDLE RIVER, NEW JERSEY

Introduction

In these tumultuous times, the bathroom has become a safe haven for peace – one good reason why restroom reading is on a roll.

Proof of this privial pursuit comes from the findings of "The Toilet Paper Report"* (subtitled "What's Happening in Today's Bathroom") which reveals that reading is the third most time-consuming activity behind that closed door, trailing only bathing and showering.

Further, the Scott Paper Company, makers of the toilet tissue, reports that bathroom reading is linked with the higher seats of learning. They conducted a recent survey which concluded that more than two-thirds of people holding master's degrees and doctorates read in the bathroom.

And so it is that we at Red-Letter Press continue to add to the loo's literary cause with our latest "Bathroom Library" book, "The Bathroom Trivia Almanac". The page per day format of quips, quizzes, facts and other fancies makes it ideal for the regular reader— the quintessential almanac for the Quincy!**

Yours flushingly,

Jack Kreismer
Publisher

*Yes, there really is such a document. It's published by the manufacturers of Quilted Northern toilet tissue.

**For those not privy to the term, the bathroom became known as the Quincy back in the days when President John Quincy Adams had a bathroom installed in the White House.

J A N U A R Y

TODAY'S THOUGHT:
"This is the year you expected so much from last year." —Ed Howe

OBSERVANCES/EVENTS—
New Year's Day . . . Beginning today are National Prune Breakfast Month, National Oatmeal Month and National Fiber Focus Month. Since you're reading "The Bathroom Trivia Almanac", you're right on top of things!

BIRTHDAYS—
Paul Revere, 1735; Betsy Ross, 1752; J. Edgar Hoover, 1895; Xavier Cugat, 1900; Dana Andrews, 1909; J. D. Salinger, 1919; Frank Langella, 1940; Don Novello (Father Guido Sarducci), 1943

NEW WORD—
manumit - verb: to release from slavery

QUIZ—
What day preceded January 1st as New Year's Day in English speaking countries?

TRIVIA
All race horses celebrate their birthdays on New Year's Day, no matter when they were born. . . . The average American adult logs about 2,920 hours of shut-eye a year. Wonder how much that is in winks? . . . A wink takes $1/10$ of a second.

HISTORY—
On this date in 1863 President Lincoln issued the Emancipation Proclamation, a document freeing all slaves in areas still in rebellion.

GRAFFITI
Don't take life too seriously - you'll never get out of it alive!

Quiz Answer: January 1st has kicked off the New Year in English speaking countries since the adoption of the British Calendar Act of 1751. Prior to that, the New Year began on March 25th.

JANUARY

TODAY'S THOUGHT:
"Never raise your hand to your children — it leaves your midsection unprotected." —Fred Allen

OBSERVANCES/EVENTS—
It's Ancestor's Day in Haiti and time for the Kakizome festival in Japan.

BIRTHDAYS—
Nathaniel Bacon, 1647; Isaac Asimov, 1920; Dabney Coleman, 1932; Roger Miller, 1936; James Orsen (Jim Bakker), 1939

NEW WORD—
prolix - adjective: extended to tedious or unnecessary length, wordy and long

QUIZ—
A certain southpaw pitcher was given a tryout by the Washington Senators in the 1950's. He didn't make the team and he's been having nothing but trouble with Washington ever since. Who is he?

TRIVIA
If you like to engage in many sesquipedalianisms, you like to use big words. . . . In Africa it is estimated that there are over 1,000 languages spoken. . . .The stuffing you find inside bedding or furniture is called kapok. It is a fiber that is extracted from the seeds in the pods of the kapok tree.

HISTORY—
On this date in 1959 Soviet space probe Luna I missed the moon and went into orbit around the sun. All those years we sweated their missiles and these guys missed the MOON!!

GRAFFITI
Possessiveness is a state of MINE.

Quiz Answer: Fidel Castro

J A N U A R Y

TODAY'S THOUGHT:
"Laughter is the shortest distance between two people." —Victor Borge

BIRTHDAYS—
Victor Borge, 1909; Betty Furness, 1916; Maxene Andrews, 1918; Bobby Hull, 1939; Stephen Stills, 1945; Mel Gibson, 1951

NEW WORD—
furcula - noun: a wishbone from a bird — and that's probably all that's left from that holiday turkey about now!

QUIZ—
What long running game show was pivotal in Mel Gibson's life?

TRIVIA
There is only one fish that swims upright — the sea horse. . . . The eyes of some birds weigh more than their brains. . . . Insects give off a sticky substance which is used to make shellac.

HISTORY—
On this date in 1888 the U.S. Patent Office issued a patent for artificial drinking straws.
In 1959 Alaska joined Uncle Sam's family.

GRAFFITI
Organic farming is tilling it like it is.

Quiz Answer: "Jeopardy!" — Mel was born in the States, but when the turbulent sixties came around, his dad wanted to give things a try "Down Under". He went on "Jeopardy!" to win enough money to move the family to Australia.

JANUARY

TODAY'S THOUGHT:
"Hospitals are weird. They put you in a private room and then give you a public gown." —Milton Berle

OBSERVANCES/EVENTS—
Little did you realize that by reading this book you were in keeping with the spirit of the date - it's Trivia Day. A tip of the hat to all of you spermologists out there . . . that's a "trivia expert".

BIRTHDAYS—
Sir Isaac Newton, 1642; Jacob Grimm, 1785; Louis Braille, 1809; Tom Thumb, 1838; William Bendix, 1906; Jane Wyman, 1914; Don Shula, 1930; Floyd Patterson, 1935; Dyan Cannon, 1937

NEW WORD—
springe - noun: a snare used to catch small game

QUIZ—
Bathroom Brain Teaser: Which can see better in total darkness — an owl, a raccoon or a skunk?

TRIVIA
There are 26 states named on the back of a five dollar bill. . . . Missouri and Tennessee both touch on eight other states. . . . Alaska gets the least amount of sunshine of any state; the sun shines only 30% of the time.

HISTORY—
On this date in 1493 Columbus began his journey back to Spain to report his discovery.
In 1896 Utah joined the Union.

GRAFFITI
The world is flat.
—Class of 1491

Quiz Answer: None of them can see in *total* darkness.

JANUARY

TODAY'S THOUGHT:

"If you want to talk to somebody who's not busy, call the Vice President. I get plenty of time to talk to anybody about anything."

—Walter Mondale

BIRTHDAYS—

Stephen Decatur, 1779; Konrad Adenauer, 1876; Jean-Pierre Aumont, 1913; Jeanne Dixon, 1918; Walter "Fritz" Mondale, 1928; Alvin Ailey, 1931; Robert Duval, 1931; Diane Keaton, 1946; Pamela Sue Martin, 1954

NEW WORD—

vellicate - verb: to nip, pinch, pluck or twist

QUIZ—

Benjamin Franklin was a prolific inventor who cooked up the idea for the Franklin stove and had great vision in developing bifocal spectacles. Is it true that he was also the inventor of perforated toilet paper?

TRIVIA

Duke Ellington's hit "Mood Indigo" was originally named "Dreamy Blues". . . . Mozart wrote the nursery rhyme tune "Twinkle, Twinkle, Little Star" at the age of five. . . . Albert Tilzer wrote "Take Me Out to the Ball Game" but he didn't see an actual baseball game for another twenty years.

HISTORY—

On this date in 1893 an Austrian newspaper reported the enormous potential of X-rays.

GRAFFITI
Betty Crocker was a flour child.

Quiz Answer: False — Ol' Ben wasn't even around for the invention of toilet paper which was the creation of one Joseph Gayetty in 1857. As for the perforated variety, an English manufacturer by the name of Walter James Alcock came up with the idea in the 1880's.

JANUARY

TODAY'S THOUGHT:
"Slang is a language that rolls up its sleeves, spits on his hands, and goes back to work." —Carl Sandburg

OBSERVANCES/EVENTS—
Congratulations to George and Martha Washington who were married in 1759 and, believe it or not, they haven't spoken a harsh word to one another in years!

BIRTHDAYS—
Carl Sandburg, 1878; Tom Mix, 1880; Joey Adams, 1911; Danny Thomas, 1912; Loretta Young, 1913; Lou Harris, 1921; Earl Scruggs, 1924; Bonnie Franklin, 1944

NEW WORD—
burgoo - noun: a thick oatmeal eaten by sailors (not to be confused with bird-goo)

QUIZ—
What long running classic sitcom got its start on the Danny Thomas show, "Make Room For Daddy"?

TRIVIA
Saudi Arabia refused to carry the "Muppet Show" on television because one of the stars was a pig. . . . Frank Lloyd Wright, the famous architect, also had a hand in designing one of the biggest movie stars of the fifties. Ann Baxter is his granddaughter. . . . Adam Ant was the first guest VJ on MTV.

HISTORY—
On this date in 1942 the first around-the-world trip by a commercial airliner was completed . . . but the luggage was never found.

GRAFFITI
Misers make lousy relatives but great ancestors.

Quiz Answer: The "Andy Griffith Show" - Andy Taylor, sheriff of Mayberry, was first seen on an episode of "Make Room for Daddy".

J A N U A R Y

TODAY'S THOUGHT:

"An honorable defeat is better than a dishonorable victory."

—Millard Fillmore

OBSERVANCES/EVENTS—

In Japan, the Nanakusa Festival begins, celebrating seven herbs which have great medicinal powers: parsley, chickweed, shepherd's purse, radish, cottonweed, aona and hotoke-no-za.

In Germany the fabulous Munich Fasching Carnival begins, celebrating a plant that they consider has great medicinal powers - hops!

BIRTHDAYS—

Millard Fillmore, 1850; Vincent Gardenia, 1922; William Peter Blatty, 1928; Kenny Loggins, 1948; Erin Gray, 1952

NEW WORD—

eche - verb: to increase or enlarge

QUIZ—

American soldiers have often been referred to as "G.I.'s". What does G.I. stand for?

TRIVIA

Leonardo da Vinci had an odd habit of writing all his notes backwards. . . . President James Garfield was ambidextrous and could write with both hands simultaneously. , . . F. Scott Fitzgerald was a notoriously bad speller.

HISTORY—

Moons and balloons . . .   On this date in 1610 Galileo discovered the four largest moons of Jupiter.

In 1795 the first balloon flight over the English Channel took place.

GRAFFITI

It's not whether you win or lose but how you place the blame.

Quiz Answer: "General Issue", the term stamped on their clothing, equipment and supplies

JANUARY

TODAY'S THOUGHT:
"Be true to your teeth and they won't be false to you." —Soupy Sales

OBSERVANCES/EVENTS—
It's Midwife's or Women's Day in Greece. This is an occasion for women to get out of the house, lounge around in cafes and kick up their heels in general, while men stay home, do the chores and mind the kids.

BIRTHDAYS—
Jose Ferrer, 1912; Soupy Sales, 1930; Elvis Presley, 1935; Shirley Bassey, 1937; Yvette Mimieux, 1941; David Bowie, 1947

NEW WORD—
plumcot - noun: a hybrid tree produced by crossing the plum and the apricot

QUIZ—
What do Clint Reno, Tulsa McCauley, Glenn Tyler, Josh Morgan, Vince Everett, Joe Lightcloud and Jesse Wade have in common?

TRIVIA
Elvis was once appointed Special Agent of the Bureau of Narcotics and Dangerous Drugs. . . . Ann-Margret's code name when she called Elvis at Graceland was "Bunny". . . . Elvis had a pet monkey named Scatter.

HISTORY—
On this date in 1815 the Battle of New Orleans was fought, two weeks after the war was over!
Ma Bell - R.I.P. . . In 1982 AT&T was disconnected as the only operator on the block.

GRAFFITI
Cosmetology students take makeup exams.

Quiz Answer: They were all characters that Elvis played in his movies. By the way, the name on Elvis' birth certificate reads "Elvis Aron Presley", a misspelling that was later corrected.

JANUARY

TODAY'S THOUGHT:
"I have often thought that if there had been a good rap group around in those days, I might have chosen a career in music instead of politics."
—Richard M. Nixon

BIRTHDAYS—
Sir Rudolph Bing, 1902; George Balanchine, 1904; Richard Nixon, 1913; Bob Denver, 1935; Dick Enberg, 1935; Joan Baez, 1941; Bart Starr, 1944; Crystal Gayle, 1951

NEW WORD—
lamprophony - adjective: clarity and loudness of voice

QUIZ—
How many sides are there on a dodecagon?

TRIVIA
Richard Nixon was the first president to call the moon. . . . Before "Hello" became the standard telephone greeting, folks said, "Ahoy". Thomas Edison suggested the change. . . . Actor Dustin Hoffman used to type entries for the yellow pages.

HISTORY—
On this date in 1788 Connecticut joined the Union.
In 1793 the first successful American balloon flight was made from Philadelphia to New Jersey, piloted by Jean Pierre Blanchard.

GRAFFITI
If at first you don't succeed, that pretty much does it for skydiving.

Quiz Answer: Twelve

JANUARY

TODAY'S THOUGHT:
"Boxing is sort of like jazz. The better it is, the less amount of people can appreciate it." —George Foreman

OBSERVANCES/EVENTS—
Today is the anniversary of both the League of Nations and the United Nations.

BIRTHDAYS—
Ethan Allen, 1738; Robinson Jeffers, 1887; Ray Bolger, 1904; Sal Mineo, 1939; rocker Rod Stewart, 1945; socker George Foreman, 1949

NEW WORD—
gerenuk - noun: a reddish-brown, slender-necked antelope of East Africa

QUIZ—
When is a band-aid a band-aid?

TRIVIA
It wasn't until the Civil War that specific left and right shoes were made. . . . National Park Service policy prohibits acts of violence or death scenes to be filmed in front of Mount Rushmore. In "North By Northwest" they filmed many of the shots elsewhere and crosscut them with scenes from Rushmore. . . . The inventors of Pepsi, Coke and Dr. Pepper were all Civil War veterans.

HISTORY—
On this date in 1776 Thomas Paine published "Common Sense".

GRAFFITI
Dreams don't come true until you get up and go to work.

Quiz Answer: Only when it's made by Johnson and Johnson — though we commonly refer to an adhesive bandage by that name, J & J holds the trademark on it.

JANUARY

TODAY'S THOUGHT:

"A national debt, if it's not excessive, will be to us a national blessing."
—Alexander Hamilton

BIRTHDAYS—

Alexander Hamilton, 1755; William James, 1842; Rod Taylor, 1930; Sax Machine Clarence Clemons, 1942; Darryl Dawkins, 1957

NEW WORD—

xat - noun: a carved totem pole

QUIZ—

Who was baseball's first designated hitter?

TRIVIA

Baseball's Cleveland Indians were originally called the Cleveland Spiders. . . . Hoyt Wilhelm was the first relief pitcher elected to the Baseball Hall of Fame. . . . It is 127 feet, 3³/₈ inches from home plate to second base on a big league diamond.

HISTORY—

On this date in 1813 the first pineapples were planted in Hawaii.
In 1973 the American League voted to adopt the "designated hitter" rule.

GRAFFITI

Stand for something, or you'll fall for anything.

Quiz Answer: New York Yankee Ron Blomberg, who was walked by Red Sox pitcher, Luis Tiant, on April 6, 1973

JANUARY

TODAY'S THOUGHT:
"You're only young once but you can be immature forever."
—Anonymous

OBSERVANCES/EVENTS—
It's Zanzibar Revolution Day in Tanzania.

BIRTHDAYS—
Edmund Burke, 1729; Jack London, 1876; Ray Price, 1926; Joe Frazier, 1944; Kirstie Alley, 1955

NEW WORD—
doggo - adverb: out of sight, in concealment

QUIZ—
What does "Mardi Gras" mean?

TRIVIA
The Indian on the Indian head penny was not an Indian at all. The model was Sarah Longacre, a relative of one of the mint's officials . . . . The top lottery prizes in the world come from Spain's El Gordo - the Fat One. Players can win in excess of $300 million. . . . "Mind Your Business" was the motto printed on one of the first U.S. coins.

HISTORY—
On this date in 1915 the House rejected a bill giving women the right to vote.
In 1922 Hattie Caraway became the first female U.S. Senator.
And Holy Opening Night Jitters, Batman! In 1966 the Caped Crusader and Boy Wonder, Robin, debuted on ABC.
In 1971 "All In The Family" made its TV debut on CBS.

GRAFFITI
The opposite of PROgress is CON . . .

Quiz Answer: Literally translated, it means "Fat Tuesday".

JANUARY

TODAY'S THOUGHT:
"A hospital bed is a parked taxi with the meter running."
—Groucho Marx

OBSERVANCES/EVENTS—
It's Stephen Foster Memorial Day. So whether you are "Way Down Upon the Swanee River" or at the "Camptown Races" or you just "Dream of Jeannie With the Light Brown Hair", place one hand over your heart and the other on your doo-dah and hum your favorite Foster ditty.

BIRTHDAYS—
Horatio Alger, 1834; Sophie Tucker, 1884; Robert Stack, 1919; Gwen Verdon, 1925; Charles Nelson Reilly, 1931

NEW WORD—
quidnunc - noun: a busybody or a gossip

QUIZ—
During the course of a lifetime, the average American . . .
    A: eats 269 gallons of ice cream   D: all of the above
    B: makes nearly 200,000 phone calls E: none of the above
    C: sleeps about 23 years

TRIVIA
You would have to climb 150 feet to reach the lower branch of a Redwood tree. . . . The banana tree is an herb, not a tree. . . . Americans eat about 12 billion bananas each year.

HISTORY—
On this date in 1920 a "New York Times" editorial opined that rockets would never fly.
In 1967 the U.S. population made it over the 200 million mark.

GRAFFITI
The best way to save face is to keep the bottom half shut.

Quiz Answer: D - And they take about 10,000 stupid multiple choice tests!!

JANUARY

TODAY'S THOUGHT:
"Go to bed. What you're staying up for isn't worth it." —Andy Rooney

OBSERVANCES/EVENTS—
It's Vinegrower's Day in Bulgaria. There are feasts, festivals and the coronation of the Vine King, so grab the first flight out to the old country and party down!

BIRTHDAYS—
Benedict Arnold, 1741; Albert Schweitzer, 1875; Andy Rooney, 1919; Julian Bond, 1940; Faye Dunaway, 1941; Jason Bateman, 1969

NEW WORD—
syndet - noun: a synthetic detergent

QUIZ—
EWR, LAX, DFW and ORD are flighty abbreviations for what?

TRIVIA
Adolf Hitler was a vegetarian. . . . Before getting into politics, Fidel Castro was a movie extra in Hollywood and made a film with Esther Williams. . . . Robert Todd Lincoln was present at three presidential assassinations — his father's, President Garfield's and President McKinley's. After the last shooting he refused to attend any more state affairs.

HISTORY—
On this date in 1784 the Revolutionary War formally ended.
In 1952 the "Today" show premiered on NBC.

GRAFFITI
Support the right to arm bears.

Quiz Answer: Airports — EWR is Newark Airport; LAX is Los Angeles; DFW is Dallas-Fort Worth; and ORD is for O'Hare in Chicago (from the old Orchard Field).

JANUARY

TODAY'S THOUGHT:
"If women didn't exist, all the money in the world would have no meaning." —Aristotle Onassis

BIRTHDAYS—
Aristotle Onassis, 1906; Gene Krupa, 1909; Lloyd Bridges, 1913; Chuck Berry, 1926; Dr. Martin Luther King, 1929; Charo, 1951

NEW WORD—
zarf - noun: an ornamental holder for coffee cups without handles

QUIZ—
One-day-wonder George Willig climbed the 110 story south tower of the World Trade Center in New York in 1977. Then Mayor Abraham Beame fined him for his misconduct. How much was he fined?
   A: $110,000   B: $11,000   C: $1,100   D: $1.10

TRIVIA
The world's first skyscraper was the Auditorium Building in Chicago. Built in 1889, it was ten stories tall. . . .If you want to go from the ground floor to the top of the Empire State Building on foot, get ready for 1,575 steps. . . . Toronto is the home of the world's largest free-standing tower. It is 1,822 feet high.

HISTORY—
On this date in 1861 Elisha Otis climbed to the top when he patented the elevator.
In 1870 "Harper's Weekly" introduced the donkey as the symbol of the Democratic Party.

—— GRAFFITI ——
I'd like to help you out; which way did you come in?

Quiz Answer: D - Willig was fined a penny for every floor.

JANUARY

TODAY'S THOUGHT:
"My father told me all about the birds and the bees. The liar - I went steady with a woodpecker till I was twenty-one." —Bob Hope

OBSERVANCES/EVENTS—
It's National Nothing Day, a day to sit back, relax and do nothing. Observed by the public since 1973, it's a much older tradition with Congress.

BIRTHDAYS—
Andre Michelin, 1888; Ethel Merman, 1909; Dizzy Dean, 1911; A. J. Foyt, 1935; Ronnie Milsap, 1944; Debbie Allen, 1950

NEW WORD—
geck - noun: a contemptible person

QUIZ—
What is the plural of praying mantis?

TRIVIA
Children under age 4 and adults over 50 rarely blush. . . . Kleenex tissues were first used as a filter in gas masks during World War I. . . . At the outbreak of WWI, the American Air Force consisted of only 50 men. Of course that wasn't so bad considering they only had one plane!

HISTORY—
On this date in 1920 prohibition became the law of the land and America went dry.
In 1991 Saddam Hussein's (see NEW WORD — above) throat went dry as "Desert Storm" blew into Kuwait and Iraq.

GRAFFITI
Why be difficult? With a bit more effort, you could be impossible.

Quiz Answer: Praying mantid

JANUARY

TODAY'S THOUGHT:
"Anger is never without a Reason, but seldom with a good One."
—Benjamin Franklin

BIRTHDAYS—
Benjamin Franklin, 1706; Noah Beery, 1884; Jerome Kern, 1885; Betty White, 1925; James Earl Jones, 1931; Shari Lewis, 1934

NEW WORD—
boudeuse - noun: a sofa having two seats with a common backrest between them

QUIZ—
What popular beverage was introduced in 1929 as Bib-Label Lithiated Lemon-Lime soda?

TRIVIA
Snickers is America's most popular candy bar. . . . The average American eats 1,483 pounds of candy while living the sweet life. . . . The world's record for keeping a Lifesaver in the mouth with the hole intact is 7 hours and 10 minutes.

HISTORY—
On this date in 1871 Andrew Hallidie was issued a patent for the first cable car.
In 1929 "Popeye" made his first appearance in E.C. Segar's comic strip "Thimble Theatre".

GRAFFITI
Just when you think you've won the race, along come faster rats.

Quiz Answer: Imagine having to write a jingle for that name! Fortunately the bottlers wised up and rechristened the drink 7-Up.

JANUARY

TODAY'S THOUGHT:

"It's no longer a question of staying healthy. It's a question of finding a sickness you like." —Jackie Mason

BIRTHDAYS—

Peter Mark Roget, 1779; Daniel Webster, 1782; Oliver Hardy, 1892; Cary Grant, 1904; Danny Kaye, 1913; Curt Flood, 1938; Kevin Costner, 1955

NEW WORD—

etiolate - verb: to bleach; to cause a plant to whiten by excluding light

QUIZ—

Does a zebra have white or black stripes?

TRIVIA

If all the ice in Antarctica melted it would raise the water level of the world's oceans over two hundred feet. . . . In the next sixty seconds about 960 million tons of rain will fall worldwide. . . . Every day a thousand tons of meteor dust fall to earth.

HISTORY—

On this date in 1919 the Peace Conference at Versailles began. The conference eventually settled World War I but set the stage for World War II.

In 1986 it was the first observance of Martin Luther King Jr.'s birth as a legal public holiday.

GRAFFITI

The weather is here . . . wish you were beautiful.

Quiz Answer: It has black stripes on a white or tawny body.

J A N U A R Y

TODAY'S THOUGHT:

"The way I see it, if you want the rainbow, you gotta put up with the rain."
—Dolly Parton

BIRTHDAYS—

James Watt, 1736; Isaiah Thomas, 1749; Robert E. Lee, 1807; Edgar Allen Poe, 1809; Robert MacNeil, 1931; Phil Everly, 1939; Shelley Fabares, 1944; Dolly Parton, 1946; Desi Arnaz Jr., 1953

NEW WORD—

oppilate - verb: to obstruct; to stop up

QUIZ—

What job did Robert E. Lee turn down to accept command of the Confederate forces?

TRIVIA

Edgar Allen Poe was expelled from West Point in 1831 when he appeared at a parade in his birthday suit (See above). . . . Sandhurst is the British equivalent of West Point. Ian Fleming and David Niven were graduates. . . . When George Washington made the Marquis de Lafayette a major general in the Continental Army, the Frenchman was just nineteen years old.

HISTORY—

On this date in 1825 tin cans were patented.
In 1903 the first transatlantic radio broadcast took place. (The tin cans with string never caught on for intercontinental communication.)
In 1977 President Ford pardoned Tokyo Rose. She had been convicted of treason for her broadcasts during World War II.

GRAFFITI

Since I gave up hope, I feel much better.

Quiz Answer: Lee declined command of the Union forces. He apparently felt his loyalty was to his home state of Virginia.

J A N U A R Y

TODAY'S THOUGHT:
"By the time you're eighty years old, you've learned everything. You only have to remember it." —George Burns

OBSERVANCES/EVENTS—
It is San Sebastian's Day in Brazil honoring the patron saint of Rio De Janeiro.

BIRTHDAYS—
George Burns, 1896; Federico Fellini, 1920; Edwin "Buzz" Aldrin, 1930; Arte Johnson, 1934; David Lynch, 1946; Lorenzo Lamas, 1958

NEW WORD—
rhetor - noun: an orator

QUIZ—
Don't get a headache over it, but can you figure out the common name for $C_9H_8O_4$?

TRIVIA
George Burns was born Nathan Birnbaum. . . . Hot Foot Teddy was Smokey the Bear's original name. . . . In 1952 Queen Elizabeth was named "Time" magazine's "Man of the Year".

HISTORY—
On this date in 1265 the first English Parliament was called to session. In 1981 Ronald Reagan became president on the same day the Iranian crisis ended with the release of 52 American hostages.

GRAFFITI
Get even . . . Live long enough to be a problem to your children.

Quiz Answer: Aspirin (acetylsalicylic acid)

J A N U A R Y

TODAY'S THOUGHT:
"It's hard not to play golf that's up to Jack Nicklaus standards when you *are* Jack Nicklaus." —Jack Nicklaus

BIRTHDAYS—
Stonewall Jackson, 1824; Wolfman Jack, 1939; Jack Nicklaus, 1940; Placido Domingo, 1941; Mac Davis, 1942; Jill Eikenberry, 1947; Robby Benson, 1956; Geena Davis, 1957

NEW WORD—
hyposmia - noun: impaired sense of smell

QUIZ—
What real life situation inspired the character of the Mad Hatter in "Alice in Wonderland"?

TRIVIA
Up until 1850, golf balls were made of leather and stuffed with feathers. . . . Miniature golf was originally called "Tom Thumb Golf". . . . Before wooden tees were invented, golfers used sand which was kept in a box near the tee area.

HISTORY—
On this date in 1908 New York City passed a regulation making it illegal for women to smoke in public.

GRAFFITI
When you're over the hill, you pick up speed.

Quiz Answer: The phrase "as mad as a hatter" was very common at the time the book was written. The reason was that mercury was used in the production of felt hats and since it can be absorbed through the skin, many in the industry became afflicted with mercury poisoning which can cause nerve damage and mental breakdown.

J A N U A R Y

TODAY'S THOUGHT:
"The cat could very well be man's best friend but would never stoop to admitting it." —Doug Larson

OBSERVANCES/EVENTS—
It's Answer Your Cat's Question Day. Ever notice that quizzical way your cat looks at you? The organizers of the event suggest that you meditate on your cat awhile and then take your best shot at answering its question.

BIRTHDAYS—
Sir Francis Bacon, 1561; poet Lord Byron, 1788; Piper Laurie, 1932; Bill Bixby, 1934; Joseph Wambaugh, 1937; John Hurt, 1940; Linda Blair, 1959

NEW WORD—
pavonine - adjective: resembling the feathers of a peacock

QUIZ—
Bathroom Brain Teaser: A man rode a horse from New York to Los Angeles. He left on Wednesday and arrived on the very same Wednesday. How is that?

TRIVIA
The ten most popular cat names, in order, are: Kitty, Smokey, Shadow, Tiger, Boo, Boots, Molly, Tigger, Spike and Princess. . . . The longest recorded life span of a cat is 34 years. . . . There are close to 60 million cats in the United States.

HISTORY—
On this date in 1901 the Victorian era ended when the Queen died at age 82.
In 1970 the jumbo jet era began as Boeing 747s took to the sky in commercial flights for the first time.

GRAFFITI
Horse lovers are stable people.

Quiz Answer: The horse's name was Wednesday.

J A N U A R Y

TODAY'S THOUGHT:
"A medium, so called because it is neither rare nor well done."
—Ernie Kovacs, on television

OBSERVANCES/EVENTS—
It is National Handwriting Day so give more than a cursory thought to cursive writing. Naturally the day is observed annually on the anniversary of John Hancock's birth.

BIRTHDAYS—
John Hancock, 1737; Randolph Scott, 1898; Humphrey Bogart, 1899; Ernie Kovacs, 1919; Chita Rivera, 1933; Rutger Hauer, 1944; Richard Dean Anderson, 1950; Princess Caroline, 1957

NEW WORD—
gunyah - noun: an aboriginal hut in Australia

QUIZ—
Everybody knows that Humphrey Bogart's character in "Casablanca" was named Rick, but what was his last name?

TRIVIA
There are no armed forces in the nations of Iceland, Costa Rica or Lichtenstein. . . . Excalibur was the name of King Arthur's sword. . . . During the Civil War undertakers were called doctors.

HISTORY—
On this date in 1849 Elizabeth Blackwell became the first female medical doctor.
In 1968 the U.S. Navy ship Pueblo and its 83 man crew were seized by North Korea.

GRAFFITI
Humpty Dumpty was pushed.

Quiz Answer: You must remember this . . . the name was Blaine.

JANUARY

TODAY'S THOUGHT:
"Start every day with a smile and get it over with." —W. C. Fields

BIRTHDAYS—
Jack Brickhouse, 1916; Ernest Borgnine, 1917; Neil Diamond, 1941; John Belushi, 1949; Nastassja Kinski, 1961; Mary Lou Retton, 1968

NEW WORD—
nemoricole - adjective: living in a grove

QUIZ—
Who was the first woman to appear on the cover of a Wheaties Box?

TRIVIA
There are 450 to 600 active volcanos around the world. . . . Some species of bamboo can grow up to three feet in a single day. . . . There are 685 drinking fountains in the Pentagon.

HISTORY—
On this date in 1848 the California gold rush began when nuggets were discovered at Sutter's Mill.
In 1925 New York City had its original "Great Blackout" with a total solar eclipse.

GRAFFITI
Old musicians never die, they just decompose.

Quiz Answer: Today's birthday girl, Mary Lou Retton - The Olympic gold medal gymnast made her "Breakfast of Champions" appearance in 1984.

J A N U A R Y

TODAY'S THOUGHT:

"They should put expiration dates on clothes so we would know when they go out of style." —Garry Shandling

BIRTHDAYS—

Robert Burns, 1759; Somerset Maugham, 1874; Ernie Harwell, 1918; Edwin Newman, 1919; Dean Jones, 1931; Mark "Super" Duper, 1959

NEW WORD—

oligophagous - adjective: feeding on only a few particular types of food, especially insects

QUIZ—

If you were heading south from Detroit, what is the first foreign country you would arrive in?

TRIVIA

Mayberry deputy Barney Fife's middle name was Oliver. . . . The very first group to appear on Dick Clark's "American Bandstand" was the Chordettes. . . . Fred Gwynne's first hit TV series of the sixties was "Car 54, Where Are You?"

HISTORY—

On this date in 1533 Anne Boleyn married Henry VIII.
In 1940 the first Social Security checks went out in the mail. Most of them have probably been delivered by now.

GRAFFITI

If you think the system is working, ask someone who isn't.

Quiz Answer: Canada

JANUARY

TODAY'S THOUGHT:
"My wife's final decision seldom tallies with the one immediately following it." —Paul Newman

OBSERVANCES/EVENTS—
It's a national holiday in the Dominican Republic celebrating the birth of founding father Juan Pablo Duarte.
There are also big doings in India where it's Republic Day.

BIRTHDAYS—
First Lady Julia Dent Grant, 1826; Douglas MacArthur, 1880; Paul Newman, 1925; Jules Feiffer, 1929; Angela Davis, 1944

NEW WORD—
aposiopesis - noun: a sudden breaking off in the middle of a senten . . .

QUIZ—
Can you identify the foreign capital named after the fifth U.S. president and the country where it's located?

TRIVIA
Some laws which were (and may still be!) on the books— In Memphis, Tennessee it's against the law for frogs to croak after 11 P.M. . . . It's illegal to ride a bike into a swimming pool in Baldwin Park, California. . . . You're not allowed to remove your shoes if your feet smell while you're in the theater in Winnetlea, Illinois.

HISTORY—
On this date in 1784 Benjamin Franklin declared that he wanted the turkey, rather than the eagle, as the U.S. symbol.
In 1837 Michigan joined up with the other 25 United States.

GRAFFITI
Censors stick their "nos" in other peoples' business.

Quiz Answer: Monrovia, Liberia

The Bathroom Trivia Almanac

JANUARY

TODAY'S THOUGHT:

"Early to rise and early to bed, makes a man healthy, wealthy and dead."
—James Thurber

OBSERVANCES/EVENTS—

It's Thomas Crapper Day, marking the anniversary of the death of the inventor of the modern toilet.

BIRTHDAYS—

Wolfgang Amadeus Mozart, 1756; Lewis Carroll, 1832; Jerome Kern, 1885; Hyman Rickover, 1900, Skitch Henderson, 1918; Donna Reed, 1921; Troy Donahue, 1936; Mikhail Baryshnikov, 1948

NEW WORD—

gride - verb: to scrape harshly; make a grating sound

QUIZ—

Will the year 2000 be a leap year?

TRIVIA

Thomas Adams invented chewing gum while looking for a replacement for rubber. . . . Grover Cleveland had an artificial jaw made out of rubber. All politicians have been known to stretch a point, but this was ridiculous! . . . Stephen Perry invented the rubber band in 1845.

HISTORY—

On this date in 1880 Thomas Edison got his patent for one of his brightest ideas - the electric light bulb!
In 1973 the United States signed a peace accord with North Vietnam in Paris.

GRAFFITI
Fishermen make net profits.

Quiz Answer: Leap year comes every four years except in years that end with "00". But wait! There's another little known rule that says that every year evenly divisible by 400 is also a leap year. So, yes, 2000 will be a leap year.

JANUARY

TODAY'S THOUGHT:
"There are only three basic jokes, but since the mother-in-law is not a joke but a very serious question, there are only two." —George Ade

BIRTHDAYS—
Charlemagne, 742; Sir Francis Drake, 1545; Colette, 1873; Arthur Rubinstein, 1887; Susan Sontag, 1933; Alan Alda, 1936

NEW WORD—
sapor - noun: flavor, the quality of a substance that excites the sense of taste

QUIZ—
Knowing that the Addams family is a little weird, what do you think little Wednesday's middle name is?

TRIVIA
Natural gas has no odor. That distinctive aroma is added so people can detect leaks. . . . Most of the germs that get into your body enter through your mouth. . . . The blood of a spider is transparent.

HISTORY—
On this date in 1986 the space shuttle "Challenger" exploded, 74 seconds into flight, killing the seven crew members.

GRAFFITI
Hypochondria is the only disease I haven't got.

Quiz Answer: Thursday —Just think, if she married Joe Friday, she'd be . . .

JANUARY

TODAY'S THOUGHT:
"I was born into it and there was nothing I could do about it. It was there, like air or food, or any other element. The only question with wealth is what you do with it." —John D. Rockefeller, Jr.

OBSERVANCES/EVENTS—
It's Backwards Day! That's right, a day to do everything sdrawkcab.

BIRTHDAYS—
Thomas Paine, 1737; William McKinley, 1843; John D. Rockefeller, Jr., 1906; John Forsythe, 1918; Katherine Ross, 1943; Tom Selleck, 1945; Ann Jillian, 1951; Oprah Winfrey, 1954; Stacey King, 1967

NEW WORD—
kakapo - noun: a large, nocturnal parrot of New Zealand, no doubt named by enraged natives who were under the wrong branch at the wrong time . . .

QUIZ—
Within a hundred pounds or so, if you wanted to steal a billion dollars in $100 bills, how much weight would you have to be prepared to carry?

TRIVIA
Martha Washington was the first woman to appear on American paper currency. . . . . The average dollar bill has a life span of eighteen months. . . . There are 293 ways to make change for a dollar.

HISTORY—
On this date in 1845 "The Raven", by Edgar Allen Poe, was published in the "New York Mirror".
In 1900 baseball's American League got its start.

GRAFFITI
If you drink like a fish, swim, don't drive.

Quiz Answer: A billion bucks in C-notes would be some seriously heavy bread. In fact, it would weigh about 10 tons!

JANUARY

TODAY'S THOUGHT:
"I belong to Bridegrooms Anonymous. Whenever I feel like getting married, they send over a lady in a housecoat and hair curlers to burn my toast for me." —Dick Martin

BIRTHDAYS—
Franklin Delano Roosevelt, 1882; John Ireland, 1915; Dick Martin, 1922; Gene Hackman, 1930; Tammy Grimes, 1934; Vanessa Redgrave, 1937

NEW WORD—
refulgent - adjective: radiant; glowing; shining ("Why, my dear, you look positively refulgent!" Slap!)

QUIZ—
What was the first U.S. network show to introduce the Beatles to America?

TRIVIA
The original name for the portrait "Whistler's Mother" was "Arrangement in Grey and Black". . . . DaVinci's masterpiece, "Mona Lisa", took ten years to complete. . . . A Matisse, "Le Bateau", was hung upside down for a month and a half in the Museum of Modern Art in New York before anyone noticed.

HISTORY—
On this date in 1958 the first moving sidewalk appeared in Dallas.
In 1969 the Beatles played together publicly for the final time on the roof of their Apple Studios. The concert came to an abrupt end when London bobbies broke up the event after neighbors called to complain about the noise. ("You say you want a revolution, well, you know . . .")

GRAFFITI
A sneeze is much achoo about nothing.

Quiz Answer: That's right; it wasn't the "Ed Sullivan Show". The Fab Four were actually featured on tape early in January, 1964 on 'The Jack Paar Show".

JANUARY

TODAY'S THOUGHT:
"There are two great rules of life: never tell everything at once."
—Ken Venturi

BIRTHDAYS—
Franz Schubert, 1797; Eddie Cantor, 1892; Jackie Robinson, 1919; Carol Channing, 1923; Ernie "Mr. Cub" Banks, 1931; Suzanne Pleshette, 1937; Nolan Ryan, 1947

NEW WORD—
nide - noun: a brood or nest, especially of pheasants

QUIZ—
They are manufactured in Topeka, Kansas. They measure eleven and one half feet across, weigh 12,500 pounds and cost over $50,000. What are they?

TRIVIA
Alaska was bought from Russia for about two cents an acre. . . . Lenin was the pseudonym taken by Vladimir Ilich Ulyanov. . . . Russia is the home of the world's longest escalator. It is part of the Leningrad subway system and goes down nearly 195 feet. Some really dumb tourists once got stuck on it for three hours during a power failure.

HISTORY—
On this date in 1958 in response to the new space race with the Russians, the U.S. launched its first satellite, Explorer I, an event that lead directly to our modern world of defense, weather and communications satellites.

GRAFFITI
Hospitality is making your guests feel at home, even when you wish they were.

Quiz Answer: The largest tires that Goodyear makes, they fit on giant dump trucks. Wonder how many cans of fix-a-flat you'd need to get those puppies rolling again??

FEBRUARY

TODAY'S THOUGHT:
"If your parents didn't have any children, there's a good chance that you won't have any." —Clarence Day

BIRTHDAYS—
Victor Herbert, 1859; John Ford, 1895; Clark Gable, 1901; Don Everly, 1937; "Saturday Night Live's" Garrett Morris, 1937; Sherman Hemsley, 1938; "Monty Python's" Terry Jones, 1942; Lisa Marie Presley, 1968

NEW WORD—
zugzwang - noun: in chess, a situation where the only move a player can make will damage his position

QUIZ—
Admiral Byrd took along a refrigerator on his expedition to the Antarctic. Why?

TRIVIA
Julius Caesar's autograph is worth $2 million. . . . Creative people have some strange habits. Ernest Hemingway wrote many of his best novels while standing up. Victor Hugo would have his clothes taken away so he would have to stay in and write! . . . Glenn Ford and Nelson Eddy are both descendants of President Martin Van Buren.

HISTORY—
On this date in 1862 Julia Howe's "Battle Hymn of the Republic" was published.
In 1892 the term "400" first came into use in snobbery circles when the queen of New York's social scene, Mrs. William Astor, held a ball at her mansion. Four hundred was the maximum number that her ballroom could accommodate.

GRAFFITI
Fads are in one year and out the other.

Quiz Answer: To keep the crew's food from freezing since the refrigerator was warmer than the outside temperature

FEBRUARY

TODAY'S THOUGHT:

"I'm no different from anybody else with two arms, two legs and forty-two hundred hits." —Pete Rose

OBSERVANCES/EVENTS—

It's Groundhog Day so a tip of the hat to Punxsutawney Phil, Woodrow K. Chuck IV, General Lee, Jimmy V and to meteorological mammals everywhere!

BIRTHDAYS—

James Joyce, 1882; Ayn Rand, 1905; Lorne Greene, 1915; Stan Getz, 1927; Tom Smothers, 1937; Farrah Fawcett, 1947; Christie Brinkley, 1953; Garth Brooks, 1962

NEW WORD—

encomium - noun: eulogy; formal expression of high praise

QUIZ—

February is National Weddings Month. Can you say "I do" to the following question?

Do you know what the bride walks down in church during the wedding ceremony?

TRIVIA

A man with more than one wife is a polygamist. A woman with more than one husband is a polyandrist. . . . The most married man in the monogamous world was a former Baptist minister, Glynn "Scotty" Wolfe of California who had 27 wives. . . . Less than half of the single men in the U.S. who've reached the age of 35 ever get married.

HISTORY—

On this date in 1876 eight teams joined together to form baseball's National League.

——— GRAFFITI ———
Money used to talk. Now it whispers.

Quiz Answer: Aisle? No, not quite. The aisles of a church are on the sides. The center path through the pews is called the nave.

FEBRUARY

TODAY'S THOUGHT:
"If you are ever in doubt as to whether you should kiss a pretty girl, always give her the benefit of the doubt." —Thomas Carlyle

OBSERVANCES/EVENTS—
It is "The Day The Music Died". In 1959 Buddy Holly, Richie Valens and J.P. Richardson (the Big Bopper) perished in an Iowa plane crash. Waylon Jennings gave up his seat on that ill-fated flight.

BIRTHDAYS—
Horace Greeley, 1811; Gertrude Stein, 1874; Norman Rockwell, 1894; James Michener, 1907; Joey Bishop, 1918; Shelley Berman, 1926; Fran Tarkenton, 1940; Bob Griese, 1945; Morgan Fairchild, 1950

NEW WORD—
birl - verb: to cause a log to rotate rapidly by stepping on it

QUIZ—
Norman Rockwell illustrated 317 covers over a 47 year period for what magazine?

TRIVIA
The first minimum wage, instituted in the U.S. in 1938, was 25 cents an hour. . . . George Washington earned $25,000 a year as president of the U. S. . . . John Madden makes $365,000 per game broadcasting football on the Fox network.

HISTORY—
On this date in 1913 the Sixteenth Amendment was ratified. That's what gave Congress the power to levy income taxes. Planning any celebration?

GRAFFITI
Celebrities work hard to become famous, then wear dark glasses to avoid being recognized.

Quiz Answer: "The Saturday Evening Post"

FEBRUARY

TODAY'S THOUGHT:
"I don't like to watch golf on television. I can't stand whispering."
—David Brenner

BIRTHDAYS—
Nigel Bruce, 1895; Charles Lindbergh, 1902; Eddie Foy, 1905; Ida Lupino, 1918; Betty Friedan, 1921; Conrad Bain, 1923; Isabel Peron, 1931; David Brenner, 1945; Dan Quayle, 1947; Vincent Damon Furnier (Alice Cooper), 1948

NEW WORD—
lucubrate - verb: to work or study very hard, especially at night

QUIZ—
Buffalo Bill Cody gave what sharpshooter the nickname "Little Sure Shot"?

TRIVIA
Charles Lindbergh was not the first person to cross the Atlantic in an airplane. Sixty-six people made the trip before he did. He was the first to fly alone. . . . Lindbergh was a letter carrier. He operated an airmail run from St. Louis to Chicago between 1926 and 1927. . . . Lindbergh was a Pulitzer Prize winner for his 1953 autobiography, "The Spirit of St. Louis".

HISTORY—
On this date in 1941 the USO was founded.
In 1974 the SLA kidnapped Patty Hearst.

GRAFFITI
Eat like a horse and you'll look like one, too.

Quiz Answer: Annie Oakley

FEBRUARY

TODAY'S THOUGHT:
"Flattery is alright, if you don't inhale." —Adlai Stevenson

OBSERVANCES/EVENTS—
It's Weatherman's Day, a day to give those professional prognosticators a break, even if you think that they couldn't pour slush out of galoshes if the instructions were printed on the heel!

BIRTHDAYS—
Adlai Stevenson, 1900; John Carradine, 1906; Red Buttons, 1919; Hank Aaron, 1934; Roger Staubach, 1942; Bob Morley, 1945; Spinal Tap's Christopher Guest, 1948

NEW WORD—
persiflage - noun: light talk; banter

QUIZ—
Who walks faster, a man or a woman?

TRIVIA
The Hundred Years War lasted 116 years. . . . Clark Gable's U.S. military discharge papers were signed by Major Ronald Reagan. . . . James Garner, Art Carney, Blake Edwards and James Arness all survived serious combat wounds.

HISTORY—
On this date in 1985 the longest war in history ended. The Third Punic War, between Rome and Carthage, was officially settled with a treaty - 2,131 years after it began.

GRAFFITI
If ignorance is bliss, why aren't more people happy?

Quiz Answer: According to a University of Minnesota, Duluth study, a woman does. The average woman walks 256 feet per minute while a man walks about 245.

FEBRUARY

TODAY'S THOUGHT:
"I have never hated a man enough to give his diamonds back."
—Zsa Zsa Gabor

OBSERVANCES/EVENTS—
It is Aaron Burr Day so go out and shoot a ten dollar bill on anything you'd like!

BIRTHDAYS—
Aaron Burr, 1756; Babe Ruth, 1895; Ronald Reagan, 1911; Zsa Zsa Gabor, 1919; Francois Truffaut, 1932; Mike Farrell, 1939; Tom Brokaw, 1940; Fabian, 1943; Michael Tucker, 1944; Natalie Cole, 1950

NEW WORD—
salmagundi - noun: a mixture

QUIZ—
What do James I of Scotland, Henry III of France, King Edward Ironsides of England and Catherine the Great of Russia have in common?

TRIVIA
As many as 100 pearls have been found in a single oyster. . . . The shark in the movie "Jaws" was nicknamed Bruce. . . . The ice covering the Arctic Ocean is 7 to 10 feet thick.

HISTORY—
On this date in 1971 Alan Shepard played golf on the moon.

GRAFFITI
You join the navy to see the world . . .
and then spend two years on a submarine.

Quiz Answer: The last throne they ever sat upon was in a bathroom. By the way, Charles I of Spain was the only king ever born in a bathroom.

FEBRUARY

TODAY'S THOUGHT:
"Somebody said to me, 'But the Beatles were antimaterialistic.' That is a huge myth. John and I literally used to sit down and say, 'Now, let's write a swimming pool.' " —Paul McCartney

OBSERVANCES/EVENTS—
It's National Hangover Awareness Day.

BIRTHDAYS—
Charles Dickens, 1812; Eubie Blake, 1883; Sinclair Lewis, 1885; Buster Crabbe, 1908; Eddie Bracken, 1920; Gay Talese, 1932; Dan Quisenberry, 1953; Ashley Walker Bush, 1989

NEW WORD—
temblor - noun: an earthquake; a tremor

QUIZ—
Dr. Benjamin Spock, American child care guru, achieved quite a distinction in sports in his youth. Any idea what it was?

TRIVIA
Shirley Temple had exactly 56 curls in her hair. . . . Amy Carter's Secret Service code name was Dynamo. . . . While you are reading this item, three more babies have been born into the world.

HISTORY—
On this date in 1964 the British invasion began as those lovable moptops from Liverpool, the Beatles, landed on U.S. shores.

GRAFFITI
Money is called "cold cash"
because it is never in your pocket long enough to get warm.

Quiz Answer: Strangely enough, the great opponent of paddling was a member of the American Rowing Team in the 1924 Paris Olympics.

FEBRUARY

TODAY'S THOUGHT:
"If you think it's hard to meet new people, try picking up the wrong golf ball." —Jack Lemmon

BIRTHDAYS—
General William Tecumseh Sherman, 1820; Jules Verne, 1828; John Uhler III (Jack Lemmon), 1925; James Dean, 1931; John Williams of the Boston Pops, 1932; Ted Koppel, 1940; Robert Klein, 1942; Nick Nolte, 1942

NEW WORD—
icosahedron - noun: a solid figure having twenty faces

QUIZ—
Take a good look at the birthday list and see if you can guess which one of these prominent Americans was actually born in Lancashire, England.

TRIVIA
Erma Bombeck began her career as an obituary writer for Ohio's "Dayton Journal-Herald". . . . Jerry Seinfeld sold light bulbs by telephone. . . . "The Far Side's" Gary Larson once ran over a dog on his way to a job interview with the Seattle Humane Society. He got the job and became an animal abuse investigator.

HISTORY—
On this date in 1910 the Boy Scouts of America did their first good deed as they were founded.

GRAFFITI
A disc jockey works for the love of mike.

Quiz Answer: Born "across the pond" in jolly Olde England was none other than "Nightline" anchorman, Ted Koppel.

FEBRUARY

TODAY'S THOUGHT:
"I have everything now I had twenty years ago - except now it's all lower."
—Gypsy Rose Lee

BIRTHDAYS—
William Henry Harrison, 1773; Ronald Colman, 1891; Gypsy Rose Lee, 1914; Roger Mudd, 1928; Carole King, 1942; Maria de Lourdes Villers (Mia Farrow), 1945; Judith Light, 1949

NEW WORD—
farinaceous - adjective: made from flour or meal; starchy

QUIZ—
What is birthday boy William Henry Harrison's chief distinction as Chief Executive?

TRIVIA
Mia Farrow was on the first cover of "People" magazine in 1974. . . . A giraffe has the highest blood pressure of any animal and its heart can weigh up to 25 pounds. . . . A chow is the only dog without a pink tongue; it is black.

HISTORY—
On this date in 1895 volleyball, the national pastime of nudist colonies, was invented by W.G. Morgan of Holyoke, Massachusetts.

GRAFFITI
A politician puts his best foot forward - into his mouth.

Quiz Answer: He served the shortest time of any elected president - 32 days. Harrison was also the only president to study to be a doctor. He should have finished. He died of pneumonia contracted during his dank and cold inauguration.

FEBRUARY

TODAY'S THOUGHT:
"Never try to impress a woman, because if you do she'll expect you to keep up to the standard for the rest of your life." —W.C. Fields

BIRTHDAYS—
W. C. Fields, 1880; Jimmy Durante, 1893; Dame Judith Anderson, 1898; Larry Adler, 1914; Leontyne Price, 1927; Roberta Flack, 1940; Peter Allen, 1944; Mark Spitz, 1950; Greg Norman, 1955; Lenny Dykstra, 1963

NEW WORD—
biltong - noun: in South Africa, strips of meat dried in the open air

QUIZ—
February is the second month. Can you name these other seconds?
- A: Paris is the largest French speaking city in the world. Which city is second?
- B: John Glenn was the first American astronaut to orbit the earth. Who was second?
- C: John Hancock was the first to sign the Declaration of Independence. Who was second?

TRIVIA
Elephants sleep only two or three hours a night. . . . The average person spends a total of about two years on the phone during their lifetime. . . . Two states are the most "neighborly" of all; Missouri and Tennessee both touch on eight other states.

HISTORY—
On this date in 1897 the "New York Times" introduced its slogan, "All The News That's Fit To Print".

GRAFFITI
Jogging is a change of pace.

Quiz Answer: A - Montreal; B - Scott Carpenter; C - Samuel Adams

FEBRUARY

TODAY'S THOUGHT:

"You can only hold your stomach in for so many years." —Burt Reynolds

OBSERVANCES/EVENTS—

It's White Shirt Day in Flint, Michigan, an observance in which blue-collar workers wear white shirts. Tomorrow, it's Ring-Around-The-Collar Day.

BIRTHDAYS—

Thomas Edison, 1847; Sidney Sheldon, 1917; Lloyd Bentsen, 1921; Eva Gabor, 1921; Leslie Nielsen, 1922; Mary Quant, 1934; Burt Reynolds, 1936; Sergio Mendes, 1941

NEW WORD—

kyle - noun: a narrow strait of water between two islands or between an island and the mainland

QUIZ—

Before he got into steamy novels of lust and lies, what sixties sitcoms did Sidney Sheldon create and write?

TRIVIA

The last breath of Thomas Edison is preserved in a tube at Greenfield Village in Deerborn, Michigan. . . . Edison's formal schooling was limited to three months. . . . In his lifetime Thomas Edison patented 1,093 inventions.

HISTORY—

On this date in 1960 Jack Paar walked off his show in protest of the network's censoring of a mild "water closet" gag he had done the night before. After almost a month of negotiations, the show was back up to "Paar" as the host returned to his post.

GRAFFITI
Bigamy's penalty is two mothers-in-law.

Quiz Answer: He dreamed up "I Dream of Jeannie" and saw double with "The Patty Duke Show".

FEBRUARY

TODAY'S THOUGHT:
"My theory of evolution? I think Darwin was adopted." —Steven Wright

OBSERVANCES/EVENTS—
It's Oglethorpe Day, commemorating the founding of Georgia in 1733.

BIRTHDAYS—
Abe Lincoln, 1809; General Omar Bradley, 1893; R. Buckminster Fuller, 1895; Joe Garagiola, 1926; Bill Russell, 1934; Joanna Kerns, 1953; Arsenio Hall, 1955

NEW WORD—
vitiate - verb: to spoil or mar

QUIZ—
Another of the greatest men of the 19th century was born the exact same day as Lincoln, half a world away. Any guesses?

TRIVIA
The word "duke" is repeated 132 times in the 1962 Gene Chandler hit "Duke of Earl". . . . Abraham Lincoln's "Gettysburg Address" contained 272 words. . . . The word "caper" appeared in every episode title of "77 Sunset Strip".

HISTORY—
On this date in 1709 Scottish seaman Alexander Selkirk, whose adventures were the source of inspiration for "Robinson Crusoe" by Daniel Defoe, was taken off Juan Fernandez Island after more than four years of living there alone.

GRAFFITI
If Darwin wasn't right,
how come it's so easy to make a monkey out of a man?

Quiz Answer: Charles Darwin - While Abe was destined to deal with revolution, Charles worked out evolution.

FEBRUARY

TODAY'S THOUGHT:
"Never slap a man who chews tobacco." —Willard Scott

BIRTHDAYS—
Bess Truman, 1885; Grant Wood, 1892; Tennessee Ernie Ford, 1919; Chuck Yeager, 1923; Kim Novak, 1933; George Segal, 1934; Carol Lynley, 1942; Stockard Channing, 1944

NEW WORD—
transmogrify - verb: to transform; to grotesquely change in appearance.

QUIZ—
Can you identify the following famous folks by their given names?
- A: Joe Yule, Jr.
- C: Michael Douglas
- B: Walter Palahnuik
- D: Mary Cathleen Collins

TRIVIA
Jay North starred as "Dennis the Menace" for years but he was also the voice of Bamm Bamm Rubble. . . . Alice Kramden was known as Alice Gibson before she married Ralph. . . . Packy East, an amateur boxer, is better known as Bob Hope.

HISTORY—
On this date in 1741 the first American magazine, appropriately titled "The American Magazine", was published by Andrew Bradford. Of course, back then the Publisher's Clearinghouse Sweepstakes Grand Prize was only 10 cents . . .

GRAFFITI
Have you hugged your porcupine today?

Quiz Answer:
- A: Mickey Rooney
- C: Michael Keaton
- B: Jack Palance
- D: Bo Derek

F E B R U A R Y

TODAY'S THOUGHT:

"Never sign a valentine with your own name." —Charles Dickens

OBSERVANCES/EVENTS—

It's Valentine's Day as well as National Have-A-Heart Day, sponsored by vegetarians who want to raise the public's consciousness.

BIRTHDAYS—

Jack Benny, 1894; Thelma Ritter, 1905; Jimmy Hoffa, 1913; Mel Allen, 1913; Hugh Downs, 1921; Florence Henderson, 1934; Carl Bernstein, 1944; Gregory Hines, 1946

NEW WORD—

osculate - verb: to kiss; to touch closely

QUIZ—

How many pennies are in a pound?

   A: 54   B: 100   C: 123   D: 181

TRIVIA

The post office in Loveland, Colorado is very busy today. It handles about 200,000 valentines every year. . . . A survey among florists revealed that men tend to buy red flowers more than any other color. . . . Another survey found that females visit florists an average of 2.8 times a year while males do so an average of 3.8 times.

HISTORY—

On this date in 1849 President James Polk became the first U.S. president to be photographed while in office.

Valentine's Day was a heartbreaking one for Teddy Roosevelt. The former president's mother and wife both died on this date in 1884.

GRAFFITI

**If men are God's gift to women,
then God must really be into gag gifts!**

Quiz Answer: D - Were you "penny-wise" or "pound-foolish"?

F E B R U A R Y

TODAY'S THOUGHT:

"Middle age is when your old classmates are so grey and wrinkled and bald they don't recognize you." —Bennett Cerf

BIRTHDAYS—

Galileo, 1564; Henry Steinway, 1797; Susan B. Anthony, 1820; John Barrymore, 1882; Harvey Korman, 1927; Melissa Manchester, 1951; Jane Seymour, 1951; Bart Simpson's creator, Matt Groening, 1954

NEW WORD—

gustatory - adjective: pertaining to taste

QUIZ—

Famous Last Words: The quotes below were the last ever heard from the lips of the following people. Can you match them up?

1. "I have a terrific headache."
2. "Strike my tent!"
3. "Dying is a very dull, dreary affair. And my advice to you is to have nothing whatever to do with it."
4. "I've never felt better!"

A: Douglas Fairbanks, Sr.   B: W. Somerset Maugham
C: Robert E. Lee   D: Franklin Delano Roosevelt

TRIVIA

Do you flush the toliet while sitting on it? One out of every three Americans does. . . . In 1893 the ferris wheel was introduced at the Chicago Columbian Exposition. It was 250 feet high with 36 cars. . . . Henry F. Phillips invented the Phillips screw in 1936.

HISTORY—

On this date in 1842 the first adhesive-backed postage stamp was introduced.
In 1903 the first Teddy Bear made its appearance.

GRAFFITI
The meek shall inherit the work.

Quiz Answer: 1-D;   2-C;   3-B;   4-A

F E B R U A R Y

TODAY'S THOUGHT:

"Tennis is like marrying for money. Love has nothing to do with it."
—Phyllis Diller

BIRTHDAYS—

Edgar Bergen, 1903; Patti Andrews, 1920; Sonny Bono, 1935; William Katt, 1950; LaVar Burton, 1957; John McEnroe, 1959; Mark Price, 1964; Molly Ringwald, 1968

NEW WORD—

ephemera - adjective: something short-lived or transitory

QUIZ—

Bathroom Brain Teaser:
If your doctor gave you three pills and told you to take one every half hour, how long would they last?

TRIVIA

The microwave oven is used more for reheating coffee than for any other reason. . . . Hanson Crockett invented the doughnut hole in 1847. . . . The average American eats more lettuce than any other vegetable, an average of 27.4 pounds per year.

HISTORY—

On this date in 1883 the very first issue of "The Ladies Home Journal" hit the newsstands. No doubt most of the coupons have expired by now.

——— GRAFFITI ———
A bird in the hand is better than one over head.

Quiz Answer: One hour

FEBRUARY

TODAY'S THOUGHT:
"In spite of the cost of living, it's still popular." —Kathleen Norris

OBSERVANCES/EVENTS—
It's National P.T.A. Founder's Day, celebrating the founding of the P.T.A. in 1897 by Phoebe Apperson Hearst and Alice McLellan Birney.

BIRTHDAYS—
A. Montgomery Ward, 1843; industrialist H. L. Hunt, 1889; Marion Anderson, 1902; Red Barber, 1908; Margaret Truman, 1924; Hal Holbrook, 1925; Alan Bates, 1934; Jim Brown, 1936; Michael Jordan, 1963

NEW WORD—
ariose - adjective: songlike

QUIZ—
Who are Moses Horwitz, Jerome Horwitz and Larry Feinberg?

TRIVIA
In 1902 Theodore Roosevelt became the first president to ride in an automobile. . . . 88 out of 100 people put on their right shoe first. . . . Thomas Jefferson was the first man to be defeated in a presidential election.

HISTORY—
On this date in 1867 the first ship passed through the Suez Canal. In honor of the occasion the band was playing "Is Suez or is Su-ain't my baby?" So it's a horrible pun . . . so Suez!

GRAFFITI
In politics, after all is said and done, a lot more is said than done.

Quiz Answer: They are the Three Stooges: Moe, Curley and Larry.

FEBRUARY

TODAY'S THOUGHT:

"It's not the most intellectual job in the world, but I do have to know the letters." —Vanna White

BIRTHDAYS—

Louis Tiffany, 1848; Wendell Wilkie, 1892; Bill Cullen, 1920; Jack Palance, 1920; Helen Gurley Brown, 1922; George Kennedy, 1927; Yoko Ono, 1933; Cybill Shepherd, 1950; John Travolta, 1955; Vanna White, 1957

NEW WORD—

bifurcate - verb: to divide or fork into 2 branches

QUIZ—

True or False?
Prince Charles is an avid collector of toilet seats.

TRIVIA

What is a billion? Let me count the ways . . . 1 billion seconds equals about 31.7 years. . . . 1 billion days is more than 2.7 million years. . . . 1 billion miles per hour is 1 1/2 times the speed of light.

HISTORY—

On this date in 1930 Pluto was discovered. He was sitting on a stool at Schwab's when Walt Disney came in . . . actually it was the planet Pluto, the smallest, farthest and coldest in the solar system.

GRAFFITI

The only way to make ends meet is to get off YOURS!

Quiz Answer: True

FEBRUARY

TODAY'S THOUGHT:
"A tourist is a fellow who drives thousands of miles so he can be photographed standing in front of his car." —Emile Ganest

BIRTHDAYS—
Nicolaus Copernicus, 1473; Merle Oberon, 1911; Eddie Arcaro, 1916; Lee Marvin, 1924; Smokey Robinson, 1940; Mama Cass Elliott, 1941; Prince Andrew, Duke of York, 1960; Justine Bateman, 1966

NEW WORD—
mesodont - adjective: having medium-sized teeth

QUIZ—
Which state has the longest coastline?

TRIVIA
The name of the dog shown on a Cracker Jack box is Bingo. The little sailor boy is, of course, Jack. . . . Since 1912 more than 16 million toys have been given away in Cracker Jack boxes. . . . The average kid eats 33 quarts of popcorn per year.

HISTORY—
On this date in 1884 the phonograph was patented and the phrase "Turn that down or you're grounded!" entered the language.

GRAFFITI
Money can't buy happiness . . . but at least you can go sulk in Aruba!

Quiz Answer: By far, the state with the longest coastline is Alaska. In fact, its coastline is longer than that of *all* the other coastal states combined! Strange that it never became a beach resort . . .

F E B R U A R Y

TODAY'S THOUGHT:

"Work banishes those three great evils — boredom, vice and poverty."

—Voltaire

BIRTHDAYS—

Voltaire, 1694; Ansel Adams, 1902; John Daly, 1914; Gloria Vanderbilt, 1924; Robert Altman, 1925; Sidney Poitier, 1927; Bobby Unser, 1934; Sandy Duncan, 1946; Peter Strauss, 1947; Jennifer O'Neill, 1949; Edward Albert, 1951; Charles Barkley, 1963

NEW WORD—

yegg - noun: a thug; a petty burglar

QUIZ—

Here's a double extra super killer trivia question for you just to shake the cobwebs off your cranium:

What's Donald Duck's middle name?

TRIVIA

Mickey Mouse's nephews are Morty and Ferdy. . . . The original voice of Mickey Mouse was Walt Disney. . . . Mussolini's favorite cartoon character was Donald Duck.

HISTORY—

On this date in 1962 Lt. Colonel John Glenn became the first American in orbit as he circled the earth three times in Friendship 7.

GRAFFITI

**An optimist invented the boat;
a pessimist invented the life preserver.**

Quiz Answer: Fauntleroy

FEBRUARY

TODAY'S THOUGHT:
"If a man watches three football games in a row, he should be declared legally dead." —Erma Bombeck

BIRTHDAYS—
W. H. Auden, 1907; Sam Peckinpah, 1925; Erma Bombeck, 1927; Hubert de Givenchy, 1927; Barbara Jordan, 1936; Tricia Nixon, 1946; Tyne Daly, 1947; Christopher Atkins, 1961

NEW WORD—
susurrus - adjective: full of whispering or rustling sounds

QUIZ—
What "first" do baseball luminaries Babe Ruth, Sparky Anderson and Tom Seaver share?

TRIVIA
All llamas have bad breath — probably from yakking too much! . . . A dog's nose print is as individual as a person's fingerprint. . . . A squirrel's nest is a drey; home sweet home to a badger is a sett; and a rabbit lives in a warren.

HISTORY—
On this date in 1855 Lucy Hobbs became the first female to graduate from dental school in Cincinnati, Ohio. But since "Women's Lib" was more than a hundred years off, building a practice for Lucy was like pulling teeth . . .
In 1925 the first issue of "New Yorker" magazine was published.

GRAFFITI
An expert is a real knowbody.

Quiz Answer: The same first name — George

F E B R U A R Y

TODAY'S THOUGHT:
"Frankly, I don't mind not being president. I just mind that someone else is." —Edward M. Kennedy

BIRTHDAYS—
George Washington, 1732; Frederic Chopin, 1810; Sheldon Leonard, 1907; Robert Young, 1907; John Mills, 1908; Senator Edward Kennedy, 1932; Julius Erving, 1950

NEW WORD—
nugatory - adjective: worthless; insignificant, not of real value

QUIZ—
Who was the originator of the military decoration known as "The Purple Heart"?

TRIVIA
George Washington gave New York the nickname the "Empire State". . . . The only state in the United States to be named after a president is Washington. . . . A check of today's birthday list shows that Ted Kennedy was born exactly 200 years after George Washington.

HISTORY—
On this date in 1879 Franklin W. Woolworth opened his first five-and-ten cent store in Utica, New York.
In 1889 four more stars were added to the flag as North and South Dakota, Montana and Washington became states.

GRAFFITI
**Washington was no fisherman;
he couldn't tell a lie.**

Quiz Answer: It was originated by none other than George Washington. Since he often soaked his false teeth in wine, he created a special decoration for the army dentists who gave him that advice: the purple tooth.

F E B R U A R Y

TODAY'S THOUGHT:
"Many a man owes his success to his first wife and his second to his success." —Jim Backus

BIRTHDAYS—
W.E.B. DuBois, 1868; Jim Backus, 1913; Elston Howard, 1929; Peter Fonda, 1939; Edward "Too Tall" Jones, 1951; Bobby Bonilla, 1963; Jason Keller, 1971; Shane Keller, 1971

NEW WORD—
irenic - adjective: peacefully calm

QUIZ—
What is the only number spelled with the exact number of letters it stands for?

TRIVIA
Instead of letters, the Chinese have a different character for every single word. . . . "Bharat" is the official name of India. . . . Iran was formerly known as Persia. Before that, it was known as Iran.

HISTORY—
On this date the United States won one and lost one . . .In 1836 the siege of the Alamo began.
In 1945 the U.S. flag was raised on Mt. Surabachi on Iwo Jima.

GRAFFITI
Tomorrow has been cancelled due to lack of interest.

Quiz Answer: Four

F E B R U A R Y

TODAY'S THOUGHT:
"Interest your kids in bowling. Get them off the streets and into the alleys."
—Don Rickles

OBSERVANCES/EVENTS—
It's Gregorian Calendar Day, commemorating the 1582 papal bull that corrected the old Julian calendar which by then was 10 days off.

BIRTHDAYS—
Winslow Homer, 1836; Honus Wagner, 1874; Chester Nimitz, 1885; "Ma Kettle" Majorie Main, 1890; Abe Vigoda, 1921; James Farentino, 1938; Barry Bostwick, 1945; Edward James Olmos, 1947; Apple co-founder Steven Jobs, 1955; Kienast Quints, 1970

NEW WORD—
katabatic - adjective: moving down a slope or valley

QUIZ—
Which word is mispelled - parallel, embarrass, assassin?

TRIVIA
Hockey superstar Wayne Gretzky and Los Angeles Kings owner Bruce McNall teamed up in 1991 to buy a Honus Wagner baseball card - for $451,000! . . . A hockey rink is up to 200 feet long and 85 feet wide. . . . A puck is one inch thick.

HISTORY—
In 1980 the U.S. Hockey team won the gold medal at the Winter Olympics.

GRAFFITI
**Most people are a lot like coffee . . .
they're either perky or drips.**

Quiz Answer: You didn't fall for this, did you? "Mispelled" was misspelled.

FEBRUARY

TODAY'S THOUGHT:
"As far as I'm concerned, there won't be a Beatles reunion as long as John Lennon remains dead." —George Harrison

BIRTHDAYS—
Buffalo Bill Cody, 1846; Enrico Caruso, 1873; Zeppo Marx, 1901; Adelle Davis, 1905; Jim Backus, 1913; Tom Courtenay, 1937; George Harrison, 1943; Sally Jessy Raphael, 1943; Karen Grassle, 1944

NEW WORD—
magniloquent - adjective: boastfully pompous

QUIZ—
Which of the following statements is false?
    A: Ships travel faster in cold water than warm.
    B: Attila the Hun dropped dead on his wedding night.
    C: The Oscar winning sci-fi film "Forbidden Planet" was based on a Shakespearean play.
    D: None of the above

TRIVIA
Honorificabilitudinitatibus is the longest word in the works of William Shakespeare. . . . Salvador Dali once wrote a script for the Marx Brothers called "The Marx Brothers on Horseback Salad". . . . During her lifetime only seven of Emily Dickinson's poems were published. Approximately 1,770 completed and fragmented poems were found after her death in 1886.

HISTORY—
On this date in 1836 government officials issued the patent for the Colt revolver.

GRAFFITI
A waist is a terrible thing to mind.

Quiz Answer: D - Believe it or not, they are all true. By the way, the Shakespearean play was "The Tempest".

F E B R U A R Y

TODAY'S THOUGHT:
"Thin people are beautiful but fat people are adorable." —Jackie Gleason

BIRTHDAYS—
Victor Hugo, 1802; Buffalo Bill Cody, 1846; John Harvey Kellogg, 1852; Jackie Gleason, 1916; Tony Randall, 1920; Fats Domino, 1928; Johnny Cash, 1932; Godfrey Cambridge, 1933

NEW WORD—
pellucid - adjective: translucent; able to be seen through

QUIZ—
In Britain the game is called "draughts". What is it called in the U.S.A.?

TRIVIA
"Jack" is the most common name in nursery rhymes. . . . The only one of the seven dwarfs who's beardless is Dopey. . . . Employees at Disney World are not allowed to wear mustaches.

HISTORY—
On this date in 1881 the S.S. Ceylon sailed from Liverpool, England on the very first around-the-world cruise.
In 1951 James Jones' novel "From Here to Eternity" was published in New York.
On this same day the 22nd amendment to the U.S. Constitution was ratified. It stipulated that no person can be elected to the presidency for more than two terms.

GRAFFITI
Communicate with a fish - drop him a line.

Quiz Answer: Checkers

FEBRUARY

TODAY'S THOUGHT:
"Success is a great deodorant. It takes away all your past smells."
—Elizabeth Taylor

BIRTHDAYS—
Henry Wadsworth Longfellow, 1807; John Steinbeck, 1902; Joanne Woodward, 1930; Elizabeth Taylor, 1932; consumer crusader Ralph Nader, 1934; Howard Hesseman, 1940; Mary Frann, 1943; physicist Alan Guth, 1947

NEW WORD—
farrago - noun: mixture; jumbled; hodge-podge

QUIZ—
What was the original purpose of cuffs on men's trousers?

TRIVIA
Although their business has often gone on the rocks, Justerini and Brooks continue to make a famous product - J & B Scotch. . . . The Oscars are manufactured by the Dodger Trophy Company. . . . The world's largest manufacturer of feminine apparel is Mattel, the toymaker. The company sells about twenty million Barbie doll costumes annually.

HISTORY—
On this date in 1883 Oscar Hammerstein obtained a patent for the first cigar rolling machine. By the way, it was Oscar Hammerstein II who rolled out the lyrics for Richard Rodger's music.

GRAFFITI
Smoking is the leading cause of statistics.

Quiz Answer: They were originally added to catch cigar ashes.

FEBRUARY

TODAY'S THOUGHT:
"I don't jog. It makes the ice jump right out of my glass." —Martin Mull

BIRTHDAYS—
Linus Pauling, 1901; Jimmy Dorsey, 1904; Vincente Minnelli, 1913; Zero Mostel, 1915; Charles Durning, 1923; Gavin MacLeod, 1930; Tommy Tune, 1939; Mario Andretti, 1940; Bernadette Peters, 1944; Charles "Bubba" Smith, 1945; Cristina Raines, 1952

NEW WORD—
contumacious - adjective: stubbornly rebellious

QUIZ—
What does M*A*S*H stand for?

TRIVIA
Prop glass in the movies is made out of boiled sugar water and corn syrup, the same as many lollipops. . . . Jack Nicholson single-handedly rescued five drowning people from the New Jersey surf back in the fifties. . . . The first drive-in theater was opened in 1932 in Camden, New Jersey.

HISTORY—
On this date in 1983 Hawkeye Pierce, B.J. Hunnicut and the rest of the 4077 struck their tents and hit the road in the final episode of "M*A*S*H". It registered one of the highest ratings ever as 77 out of 100 people watching TV at the time tuned in.

GRAFFITI
On Wall Street every bull has a bear behind.

Quiz Answer: Mobile Army Surgical Hospital

FEBRUARY

TODAY'S THOUGHT:
"Be yourself is the worst advice you can possibly give some people."
—Tom Masson

OBSERVANCES/EVENTS—
Everybody gets an extra day to scrounge up their rent or mortgage.

BIRTHDAYS—
Louis Montcalm, 1712; Ann Lee, 1736; Navy commander French Chadwick, 1844; Jimmy Dorsey, 1904

NEW WORD—
scrutator - noun: one who investigates

QUIZ—
True or False?
There is a town called Leap, Oregon which was named in a leap year.

TRIVIA
Superman was born on February 29. . . . Heavyweight boxing champ Jack Dempsey bought a Rolls-Royce after each successful title fight - six in all. . . . The game "Simon Says" was first called "Do This, Do That" but was renamed after a social director popularized it in New York's Catskill Mountains.

HISTORY—
On this date in 1904, the very first February 29th of the century, President Theodore Roosevelt appointed the Panama Canal Commission.
In 1944 General Douglas MacArthur led the attack on the Admiralty Isles.

GRAFFITI
Wars don't decide who's right, only who's left.

Quiz Answer: True

M A R C H

TODAY'S THOUGHT:
"Never eat more than you can lift." —Miss Piggy

OBSERVANCES/EVENTS—
It is National Pig Day, a day to salute our friends, the pigs. So take a pig to lunch; just don't *have* a pig for lunch!

BIRTHDAYS—
Glenn Miller, 1904; Dinah Shore, 1917; Harry Caray, 1919; astronaut Deke Slayton, 1924; Harry Belafonte, 1927; Sonny James, 1929; Robert Conrad, 1935; Dirk Benedict, 1944; Alan Thicke, 1947; Catherine Bach, 1954; Ron Howard, 1954

NEW WORD—
younker - noun: a young gentleman

QUIZ—
On the TV show "Green Acres", why did they replace Arnold the Pig?

TRIVIA
Austria was the first country to send postcards. . . . In India playing cards are round. . . . All of Israel's cattle have been issued their own identity cards. Apparently it's an attempt to *beef* up security.

HISTORY—
On this date in 1872 Yellowstone became our first national park. In 1961 John F. Kennedy established the Peace Corps.

GRAFFITI
Do pigs go through a mud-life crisis?

Quiz Answer: Arnold, the second or third hammiest actor on "Green Acres", was secretly switched when he became too fat!

MARCH

TODAY'S THOUGHT:
"Nothing in life is 'fun for the whole family'." —Jerry Seinfeld

OBSERVANCES/EVENTS—
It's day 2 of National Noodle Month. Just thought you'd like to know . . .

BIRTHDAYS—
Sam Houston, 1793; Dr. Seuss, 1904; Desi Arnaz, 1917; Mikhail Gorbachev, 1931; Tom Wolfe, 1931; John Irving, 1942; Eddie Money, 1949; Laraine Neumann, 1952; Jon Bon Jovi, 1962

NEW WORD—
autochthon - noun: an original inhabitant

QUIZ—
Bathroom Brain Teaser:
John Smith was eight years old on his first birthday. How is that?

TRIVIA
Abel and Baker were the chimpanzees sent into space on May 28, 1959, becoming the first primates to return to Earth. . . . A rockoon is a rocket and balloon hybrid used by weathermen to launch measuring instruments sixty miles high. . . . The Association of Space Explorers is an exclusive 150 member club of space travelers from eighteen countries who have made at least one orbit around the earth. If you think you qualify, you can write to them at 35 White Street, San Francisco, CA 94109.

HISTORY—
On this date in 1836 Texas declared its independence from Mexico.

GRAFFITI
All the world's a stage and most of us are bit part players.

Quiz Answer: He was born on February 29, 1896. The year 1900 was not a leap year (only centuries divisible by 400 are leap years) so Smith's first birthday was in 1904.

MARCH

TODAY'S THOUGHT:
"Television is more interesting than people. If it were not, we should have people standing in the corners of our rooms." —Alan Coren

OBSERVANCES/EVENTS—
It's National Anthem Day, honoring "The Star-Spangled Banner".

BIRTHDAYS—
Alexander Graham Bell, 1847; Ring Lardner, 1885; Jean Harlow, 1911; Julius Boros, 1920; Princess Radziwill, 1933; Jackie Joyner-Kersee, 1962; Herschel Walker, 1962

NEW WORD—
oniomania - noun: an uncontrollable urge to buy things

QUIZ—
On the sitcom "Cheers", when was "Mayday" Malone Rookie of the Year?

TRIVIA
Alexander Graham Bell refused to keep a phone in his study because the ringing distracted him. . . . Don Ameche was so renowned for his portrayal of Alexander Graham Bell that "ameche" became a slang word for the telephone. . . . Giraffes make it necessary for the telephone poles in Kenya and Uganda to be much higher than those to which we are accustomed.

HISTORY—
On this date in 1634 the first tavern in Boston opened its doors and its taps . . . a guy in a tri-cornered hat named Norm claimed the corner stool. In 1931 the "Star-Spangled Banner", originally called "The Defense of Fort McHenry", by Francis Scott Key was officially proclaimed the national anthem of the United States.

GRAFFITI
Square bathtubs don't have rings.

Quiz Answer: Of course only a true connoisseur would know that Sam was Rookie of the Year in 1972.

M A R C H

TODAY'S THOUGHT:
"Diplomacy is the art of saying 'Nice doggie' until you can find a rock."
—Will Rogers

OBSERVATIONS/EVENTS—
It is old Inauguration Day. Presidential terms began and ended on March 4 until 1933.

BIRTHDAYS—
Prince Henry, 1394; Antonio Vivaldi, 1678; Casimir Pulaski, 1748; Knute Rockne, 1888; John Garfield, 1913; Paula Prentiss, 1939; Catherine O'Hara, 1954; Kevin Maurice Johnson, 1966; Chastity Bono, 1969

NEW WORD—
firkin - noun: small, wooden tub to hold butter

QUIZ—
Which of the following is not an actual law that was or is on the books somewhere in this country?
- A: In Pennsylvania, if a horse is afraid of passing your car, you have to dismantle it and hide it in the bushes until he passes.
- B: In Gold Beach, Oregon, dogs called in public must be addressed by "Mister" or "Miss".
- C: In California, it is against the law to shoot at game from a moving automobile unless it is a whale.

TRIVIA
A Virginia law requires all bathtubs be kept in the yard and not in the house. . . . Washington, D.C. has the highest ratio of lawyers per resident: 1 for every 19 people. . . . It's against the law for a woman to dress as Santa in Minnesota.

HISTORY—
On this date in 1952 Ronald Reagan married Nancy Davis.

GRAFFITI
There is one law we don't have to enforce - the law of gravity.

Quiz Answer: B — But now that we've suggested it. . .

M A R C H

TODAY'S THOUGHT:

"I like a woman with a head on her shoulders. I hate necks."

—Steve Martin

BIRTHDAYS—

Rex Harrison, 1908; Jack Cassidy, 1927; Dean Stockwell, 1936; Samantha Eggar, 1939; Eddie Hodges, 1947; Eugene Fodor, 1950

NEW WORD—

pandiculation - noun: the act of stretching

QUIZ—

Who was Sherlock Holmes named after? Actually, it's elementary, my dear Watson . . .

TRIVIA

In the writings of Arthur Conan Doyle, at no time did Sherlock Holmes utter the phrase, "Elementary, my dear Watson" . . . . There are no photographs which show Abraham Lincoln smiling. . . . There is no word in the English language which rhymes with purple.

HISTORY—

On this date in 1953 Soviet premier Joseph Stalin died in Moscow. His funeral was one of the largest affairs in Russian history.

GRAFFITI

Old postmen never die. They just lose their zip.

Quiz Answer: Sir Arthur Conan Doyle borrowed the name of his favorite American poet, Oliver Wendell Holmes.

MARCH

TODAY'S THOUGHT:
"The trouble with children is that they are not returnable."
—Quentin Crisp

BIRTHDAYS—
Michelangelo, 1475; Cyrano de Bergerac, 1619; Lou Costello, 1908; Ed McMahon, 1923; astronaut L. Gordon Cooper, 1927; Marion Berry, 1936; Valentina Tereshkova, 1937; Rob Reiner, 1945; Andrea Elson, 1969

NEW WORD—
battology - noun: wearisome repetition of words in writing or speaking

QUIZ—
What was the largest volcanic eruption in recorded history?

TRIVIA
A bolt of lightning can be miles long and only inches wide. . . . If you count the seconds between seeing the lightning and hearing the thunder, you can tell how far away the storm is. Every five seconds equals approximately one mile. . . . During a single storm, the Empire State Building may be struck by lightning twenty times.

HISTORY—
On this date in 1836 Davy Crockett and Jim Bowie were killed as the Alamo fell to the Mexicans.
In 1930 Clarence Birdseye put the first individually packaged frozen foods on sale — mothers throughout the country rejoiced.

GRAFFITI
Sunbathers have a constitutional right to bare arms.

Quiz Answer: If you said Mt. St. Helens, you aren't even close. That was a comparative firecracker compared to the eruption of Mt. Tambora which blew 220 million tons of dust and ash into the stratosphere in 1815, causing the "year without a summer".

M A R C H

TODAY'S THOUGHT:
"A nickel ain't worth a dime anymore." —Yogi Berra

BIRTHDAYS—
Luther Burbank, 1849; Maurice Ravel, 1875; Anthony Armstrong-Jones, 1930; Daniel J. Travanti, 1940; Michael Eisner, 1942; Franco Harris, 1950; Joe Carter, 1960

NEW WORD—
uliginous - adjective: growing in muddy places or swamps

QUIZ—
Bathroom Brain Teaser:
Suppose that 14% of the people in Detroit, Michigan have unlisted telephone numbers. Now suppose you randomly pick two hundred names from the phone book for that city. Assuming that the 14% figure holds true, how many of those names you've selected will have unlisted numbers?

TRIVIA
Little Lulu's last name was Moppet. . . . "Guess who?" were the first words spoken by Woody Woodpecker and later became his trademark. . . . Popeye's sailing vessel was named Olive after his girlfriend, Olive Oyl.

HISTORY—
On this date in 1876 Alexander Graham Bell patented the telephone. In 1897 the first bowl of corn flakes was served by Dr. John Kellogg to one of his patients at a mental hospital in Battle Creek, Michigan.

GRAFFITI
Health food is sickening.

Quiz Answer: None will be unlisted.

MARCH

TODAY'S THOUGHT:
"Being a living legend is better than being a dead legend."
—George Burns

OBSERVANCES/EVENTS—
Celebrate International Woman's Day in the United States as well as Finland, Russia and the People's Republic of China.

BIRTHDAYS—
Oliver Wendell Holmes, 1841; Sam Jaffee, 1891; Tula Finklea (Cyd Charisse), 1923; Charley Pride, 1938; Lynn Redgrave, 1943; Monkee Mickey Dolenz, 1945

NEW WORD—
mussitate - verb: to mutter; to mumble; to talk under your breath

QUIZ—
Time for a little Monkee business: What TV show did Mickey Dolenz star in before he joined up with Peter, Mike and Davy?

TRIVIA
Caroline Kennedy owned a horse which she rode on the White House grounds. Its name was Macaroni. . . . Eleven dogs played "Lassie" in the movie and TV series. Only one was female. . . . The only animal to be awarded both the Purple Heart and Silver Star during World War II was Chips, a K-9 dog.

HISTORY—
On this date in 1894 bureaucracy caught up to man's best friend as New York City passed its first dog licensing law.

GRAFFITI
A dog is the only friend you can buy for money.

Quiz Answer: As a child actor working under the name of Mickey Braddock, he starred in "Circus Boy".

M A R C H

TODAY'S THOUGHT:

"An economic downturn is when they don't have money. A recession is when you don't have money and a depression is when I don't have money." —Sanford Mims

BIRTHDAYS—

Amerigo Vespucci, 1451; Frank Morrison (Mickey Spillane), 1918; Yuri Gagarin, 1934; Marty Ingels, 1936; Bobby Fischer, 1943; Brian Bosworth, 1965; "Webster" Emmanuel Lewis, 1971

NEW WORD—

inspissate - verb: to thicken, especially a liquid, by evaporation

QUIZ-

What is the average life expectancy of a one dollar bill?
- A: 2 years
- B: 9 months
- C: 5 years
- D: 1½ years

TRIVIA

U.S. Patent Office records show that Thomas Jefferson invented the first hideaway bed. . . . The name James Ritty should ring a bell — he invented the cash register in 1884. . . . Nathan Ames invented the escalator in 1859.

HISTORY—

On this date in 1822 the first U.S. patent for artificial teeth was issued to Charles Graham of New York City. (No doubt the only guy who ever wanted to be an "in-denture-d servant"!)

GRAFFITI
An inventor is a crackpot who becomes a genius when his ideas catch on.

Quiz Answer: D — Not only doesn't a dollar go as far as it used to, it doesn't *last* as long as it used to.

M A R C H

TODAY'S THOUGHT:
"Sports do not build character. They reveal it." —Heywood Broun

BIRTHDAYS—
Barry Fitzgerald, 1888; Heywood Hale Broun, 1918; Pamela Mason, 1922; Chuck Norris, 1940; Austin Carr, 1948; Prince Edward, 1964

NEW WORD—
dactylogram - noun: a fingerprint

QUIZ—
What do the following celebrities have in common: Mel Allen, Hoagy Carmichael, John Cleese, Howard Cosell, Julio Iglesias, Ozzie Nelson and Geraldo Rivera?

TRIVIA
"You dirty rat" is a line attributed to James Cagney, but never used by him in any movie. . . . Roy Rogers is the only person ever elected to the Country Music Hall of Fame twice. . . . Rocky Lane, a cowboy film actor, was the voice of that talking horse, Mr. Ed.

HISTORY—
On this date in 1862 the first paper currency in the U.S. was issued - a $5 Hamilton, $10 Lincoln and $20 Liberty certificate.
In 1876 Alexander Graham Bell transmitted the very first telephone call to his assistant, Mr. Watson.

GRAFFITI
Lawyers wear legal briefs.

Quiz Answer: At one time, they were all lawyers but early in their careers decided to go straight.

M A R C H

TODAY'S THOUGHT:

"Is sloppiness in speech caused by ignorance or apathy? I don't know and I don't care." —William Safire

OBSERVANCES/EVENTS—

Today is Johnny Appleseed Day. On this date in 1847 John Chapman, famed as a planter of trees and an early environmentalist, went to the Big Apple in the Sky.

BIRTHDAYS—

Dorothy Gish, 1898; Lawrence Welk, 1903; Harold Wilson, 1916; Ralph Abernathy, 1926; Rupert Murdoch, 1931; Sam Donaldson, 1934; Dock Phillip Ellis, 1945; Bobby McFerrin, 1950

NEW WORD—

galimatias - noun: gibberish

QUIZ—

What hugely popular book took ten years to write and was the only one ever completed by its author?

TRIVIA

"Calcutta" was Lawrence Welk's only number one hit record, topping the charts in 1961. . . . "The Lawrence Welk Show" was originally called "The Dodge Dancing Party". . . . The total footage of film shot for "Gone With the Wind" was 449,512 feet or about 85 miles.

HISTORY—

On this date in 1888 the "Blizzard of '88" struck the northeast and became the greatest storm of the century.

GRAFFITI
Success is relative. The more success, the more relatives.

Quiz Answer: "Gone With the Wind" was the famous novel by Margaret Mitchell. Titles for this famous work included "Bah! Bah! Black Sheep", "Not In Our Stars" and "Bugles Sang True".

M A R C H

TODAY'S THOUGHT:

"A gold rush is what happens when a line of chorus girls spot a man with a bank roll." —Mae West

BIRTHDAYS—

Gordon MacRae, 1921; Wally Schirra, 1923; Edward Albee, 1928; Andrew Young, 1932; Agent 99 Barbara Feldon, 1941; Liza Minelli, 1946; James Taylor, 1948; Darryl Strawberry, 1962

NEW WORD—

saponaceous - adjective: soapy

QUIZ—

Au H_2O was a popular bumper sticker for which 1960's U.S. presidential candidate?

TRIVIA

The strawberry is a member of the rose family. . . . The only fruit to have its seeds on the outside is the strawberry. . . . The biggest strawberry on record was found in Folkestone, Great Britain in 1983 and tipped the scales at 8.17 ounces.

HISTORY—

On this date in 1850 the U.S. issued its first $20 gold piece.
In 1912 Juliet Low earned some big time brownie points as she organized the first Girl Scout troop in Savannah, Georgia.
In 1933 FDR gave his first fireside chat on the radio.

GRAFFITI
If money talks, then why is silence golden?

Quiz Answer: Barry Goldwater (Au is the chemical symbol for gold and H_2O is, of course, water.)

M A R C H

TODAY'S THOUGHT:
"My wife and I were happy for twenty years. Then we met."
—Rodney Dangerfield

OBSERVANCES/EVENTS—
It is Plant a Flower Day, a day to help offset all those other special days that result in flowers being picked.

BIRTHDAYS—
Astronomer Percival Lowell, 1855; publisher Walter Annenberg, 1908; Sammy Kaye, 1910; L. Ron Hubbard, 1911; Neil Sedaka, 1939; Deborah Raffin, 1953

NEW WORD—
napiform - adjective: shaped like a turnip

QUIZ—
How many calories does one Hershey's Kisses chocolate contain?

TRIVIA
English muffins were first made in America. . . . Venetian blinds were invented by the Chinese. . . . The Belgians were the first to make French fries.

HISTORY—
On this date in 1852 "Uncle Sam" was born in an editorial cartoon in the New York "Lantern". The character was based on an officer from the War of 1812, Sam Wilson.
Hear ye! Hear ye! In 1887 Chester Greenwood was issued a patent for earmuffs.

GRAFFITI
Gore is Clinton's vice.

Quiz Answer: 25 calories

MARCH

TODAY'S THOUGHT:
"If I had my life to live over again, I'd be a plumber." —Albert Einstein

OBSERVANCES/EVENTS—
Moth-er Day is celebrated today in museums and libraries with moth collections.

BIRTHDAYS—
Casey Jones, 1864; Albert Einstein, 1879; Hank Ketchum, 1920; Michael Caine, 1933; Quincy Jones, 1933; Billy Crystal, 1947; Prince Albert of Monaco, 1958

NEW WORD—
ulotrichichous - adjective: having short curly or wooly hair

QUIZ—
What is comedian Albert Brooks' real name?

TRIVIA
Sources say that Albert Einstein never wore socks. . . . Einstein was offered the presidency of Israel in 1952 but turned it down. . . . In his last will, after disposition of an estate of $65,000, Einstein left his manuscripts to Hebrew University and his violin to his grandson.

HISTORY—
On this date in 1923 Warren G. Harding became the first president to file an income tax.

GRAFFITI
The Upper Crust has a lot of Crumbs.

Quiz Answer: He was born Albert Einstein. His brother is Bob Einstein, Officer Judy of the old "Smothers Brothers' Comedy Hour", who nowadays wears a crash helmet as Super Dave Osborne. Brooks' father, Harry, was a famous radio comedian whom old-timers may remember as Parkyakarkas.

M A R C H

TODAY'S THOUGHT:
"One man with courage makes a majority." —Andrew Jackson

OBSERVANCES/EVENTS—
Forget the swallows coming back to Capistrano. Today is Buzzard's Day which marks the return of turkey vultures to Hinckley, Ohio.

BIRTHDAYS—
Andrew Jackson, 1767; Macdonald Carey, 1913; Harry James, 1916; Alan Bean, 1932; Judd Hirsch, 1935; Beach Boy Mike Love, 1941; Sly Stone, 1944; Prince Constantin of Liechtenstein, 1972

NEW WORD—
entelechy - noun: an actuality, as opposed to a potentiality

QUIZ—
What do A.M. and P.M. stand for, anyway?

TRIVIA
The White House was originally grey. It was burned during the War of 1812 and later rebuilt and painted white to cover the smoke stains. . . . Andrew Jackson was a crack shot. He could cut crossed threads at forty yards. . . . There is no documented proof that Betsy Ross designed the United States flag.

HISTORY—
On this date in 44 B.C. Julius Caesar was told to "beware the Ides of March". He must not have kept his ides open as he was assassinated.

GRAFFITI
He who laughs last didn't get the joke.

Quiz Answer: "Ante meridiem", Latin for "before noon" and "post meridiem" for "after noon" - The custom of beginning days at midnight rather than at sunset comes to us from the Romans.

M A R C H

TODAY'S THOUGHT:
"The trouble with the average family is it has too much month left over at the end of the money." —Bill Vaughan

BIRTHDAYS—
James Madison, 1751; Pat Nixon, 1912; Jerry Lewis, 1925; Senator Daniel Patrick Moynihan, 1927; Erik Estrada, 1949; Joan Benoit, 1957

NEW WORD—
limulus - noun: a horseshoe crab

QUIZ—
Which of the following supermarket facts is false?
- A: The average supermarket has weekly receipts of about $206,000.
- B: The final profit works out to about a penny on every dollar.
- C: Features like bakeries and delis lose money and are only there for the customer's convenience.
- D: One supermarket in the south has set aside a tabloid free aisle for customers who don't want to be assailed with tawdry headlines about "Elvis' UFO Diet".

TRIVIA
James Madison was the first president to wear long pants; his predecessors all wore knickers. . . . Pink lemonade was created in 1857 by Pete Conklin who unwittingly used a bucket of water in which a circus performer had soaked his red tights. . . . Out of the 3.9 billion pounds of tomatoes eaten in the United States each year, 20.5 percent were imported.

HISTORY—
On this date in 1802 West Point Military Academy in New York was established by an Act of Congress.

GRAFFITI
Shiftless people don't get into high gear.

Quiz Answer: C is false. Those departments are by far the store's biggest money-makers.

M A R C H

TODAY'S THOUGHT:

"We have always found the Irish a bit odd. They refuse to be English."
—Winston Churchill

OBSERVANCES/EVENTS—

It's Saint Patrick's Day, a fine day for celebrating and the wearin' of the green!

BIRTHDAYS—

Gottlieb Daimler, 1834; Mercedes McCanbridge, 1918; Nat King Cole, 1919; John Sebastian, 1944; Patrick Duffy, 1949; Kurt Russell, 1951; Lesley Ann Down, 1954; Rob Lowe, 1964

NEW WORD—

coruscate - verb: to sparkle; scintillate; gleam

QUIZ—

What do Groucho Marx, Tony Bennett, Mel Brooks, Rudy Vallee and Joan Crawford have in common?

TRIVIA

The only two words in the English language that have all the vowels in their proper order are abstemiously and facetiously. . . . Speaking involves 72 muscles. . . . All Japanese words end in vowels or the letter "n".

HISTORY—

On this date in 1845 the rubber band was invented.

GRAFFITI
Ireland is Brogues' Gallery.

Quiz Answer: They were the guest lineup the night Johnny Carson took over the "Tonight Show" on October 1, 1962.

M A R C H

TODAY'S THOUGHT:
"I told my mother-in-law that my house was her house, and she said, 'Get the hell off my property.'" —Joan Rivers

BIRTHDAYS—
Grover Cleveland, 1837; Edward Everett Horton, 1887; Irving Wallace, 1916; George Plimpton, 1927; John Updike, 1932; Peter Graves, 1936; Wilson Pickett, 1941; Vanessa Williams, 1963

NEW WORD—
rugose - adjective: wrinkled; ridged

QUIZ—
From which show in the late sixties was "Happy Days" a spinoff?

TRIVIA—
The most common name for a town in the United States is Fairview. . . . When asked to name a color, the most common answer is "red". . . . The most common last name initial in the United States is "S".

HISTORY—
On this date in 1931 the electric razor was first marketed by Schick.

GRAFFITI
Never repeat yourself. Never.

Quiz Answer: "Happy Days" began as a segment on the lighthearted romance anthology "Love, American Style" and then spun off "Laverne and Shirley", "Mork and Mindy" and "Joanie Loves Chachie".

M A R C H

TODAY'S THOUGHT:
"I hate women because they always know where things are."
—James Thurber

OBSERVANCES/EVENTS—
Celebrate St. Joseph's Day when the swallows traditionally return to Capistrano.

BIRTHDAYS—
William Jennings Bryan, 1860; Earl Warren, 1891; Irving Wallace, 1916; Patrick McGoohan, 1928; Ursula Andress, 1936; Glenn Close, 1947; Bruce Willis, 1955

NEW WORD—
jactitation - noun: a false boast that causes injury to another

QUIZ—
The last name is Buonarroti. What's the first name?

  A: Madonna   C: (Tiny) Tim
  B: Michelangelo   D: Favio

TRIVIA
The only mammal that can fly is the bat. . . . Roadrunners are a member of the cuckoo family. . . . A duck has three eyelids. That way he can open it just a quack!

HISTORY—
On this date in 1931 we bet you didn't know that Nevada legalized gambling.
In 1977 the final episode of "The Mary Tyler Moore Show" aired.

GRAFFITI
A bird in hand can be an awful mess.

Quiz Answer: B

MARCH

TODAY'S THOUGHT:
"The reason lightning doesn't strike twice in the same place is that the same place isn't there the second time." —Willie Tyler

BIRTHDAYS—
Henrik Ibsen, 1828; Carl Reiner, 1922; Mr. Fred Rogers, 1928; Hal Linden, 1931; Jerry Reed, 1937; Pat Riley, 1945; Bobby Orr, 1948; William Hurt, 1950; Holly Hunter, 1958

NEW WORD—
izzat - noun: personal dignity or honor

QUIZ—
Who am I? I'm a bird that can't fly. I'm eight feet tall. I live and work and play in New York City. My street address is 123½. And, although I am ageless, today is my birthday.

TRIVIA
The first newspaper crossword puzzle, by Arthur Wynne, appeared in the "New York World" on December 21, 1913. . . . The first supermarket was established in 1916 when Clarence Saunders set up shop with the Piggley Wiggley self-service food mart in Memphis, Tennessee. . . . The first chartered railroad in the United States was the Granite Railway which made its initial run from Quincy, Massachusetts to the Neponset River (a distance of three miles) on October 7, 1826.

HISTORY—
On this date in 1859 "Uncle Tom's Cabin", by Harriet Beecher Stowe, was published.

GRAFFITI
An apiary is a bee flat.

Quiz Answer: Big Bird from "Sesame Street"

M A R C H

TODAY'S THOUGHT:
"A lawyer is a gentleman who rescues your estate from your enemies and keeps it for himself." —Lord Brougham

OBSERVANCES/EVENTS—
The United Nations celebrates International Day for the Elimination of Racial Discrimination.

BIRTHDAYS—
Johann Sebastian Bach, 1685; Florenz Ziegfeld, 1869; John D. Rockefeller III, 1906; Cesar Chavez, 1927; James Coco, 1929; Timothy Dalton, 1946; Matthew Broderick, 1962

NEW WORD—
pozzolana - noun: porous volcanic ash used to make hydraulic cement

QUIZ—
Bathroom Brain Teaser:
The man married the little boy's mother, but was not his father (in any step of the way). Who was he?

TRIVIA
When your foot falls asleep, it is called taresthesia. . . . Smell is the first of the five senses to develop. . . . Borborygmus is the technical term for a growling stomach.

HISTORY—
On this date in 1891 a Hatfield and a McCoy were married, ending a lengthy West Virginia feud. Watch for them on the next episode of "Family Feud"!

GRAFFITI
In two days, tomorrow will be yesterday.

Quiz Answer: The clergyman

MARCH

TODAY'S THOUGHT:
"You don't want no pie in the sky when you die,
You want something here on the ground while you're still around."
—Muhammad Ali

BIRTHDAYS—
Chico Marx, 1891; Karl Malden, 1913; Marcel Marceau, 1923; Stephen Sondheim, 1930; William Shatner, 1931; May Britt, 1936; Andrew Lloyd Webber, 1948; Robert Quinlan (Bob Costas), 1952

NEW WORD—
impignorate - verb: to pledge; to mortgage

QUIZ—
When is the birthday of "Star Trek's" Captain James T. Kirk?

TRIVIA
Gene Conley is the only athlete to play on world championship teams in both major league baseball and in pro basketball. . . . Transsexual Renee Richards (nee Richard Raskind) is the only tennis player to compete in both the men's and women's singles at the U.S. Open. . . . Tom Brown was the only person to ever play in both the Super Bowl and a major league baseball game.

HISTORY—
On this date in 1733 Joseph Priestley was credited with the invention of carbonated water.
In 1967 Muhammad Ali was stripped of his heavyweight title by the World Boxing Association for refusing military induction.

GRAFFITI
He was a colorful fighter - black and blue all over.

Quiz Answer: You just missed it - March 21st. Wait! Before running out to pick up a belated birthday card, cool your jets. The future captain of the USS Enterprise won't be born until the year 2228. Riverside, Iowa claims to be his future birthplace.

M A R C H

TODAY'S THOUGHT:
"Health nuts are going to feel stupid someday, lying in hospitals dying of nothing." —Redd Foxx

OBSERVANCES/EVENTS—
It is Near Miss Day. In 1989 an asteroid passed within a half million miles of Earth, a very near miss by cosmic standards. NASA estimated that had it collided with the planet, it would have released the energy of 40,000 bombs.

BIRTHDAYS—
Joan Crawford, 1908; Roger Bannister, 1929; Yvette Marie Stevens (Chaka Khan), 1953; Moses Malone, 1954; Teresa Ganzel, 1957

NEW WORD—
botryoidal - adjective: having the form of a bunch of grapes

QUIZ—
What is the abbreviation "Mrs." short for?

TRIVIA
"Spats" is short for spatterdashes. . . . The act of snapping your fingers is called "fillip". . . . A philobat is a lover of roller coasters.

HISTORY—
On this date in 1775 Patrick Henry gave his "Give Me Liberty Or Give Me Death" speech. Henry was a happy man . . . eventually he got both.

GRAFFITI
Life is wonderful. Without it you'd be dead.

Quiz Answer: Actually, it's not really an abbreviation at all because it can't be written out as a complete word. Long ago, it was short for mistress, but not anymore.

MARCH

TODAY'S THOUGHT:
"A committee is a group that keeps minutes and loses hours."
—Milton Berle

BIRTHDAYS—
Financier Andrew Mellon, 1855; Harry Houdini, 1874; Fatty Arbuckle, 1887; Norman Fell, 1924; Steve McQueen, 1930; Bob Mackie, 1940

NEW WORD—
hebetude - noun: lethargy; state of being dull

QUIZ—
A check of our birthday list reveals that Harry Houdini was born on this date. The magician made his final disappearing act in strangely coincidental fashion. Do you know the day Houdini died?

TRIVIA
Lewis Carroll wrote "Alice's Adventures in Wonderland" standing up. . . . T.S. Eliot's initials stand for Thomas Stearns. . . . Henry David Thoreau's last words, uttered on May 6, 1862 were "Moose, Indian". Their meaning is unknown.

HISTORY—
On this date in 1958 Elvis got his sideburns chopped and his head shaved as he gave a two year command performance for Uncle Sam.
In 1989 the tanker Exxon Valdez spilled over 11 million gallons of crude oil off the coast of Alaska.

GRAFFITI
Home is where the mortgage is.

Quiz Answer: On Halloween in 1926

M A R C H

TODAY'S THOUGHT:
"Sports is the toy department of human life." —Howard Cosell

OBSERVANCES/EVENTS—
It is Pecan Day, commemorating the anniversary of George Washington's planting of pecan trees at Mount Vernon, several of which are still alive and still nutty after all these years.

BIRTHDAYS—
Arturo Toscanini, 1867; Gutzon Borglum, 1867; David Lean, 1908; Howard Cosell, 1920; Gloria Steinem, 1935; Anita Bryant, 1940; Aretha Franklin, 1942; Paul Michael Glaser, 1943; Reginald Kenneth Dwight (Elton John), 1947

NEW WORD—
thaumaturge - noun: a miracle worker

QUIZ—
What does a pogonophobic fear?

TRIVIA
It was birthday boy, Gutzon Borglum, who created Mount Rushmore in South Dakota. . . . Its rock stars are George Washington, Thomas Jefferson, Theodore Roosevelt and Abraham Lincoln. Their four carved faces, from head to chin, each measure 60 feet. If they were given proportionately-sized bodies, they would be almost 500 feet tall. . . . Mount Rushmore took 14 years to complete.

HISTORY—
On this date in 1954 the NBC peacock got a feather in its cap when RCA began manufacturing color television sets.

GRAFFITI
One of these days is none of these days.

Quiz Answer: A pogonophobic finds beards to be a hair-raising experience.

M A R C H

TODAY'S THOUGHT:
"The trouble with unemployment is that the minute you wake up in the morning you're on the job." —Slappy White

BIRTHDAYS—
Robert Frost, 1874; Al Jolson, 1886; Sterling Hayden, 1916; Leonard Nimoy, 1931; Alan Arkin, 1934; James Caan, 1940; Erica Jong, 1942; Diana Ross, 1944; Vicki Lawrence, 1949; Martin Short, 1950; Marcus Allen, 1960

NEW WORD—
withershins - adverb: in a direction contrary to the normal one

QUIZ—
What is the name of the little man with the top hat and mustache in the game of Monopoly?
- A: Daddy Warbucks
- B: I.M. Rich
- C: Mr. Monopoly
- D: Rich Uncle Pennybags

TRIVIA
Four out of five people who try out a new pen will write their own name. . . . 40 out of 100 Americans eat cereal for breakfast every day. . . . One out of ten people in the U.S. is affected by influenza each year.

HISTORY—
On this date in 1953 Dr. Jonas Salk announced a new vaccine to immunize against polio.

—— GRAFFITI ——
Old gardeners never die - they just spade away.

Quiz Answer: D - Uncle Pennybags must be rich indeed. Parker Brothers has sold well over 100 million Monopoly games since its introduction in 1933.

M A R C H

TODAY'S THOUGHT:

"I've given my memoirs far more thought than any of my marriages. You can't divorce a book." —Gloria Swanson

BIRTHDAYS—

Gloria Swanson, 1899; Sarah Vaughan, 1924; David Janssen, 1930; Cale Yarborough, 1940; Michael York, 1942; Randall Cunningham, 1963

NEW WORD—

snool - noun: a meek submissive person

QUIZ—

What do approximately one million people drink as their beverage of choice at breakfast each day?

TRIVIA

The average person spends five years of their precious time on Earth waiting on lines. . . . There are more telephones than people in Washington, D.C. . . . In his lifetime, the average person will drink 23 glasses of champagne.

HISTORY—

On this date in 1917 the U.S. wrested the Stanley Cup from the Canadians for the first time as the Seattle Metropolitans defeated the Montreal Canadians.

GRAFFITI
Nudists suffer from clothes-trophobia.

Quiz Answer: Coke is it! The company estimates that about $237 million of the Real Thing is guzzled at breakfast every year. The frightening thought is that someone actually pours it over his Sugar Frosted Flakes . . .

MARCH

TODAY'S THOUGHT:
"This would be a better world for children if parents had to eat the spinach." —Groucho Marx

BIRTHDAYS—
Maxim Gorki, 1868; Edmund Muskie, 1914; Pearl Bailey, 1918; Dirk Bogarde, 1921; Freddie Bartholomew, 1924; Zbigniew Brzezinski, 1928; Ken Howard, 1944; Reba McEntire, 1954; Byron Scott, 1961

NEW WORD—
ratoon - noun: a sprout from the root of a plant after it has been cropped

QUIZ—
Relating to careers, what did Helen Hayes have in common with Steve McQueen?

TRIVIA
Spencer Tracy was once given an Academy Award engraved to "Dick Tracy". . . . Ventriloquist Edgar Bergen (and his dummy, Charlie McCarthy) received the only wooden Oscar. . . . The story most often made into a movie is "Cinderella", no less than 58 times.

HISTORY—
On this date in 1979 Three Mile Island, a reactor complex near Harrisburg, Pennsylvania blew its cool and came close to a core meltdown.

GRAFFITI
**An honest politician is like the earth;
both are flattened at the poles.**

Quiz Answer: When Helen Hayes saw the first movie in which she appeared, "The Sin of Madelon Claudet", she was so appalled at her performance that she tried to buy the film back and destroy it. She later won the Best Actress Oscar for her work. Steve McQueen never lived down his appearance in "The Blob" and, when he became a major star, attempted to buy up all the prints and have them destroyed.

M A R C H

TODAY'S THOUGHT:

"There is only one boss. The customer. And he can fire everybody in the company from the chairman on down, simply by spending his money somewhere else." —Sam Walton

BIRTHDAYS—

John Tyler, 1790; Cy Young, 1867; Eugene McCarthy, 1916; Sam Walton, 1918; Eric Idle, 1943; Earl Campbell, 1955

NEW WORD—

macerate - verb: to soften by steeping in a liquid

QUIZ—

What is the most commonly used word in the English language?

TRIVIA

A grasshopper has over 900 different muscles. A human has 792. . . . Bees and wasps are deaf. . . . A pullicologist is an expert of fleas.

HISTORY—

On this date in 1848 an ice jam formed in Lake Erie that was so bad Niagara Falls actually ran dry for a full day.

GRAFFITI
A filing cabinet is a place
where you can lose anything systematically.

Quiz Answer: Of *the* I sing - the most commonly used word is "the".

MARCH

TODAY'S THOUGHT:
"I dream my painting and then I paint my dream." —Vincent Van Gogh

OBSERVANCES/EVENTS—
Since today is Doctor's Day, those who wish to honor physicians should wear a red carnation.

BIRTHDAYS—
Vincent Van Gogh, 1853; Sean O'Casey, 1880; McGeorge Bundy, 1919; Peter Marshall, 1927; Richard Dysart, 1929; John Astin, 1930; Warren Beatty, 1938; Eric Clapton, 1945

NEW WORD—
juglandaceous - adjective: belonging to the walnut family of trees

QUIZ—
When "Rolling Stone" premiered back in 1967, what familiar face graced the cover of the first issue?

TRIVIA
If the coils of the French horn were straightened out, the instrument would be 22 feet long. . . . A clothes designer in New Jersey once designed a jacket with 89 zippers. . . . The White House is the most visited home in the United States. Second is Graceland, the former home of Elvis Presley, in Memphis, Tennessee.

HISTORY—
On this date in 1858 Philadelphian Hyman Lippman patented the first pencil with an attached eraser.
In 1981 John Hinckley shot and wounded President Ronald Reagan in Washington, D.C.

GRAFFITI
A school is a mental institution.

Quiz Answer: Although many famous faces have appeared on the cover of "Rolling Stone", John Lennon's was the first.

M A R C H

TODAY'S THOUGHT:

"We should be grateful for subways. At least they've taken crime off the street." —Will Jordan

BIRTHDAYS—

Rene Descartes, 1596; Franz Joseph Haydn, 1732; Cesar Chavez, 1927; Gordie Howe, 1928; Shirley Jones, 1934; Herb Alpert, 1935; Richard Chamberlain, 1935; Gabe Kaplan, 1946; Al Gore, 1948; Rhea Perlman, 1948

NEW WORD—

farrier - noun: a veterinarian

QUIZ—

This inventor was one of the original founders of "National Geographic". Using the pen name H. A. Largelamb, he also wrote for the magazine. His real name ought to ring a bell. Do you know it?

TRIVIA

Herb Alpert's son is named after the first notes on a musical scale — Dore. . . . Tuesday Weld was born on a Friday. . . . Had he not dropped his last name, entertainer Ray Charles would have been popularly known as Ray Robinson, the same name as famous fighter "Sugar" Ray Robinson, who, had he not changed his name, would have been known as Walker Smith.

HISTORY—

On this date in 1889 the Eiffel Tower opened for business in Paris.

GRAFFITI

He who has sharp tongue soon cuts own throat.

Quiz Answer: Alexander Graham Bell (H. A. Largelamb unscrambled is A. Graham Bell.)

APRIL

TODAY'S THOUGHT:
"The better I get to know men, the more I find myself loving dogs."
—Charles De Gaulle

OBSERVANCES/EVENTS—
Watch out - it's April Fools Day!

BIRTHDAYS—
Wallace Beery, 1886; Hans Conreid, 1915; Debbie Reynolds, 1932; Ali MacGraw, 1939; Rusty Staub, 1944; David Eisenhower, 1947

NEW WORD—
quinquagenarian - noun: one who is between 50 and 60 years old

QUIZ—
Dogs That Do It On The Funny Papers . . . See if you can name the pooches from the following comic strips:
"Peanuts"   "Dennis the Menace"   "Blondie"

TRIVIA
Bugs Bunny weighs 6⅞ pounds. . . . Splinter and Knothead were Woody Woodpecker's niece and nephew. . . . Captain Crunch's sailing vessel is the Guppy.

HISTORY—
On this date in 1889 Mrs. W. A. Cockran of Shelbyville, Indiana perfected the first dishwasher which was marketed in Chicago.

GRAFFITI
If you think today is April Fool's Day, just wait until April 15.

Quiz Answer: In "Peanuts" it is Snoopy; "Dennis the Menace" owns Ruff; and "Blondie" pets Daisy.

A P R I L

TODAY'S THOUGHT:
"Never go to a doctor whose office plants have died." —Erma Bombeck

OBSERVANCES/EVENTS—
April is National Anxiety Month, an observance which for millions culminates annually on April 15.

BIRTHDAYS—
Hans Christian Andersen, 1805; Buddy Ebsen, 1908; Sir Alec Guiness, 1914; Jack Webb, 1920; Leon Russell, 1941; Emmylou Harris, 1948

NEW WORD—
gnamma - noun: a hollow in bare rock in which water collects

QUIZ—
Four U.S. state capitals are named after presidents. How many can you name?

TRIVIA
Fairy tale writer Hans Christian Andersen was dyslexic. Others afflicted by dyslexia include Thomas Edison, Woodrow Wilson, Tom Cruise and Henry Winkler. . . . Three out of four Americans like to doodle. . . . Aesop was believed to have been a dwarf.

HISTORY—
On this date in 1792 Congress established the United States Mint in Philadelphia.
In 1978 "Dallas" rode into prime time and became one of CBS's top guns through the 80's.

GRAFFITI
Horsepower was much safer when only horses had it.

Quiz Answer: Jackson, Mississippi; Jefferson City, Missouri; Lincoln, Nebraska; Madison, Wisconsin

A P R I L

TODAY'S THOUGHT:
"When you become senile, you won't know it." —Bill Cosby

BIRTHDAYS—
Washington Irving, 1783; George Jessel, 1898; Marlon Brando, 1924; Doris Day, 1924; Marsha Mason, 1942; Wayne Newton, 1942; Michael Cassivitis (Tony Orlando), 1944; Eddie Murphy, 1961

NEW WORD—
lunt - noun: a match or a torch

QUIZ—
How is it determined on what date Easter will occur in any given year?

TRIVIA
The official state beverage of Massachusetts is cranberry juice. . . . Jousting is the official state sport of Maryland. . . . Alaska's state flower is the forget-me-not.

HISTORY—
On this date in 1860 the first Pony Express began. It hightailed between Sacramento, California and St. Joseph, Missouri.

GRAFFITI
You can always recognize old rabbits by the gray hares.

Quiz Answer: It is tied to the lunar cycle. Easter is the first Sunday after the first full moon after the vernal equinox.

A P R I L

TODAY'S THOUGHT:
"Man is the only animal, I believe, who pretends he is thinking of other things while he is eating." —Robert Lynd

BIRTHDAYS—
Arthur Murray, 1895; Robert Sherwood, 1896; William Manchester, 1922; Elmer Bernstein, 1922; Kitty Kelley, 1942; Christine Lahti, 1950

NEW WORD—
nidificate - verb: to build a nest

QUIZ—
Everyone knows that February is the shortest month but what is the *second* shortest month?

TRIVIA
People who study such things have reported that they know that birds dream. . . . An ostrich can cover 25 feet in a single stride. . . . Most hummingbirds weigh less than a penny.

HISTORY—
On this date in 1968 Martin Luther King Jr. was assassinated in Memphis, Tennessee by James Earl Ray.

GRAFFITI
**The mind is an amazing thing.
It can be totally empty and still not cave in.**

Quiz Answer: April is the second shortest month. It has only thirty days which puts it in a tie with June, September and November. The tie breaker is the fact that Daylight Savings Time cuts an extra hour out of April.

APRIL

TODAY'S THOUGHT:
"Where lipstick is concerned, the important thing is not the color, but to accept God's final decision on where your lips end." —Jerry Seinfeld

BIRTHDAYS—
Spencer Tracy, 1900; Bette Davis, 1908; Gregory Peck, 1916; Arthur Hailey, 1920; Gale Storm, 1922; Frank Gorshin, 1934; General Colin Powell, 1937; Eric Burdon, 1941; Max Gail, 1943; Judy Resnik, 1949

NEW WORD—
selenotropism - noun: growth or movement in response to moonlight

QUIZ—
Seventies Flashback:
Who was Melvin Dummar and for what did he become briefly famous in the seventies?

TRIVIA
Nero, the fire fiddling Roman Emperor, never wore the same clothes twice. . . . Loaded dice were found in the ruins of Pompeii. . . . In the days of King Henry VIII, knitting was the specialty of men, not women.

HISTORY—
On this date in 1614 John Rolfe and Pocahontas were married in Virginia. In 1972 Howard Hughes, legendary businessman, film maker and recluse, died.

GRAFFITI
Old movies never die . . .
they are just being shown at the late, late show.

Quiz Answer: Dummar was a gas station attendant in Willard, Utah who claimed that Howard Hughes had left his fortune to him.

A P R I L

TODAY'S THOUGHT:
"The scientific theory I like best is that the rings of Saturn are composed entirely of lost airline luggage." —Mark Russell

BIRTHDAYS—
Lowell Thomas, 1892; Merle Haggard, 1937; "Mama" Michelle Phillips, 1944; John "Cliff" Ratzenberger, 1947; Marilu Henner, 1952

NEW WORD—
xenophobe - noun: one who fears strange customs or foreigners

QUIZ—
In the film, "The Natural", what is the name of Robert Redford's team?

TRIVIA
Zip-a-dee-doo-dah: To bankers, ZIP is an acronym for Zero Interest Payment. . . . To psychologists, ZIP is short for Zero Intelligence Potential. . . . To postal workers, ZIP stands for Zone Improvement Plan.

HISTORY—
On this date in 1896 the first modern Olympic Games began in Athens, Greece.
In 1909 Admiral Robert E. Peary reached the North Pole. Although Peary gets credit since he was the leader of the expedition, an assistant named Matthew Henson and two of the Eskimoes in the group were the first to reach the pole. Peary arrived almost an hour later.

GRAFFITI
Never put off until tomorrow what you can put off for good.

Quiz Answer: Redford was a Johnny-come-lately player for the New York Knights.

APRIL

TODAY'S THOUGHT:

"Vote Labor and you build castles in the air. Vote Conservative and you can live in them." —David Frost

BIRTHDAYS—

Walter Winchell, 1879; Percy Faith, 1908; Billie Holliday, 1915; James Garner, 1928; Daniel Ellsberg, 1931; Wayne Rogers, 1933; Francis Ford Coppolla, 1939; David Frost, 1939; Tony Dorsett, 1954

NEW WORD—

embosk - verb: to hide or conceal with greenery or foliage

QUIZ—

What's in a name? Match these first names with the famous folk who originally carried them . . .

1. Bob Hope	A: Leon
2. Bing Crosby	B: Leslie
3. Chuck Berry	C: Harry
4. Jellyroll Morton	D: Ferdinand

TRIVIA

Confederate General Stonewall Jackson's first name was Thomas. . . . There is a club in the United States whose only membership requirement is that your name is Jim Smith. At last count there were 781 members. . . . . Greenland's official language is Danish.

HISTORY—

On this date in 1868 Mormon Church leader Brigham Young married his 27th (and final) wife.

GRAFFITI

The problem with the game of love is they keep rewriting the rule book.

Quiz Answer: 1-B; 2-C; 3-A; and 4-D

A P R I L

TODAY'S THOUGHT:
"A verbal contract isn't worth the paper it's written on."
—Samuel Goldwyn

BIRTHDAYS—
Mary Pickford, 1893; Betty Ford, 1918; Shecky Greene, 1925; John Gavin, 1935; John Havlicek, 1940; Gary Carter, 1954

NEW WORD—
avifauna - noun: the birds of a given region

QUIZ—
Bathroom Brain Teaser:
There are ten black socks and ten white socks in a drawer. If you reach into the drawer in the dark, how many socks must you take out in order to know that you have a matching pair?

TRIVIA
A butterfly flaps its wings about 300 times a minute. . . . A penguin is the only bird that can swim but not fly. . . . The largest flying bird is the albatross.

HISTORY—
On this date in 1974 Hammerin' Hank Aaron of the Atlanta Braves broke Babe Ruth's home run record, hitting his 715th lifetime round tripper in a game against the Los Angeles Dodgers.

GRAFFITI
Spelling bee: a literate insect.

Quiz Answer: Three — All three will be the same color, or two will be one color and the third will be the other color.

APRIL

TODAY'S THOUGHT:
"If three-fourths of the earth's surface is covered with water, how come it's so hard to get to the beach?" —Teresa Skelton

BIRTHDAYS—
W. C. Fields, 1879; Paul Robeson, 1898; Hugh Hefner, 1926; Carl Perkins, 1932; Jean-Paul Belmondo, 1933; Michael Learned, 1939; Dennis Quaid, 1954

NEW WORD—
dehabeah - noun: a large boat found on the Nile used to ferry passengers

QUIZ—
Which movie has won the most Oscars?

TRIVIA
W. C. Fields kept his library in his bathroom. . . . Elvis Presley had a reading chair in his bathroom. . . . While married, Sonny and Cher sometimes communicated by writing to each other in a diary - left in their bathroom.

HISTORY—
On this date in 1865 Lee surrendered to Grant at Appomatox Courthouse, ending the Civil War.
In 1953 the first issue of "TV Guide" was published.

GRAFFITI
Every year it takes less time to fly across the ocean and longer to drive to work.

Quiz Answer: "Ben Hur", 11

A P R I L

TODAY'S THOUGHT:
"Why torture yourself when life will do it for you?" —Laura Walker

BIRTHDAYS—
Joseph Pulitzer, 1847; Harry Morgan, 1915; Chuck Connors, 1924; Max Von Sydow, 1929; Michael Shalhoub (Omar Sharif), 1932; John Madden, 1936; "Dandy" Don Meredith, 1938

NEW WORD—
fusuma - noun: the sliding door in a Japanese house

QUIZ—
Which of the following is false regarding the kangaroo?
    A: If you hold a kangaroo by its tail, it cannot jump.
    B: A group of kangaroos is known as a mob.
    C: The leader of a group is referred to as the captain kangaroo.

TRIVIA
The Flintstones live at 345 Stone Cave Road in Bedrock. . . . In "I Love Lucy" the Ricardos lived at 623 East 68th Street in Manhattan. . . . 1 Cherry Street in New York City was home to George Washington as it was the first U.S. Presidential address.

HISTORY—
On this date in 1912 the "unsinkable" Titanic set sail on her ill-fated voyage.

GRAFFITI
**After two days at sea
some travelers look like their passport photograph.**

Quiz Answer: C (Yes, this was a gimme, Mate.)

A P R I L

TODAY'S THOUGHT:

"The trouble with life in the fast lane is that you get to the other end in an awful hurry." —John Jensen

BIRTHDAYS—

Charles Evans Hughes, 1862; Dean Acheson, 1893; Oleg Cassini, 1913; Ethel Kennedy, 1928; Joel Grey, 1932; Louise Lasser, 1939

NEW WORD—

penicil - noun: small, brushlike tuft of hair

QUIZ—

By what nickname did the world know Robert Stroud?

TRIVIA

The Bronx is the only part of New York City connected to the mainland. . . . There are no streets in Washington D.C. that start with the letter J because it too closely resembles the letter I. . . . If you have lost your marbles, head for the National Marbles Tournament, held annually in Wildwood, New Jersey.

HISTORY—

On this date in 1814 Napoleon Bonaparte was abdicated as Emperor of France and banished to the Island of Elba. A day later he tried to end his life but the poison he took created a terrible case of hiccups which caused him to vomit, thereby foiling his suicide attempt.

GRAFFITI

**When birds of a feather flock together,
you'd better stay out from underneath them.**

Quiz Answer: One of the most famous residents of "The Rock", Stroud was known as "The Birdman of Alcatraz".

A P R I L

TODAY'S THOUGHT:

"Be suspicious of any doctor who tries to take your temperature with his finger." —David Letterman

BIRTHDAYS—

Henry Clay, 1777; Lionel Hampton, 1913; Herbert Buckingham Khaury (Tiny Tim), 1922; Ann Miller, 1923; Herbie Hancock, 1940; David Letterman, 1947; David Cassidy, 1950

NEW WORD—

warison - noun: a note sounded to begin an attack

QUIZ—

What kind of people have never appeared in the comic strip "Peanuts"?

TRIVIA

The bite of a cobra is so deadly that it can even kill an elephant if it is bitten on the trunk tip or the base of the toenail. . . . Cleopatra tested her poisons on her slaves. . . . Tombstones were originally placed on plots over the dead so that the deceased could not come out and harm the living.

HISTORY—

On this date in 1861 Confederates fired on Fort Sumter in Charleston harbor, touching off the Civil War.

In 1945 President Franklin D. Roosevelt died in office of a cerebral hemorrhage at the age of 63.

GRAFFITI

**Old quarterbacks never die.
They just drop back and pass away.**

Quiz Answer: The strip definitely discriminates against adults. None have ever appeared with Charlie Brown and company.

APRIL

TODAY'S THOUGHT:

"Swearing was invented as a compromise between running away and fighting." —Finley Peter Dunne

BIRTHDAYS—

Thomas Jefferson, 1743; Eudora Welty, 1909; Howard Keel, 1919; Peabo Bryson, 1951; Bret Saberhagen, 1964

NEW WORD—

quetsch - noun: a variety of plum

QUIZ—

Jerry Lee Lewis, Liberace and Van Cliburn no doubt practiced this exercise written by Arthur de Lulli in 1877. What is it?

TRIVIA

You must be at least 35 years old to be a candidate for the presidency of the United States. . . . Eight United States presidents have been born in Virginia. . . . Thomas Jefferson introduced America to ice cream.

HISTORY—

On this date in 1976 the United States Mint reissued the $2 bill with the likeness of Thomas Jefferson.

GRAFFITI
What this country needs is a good five-cent nickel.

Quiz Answer: "Chopsticks"

A P R I L

TODAY'S THOUGHT:
"What counts is not necessarily the size of the dog in the fight - it's the size. of the fight in the dog." —Dwight D. Eisenhower

OBSERVANCES/EVENTS—
Pan American Day is celebrated today.

BIRTHDAYS—
Arnold Toynbee, 1889; Sir John Gielgud, 1904; Rod Steiger, 1925; Bradford Dillman, 1930; Tony Perkins, 1932; Loretta Lynn, 1935; Julie Christie, 1940; Pete Rose, 1941

NEW WORD—
ululant - adjective: howling

QUIZ—
What future president once played fourteen games as a minor league outfielder in Junction City, Kansas under an assumed name and piqued the interest of several major league scouts?

TRIVIA
Alfred Blozis set the world's record for the hand grenade toss back in 1944 when he lobbed the old pineapple 284½ feet. . . . There is a tribe of athletes in Burma called the Intha that row their longboats with their legs. . . . A Grecian urn is the award presented to "Sports Illustrated" magazine's sportsman of the year.

HISTORY—
On this date in 1865 President Lincoln was shot by John Wilkes Booth at Ford's Theater.

GRAFFITI
Florists are just petal pushers.

Quiz Answer: Dwight David Eisenhower was this budding athlete.

A P R I L

TODAY'S THOUGHT:
"Only little people pay taxes." —Leona Helmsley

OBSERVANCES/EVENTS—
The Ides of Taxes are upon you!

BIRTHDAYS—
Leonardo da Vinci, 1452; Roy Clark, 1933; Elizabeth Montgomery, 1933; Claudia Cardinale, 1938; Michael Cooper, 1956; Evelyn Ashford, 1957

NEW WORD—
onomatopoeia - noun: a word that imitates the sound with which it is associated

QUIZ—
What is the tallest tree in the world?

TRIVIA
The United States has no circulation problems with 455 billion dollars pulsing through pocket and purse at any given time. . . . There are 119 grooves on the circumference of a quarter. . . . Three women have appeared on U.S. currency: Martha Washington, on the $1 silver certificate; Pocahontas, on the back of the 1875 $20 bill; and women's suffrage leader Susan B. Anthony, on the 1979 silver dollar.

HISTORY—
On this date in 1955 Ray Kroc opened his first McDonald's restaurant. The slogan at the time was "Q.S.C.V." (Quality, Service, Cleanliness and Value)

GRAFFITI
A penny saved is a penny taxed.

Quiz Answer: You may be tempted to say Uncle Sam's Money Tree, but the tallest species is the coast redwood, the tallest example of which is in the Redwood Creek Grove, Humbolt County, California. It measures 367.8 feet!

A P R I L

TODAY'S THOUGHT:
"Comedy is simply a funny way of being serious." —Peter Ustinov

OBSERVANCES/EVENTS—
It is National Stress Awareness Day.

BIRTHDAYS—
Wilbur Wright, 1867; Charlie Chaplin, 1889; Peter Ustinov, 1921; Henry Mancini, 1924; Bobby Vinton, 1935; Kareem Abdul-Jabbar, 1947

NEW WORD—
tergiversate - verb: to continually change one's opinion; to be ambivalent

QUIZ—
Let's check out your powers of observation. Answer the following questions without peeking:
- A: Which way does Lincoln face on a penny?
- B: What are the colors of a 7-11 sign?
- C: How many wheels of an 18 wheeler are on the trailer?
- D: In which hand does the Statue of Liberty hold her torch?

TRIVIA
Rocker Rod Stewart was once a gravedigger. . . . Entertainer Victor Borge used to play the organ at funerals. . . . The inscription on actress Joan Hackett's grave marker reads, "Go Away! I'm Sleeping."

HISTORY—
On this date in 1940 an event occurred which sparked the following brain teaser. The Cleveland Indians were playing the Chicago White Sox. No one on the White Sox got a hit. Yet none of their batting averages changed. Why not? The answer: It was opening day. Hall of Famer Bob Feller threw a no-hitter, the only no-hitter on opening day in baseball history.

GRAFFITI
Gossips are the spies of life.

Quiz Answer: A: Right; B: Red, orange and green on a white background; C: 8; D: Right

A P R I L

TODAY'S THOUGHT:
"Some cause happiness wherever they go; others whenever they go."
—Oscar Wilde

OBSERVANCES/EVENTS—
It's Flag Day in American Samoa.

BIRTHDAYS—
Nikita Khrushchev, 1897; William Holden, 1918; Harry Reasoner, 1923; Don Kirshner, 1934; Norman Julius "Boomer" Esiason, 1961

NEW WORD—
dotation - noun: an endowment

QUIZ—
Here is a super killer trivia question: Name at least three of the five actors who played Sgt. Friday's partners in "Dragnet".

TRIVIA
No news is good news? TV news anchorman Peter Jennings is a high school dropout. . . . Former anchorman Walter Cronkite was a college dropout at the University of Texas. . . . Newsman John Chancellor dropped out of high school, later got a General Equivalency Diploma, then dropped out of the University of Illinois.

HISTORY—
On this date in 1961 an invasion force halfheartedly backed by the United States was repelled at Cuba's Bay of Pigs.

GRAFFITI
**The more I think of people,
the less I think of people.**

Quiz Answer: Sure you guessed Harry Morgan, and maybe even Ben Alexander. But what about those other guys . . . Barton Yarborough, Herb Ellis and Barney Phillips.

A P R I L

TODAY'S THOUGHT:

"Asthma doesn't seem to bother me any more unless I'm around cigars or dogs. The thing that would bother me most would be a dog smoking a cigar." —Steve Allen

BIRTHDAYS—

Clarence Darrow, 1857; conductor Leopold Stokowski, 1882; Barbara Hale, 1922; Catfish Hunter, 1945; Hayley Mills, 1946; James Woods, 1947; Nate Archibald, 1948

NEW WORD—

vulgus - noun: the masses; the common people

QUIZ—

What was the game of Scrabble originally called?

TRIVIA

37% of Americans own dogs. . . . 26% have cats in their household. . . . 5% own birds.

HISTORY—

On this date in 1775 Paul Revere went on his legendary midnight ride to warn the countryside that "The British are coming!" Along with Revere rode William Dawes who never got credit despite the fact that Revere was captured early on, had his horse taken away from him and was sent packing back to Boston on foot, leaving Dawes to alert the patriots.

GRAFFITI

It's amazing what fine poker hands you get when playing bridge.

Quiz Answer: Lexico

APRIL

TODAY'S THOUGHT:
"Some luck lies in not getting what you thought you wanted but getting what you have, which once you have got it you may be smart enough to see is what you would have wanted had you known." —Garrison Keillor

BIRTHDAYS—
Don Adams, 1927; Hugh O'Brian, 1930; Jayne Mansfield, 1932; Dudley Moore, 1935; Frank Viola Jr., 1960

NEW WORD—
megrim - noun: low spirits; a depression

QUIZ—
What was the largest denomination of United States currency ever minted?

TRIVIA
Mario Andretti, John Elway, Jerry Falwell, Jose Canseco and Billy Dee Williams are all twins. . . . Stephen King, Michael Douglas, Alan Ladd and Johnny Carson were all gas station attendants. . . . Julio Iglesias is so intensely superstitious that he'll leave a dinner table if salt is spilled. And if he hears really bad news, he'll remove all his clothing and dispose of it.

HISTORY—
On this date in 1897 the first Boston marathon was run.
In 1956 Grace Kelly married Prince Rainier III.

GRAFFITI
**These are the good old days
you are going to miss twenty years from now.**

Quiz Answer: A $100,000 bill which bore a portrait of Woodrow Wilson was the largest denomination.

A P R I L

TODAY'S THOUGHT:

"The quizzical expression of the monkey at the zoo comes from his wondering whether he is his brother's keeper, or his keeper's brother."

—Evan Esar

BIRTHDAYS—

Adolf Hitler, 1889; Nina Foch, 1924; Ryan O'Neal, 1941; Jessica Lange, 1949; Peter Frampton, 1950; Luther Vandross, 1951

NEW WORD—

handsel - noun: a gift for good luck

QUIZ—

What is the only way to tell a male penguin from a female penguin? (Assuming you're not a penguin)

TRIVIA

When the mood of an octopus changes, so does its color. . . . A cow spends approximately 18 out of every 24 hours chewing on something. . . . The leader of a wolf pack is always female.

HISTORY—

On this date in 1589 in Angola, Andrew Battel became the first European to see a gorilla. He named the animal a "pongo".

GRAFFITI

People may argue whether we came from the apes, but most agree that we're going to the dogs.

Quiz Answer: By autopsy

APRIL

TODAY'S THOUGHT:
"Nature never makes any blunders; when she makes a fool, she means it."
—Josh Billings

BIRTHDAYS—
Charlotte Bronte, 1816; Josh Billings, 1818; Anthony Quinn, 1916; Queen Elizabeth II, 1926; Elaine May, 1932; Charles Grodin, 1935; Iggy Pop, 1947; Tony Danza, 1951

NEW WORD—
cicerone - noun: a guide

QUIZ—
What was the name of the right fielder in Abbott and Costello's "Who's on First?" routine?

TRIVIA
Walter Hunt invented the safety pin in 1849. . . . Lawrence Welk's bubble machine was invented by N. A. Fisher. . . . In addition to inventing dynamite, Alfred Nobel was the pioneer of plywood.

HISTORY—
On this date in 753 B.C., Rome was founded — even though it wasn't built in a day!

GRAFFITI
If you don't like feeling down in the mouth, stop kissing geese.

Quiz Answer: The right fielder was not mentioned in the routine. Rounding out the lineup - Who was on first; What on second; the third baseman was I Don't Know; I Don't Give a Darn (or I Don't Care) was at shortstop; the catcher was Today; Tomorrow was the pitcher; in left field was Why; and in center was Because.

A P R I L

TODAY'S THOUGHT:
"The laziest man I ever met put popcorn in his pancakes so they would turn over by themselves." —W.C. Fields

OBSERVANCES/EVENTS—
It is Earth Day with the message "Give Earth a Chance".

BIRTHDAYS—
Philosopher Immanuel Kant, 1724; Nikolai Lenin, 1870; J. Robert Oppenheimer, 1904; Eddie Albert, 1908; Glen Campbell, 1935; Jack Nicholson, 1936; Peter Frampton, 1950

NEW WORD—
pasquinade - noun: a lampoon or satire

QUIZ—
What do First Ladies Martha Washington, Abigail Fillmore, Caroline Harrison, Florence Harding and Pat Nixon have in common?

TRIVIA
When J. C. Penney opened his first store in Ohio in 1902, it was called The Golden Rule. . . . Seventy percent of house dust is dead skin cells. . . . . It is illegal in Idaho to give a person a box of candy that weighs over fifty pounds.

HISTORY—
On this date in 1864 the phrase "In God We Trust" was first added to United States coinage. One previous slogan printed on earlier coins was "Mind Your Business".

GRAFFITI
In God We Trust - All Others Pay Cash.

Quiz Answer: They were all older than their husbands.

A P R I L

TODAY'S THOUGHT:
"Men get to be a mixture of the charming mannerisms of the women they have known." —F. Scott Fitzgerald

BIRTHDAYS—
William Shakespeare, 1564; Janet Blair, 1921; Shirley Temple Black, 1928; Lee Majors, 1940; Sandra Dee, 1942; Phil Esposito, 1942; Herve Villechaize, 1943; Joyce Dewitt, 1949; Valerie Bertinelli, 1960

NEW WORD—
gynarchy - noun: government by a woman or women

QUIZ—
What was the significance of a character named Dippy Dawg in a 1932 Disney cartoon called "Mickey's Revue"?

TRIVIA
Shakespeare was born on April 23 and died fifty-two years later on April 23. . . . There are no living descendants of William Shakespeare. . . . Shakespeare's will contained three of his six accepted signatures - "Shakspere", "Shakespeare" and "Shakspeare".

HISTORY—
On this date in 1896 the first public exhibition of moving pictures took place in New York City.

GRAFFITI
**Behind every successful man
stands a bunch of amazed coworkers.**

Quiz Answer: Dippy Dawg had not yet acquired the stage name that would carry him through over six decades of show-biz fame and fortune. Once he changed it to Goofy, the sky was the limit!

A P R I L

TODAY'S THOUGHT:
"Never have children, only grandchildren." —Gore Vidal

BIRTHDAYS—
Leslie Howard, 1893; Howard Penn Warren, 1905; Shirley MacLaine, 1934; Barbra Streisand, 1942; Vince Ferragamo, 1954

NEW WORD—
bicipital - adjective: having two heads

QUIZ—
What Apollo astronaut is the father of a soap star?

TRIVIA
"Kilroy was here" referred to James J. Kilroy, an inspector for Bethlehem Steel who used it as his certification mark. . . . The phrase "stone broke" comes from the Middle Ages custom of breaking stone benches of craftsmen who were unable to pay their debts. . . . "Knuckle under" comes from the archaic meaning of knuckle or knee. It meant to fall on one's knees.

HISTORY—
On this date in 1800 the Library of Congress was established.
In 1888 Kodak sold its first camera.

GRAFFITI
If you don't go to a friend's funeral,
don't expect him to come to yours.

Quiz Answer: Michael Collins, left behind to pilot the command module while his shipmates Neil Armstrong and Edwin "Buzz" Aldrin made history by landing on the moon, is the father of Kate Collins who, for many years, has played Natalie on "All My Children".

A P R I L

TODAY'S THOUGHT:
"Is fuel efficiency really what we need most desperately? I say what we really need is a car that can be shot when it breaks down." —Russell Baker

BIRTHDAYS—
Oliver Cromwell, 1599; Guglielmo Marconi, 1874; Harold Lloyd, 1894; Edward R. Murrow, 1908; Ella Fitzgerald, 1918; Meadowlark Lemon, 1932; Al Pacino, 1940; Talia Shire, 1946

NEW WORD—
diglot - adjective: bilingual

QUIZ—
Who is Martin Waldseemuller and why should we remember him?

TRIVIA
The first automobile to offer seat belts was the 1950 Nash. . . . The Mayflower was just over 106 feet long and carried 102 Pilgrims. . . . After the original thirteen states, Vermont was the next state admitted in 1791.

HISTORY—
On this date in 1901 New York became the first state to require license plates on cars.

GRAFFITI
**When it comes to cars,
it's tough to drive a bargain.**

Quiz Answer: Simply put, Martin Waldseemuller is the guy who gave America its name. A German mapmaker and geographer, Waldseemuller was under the impression that Amerigo Vespucci had discovered the New World and so named the land in honor of him. We should be grateful . . . he could have named us Vespucci or even after himself, in which case we would be singing "Waldseemullerland the Beautiful".

A P R I L

TODAY'S THOUGHT:
"Adolescence is one big walking pimple." —Carol Burnett

OBSERVANCES/EVENTS—
Richter Scale Day recognizes the importance of the research and development of the earthquake magnitude scale by physicist Charles Francis Richter.

BIRTHDAYS—
John James Audubon, 1785; author Anita Loos, 1893; Rudolph Hess, 1894; Carol Burnett, 1936; Duane Eddy, 1938; Bobby Rydell, 1942; Gary Wright, 1943

NEW WORD—
sphragistic - adjective: pertaining to seals or signet rings

QUIZ—
Can you identify the people who spoke these famous words?
- A: "Ich bin ein Berliner!"
- B: "Anyone who hates children and dogs can't be all bad."
- C: "If you've seen one redwood tree, you've seen them all."

TRIVIA
The four H's in the 4-H Club stand for Head, Heart, Hands and Health. . . . There are more words in the English language than any other language in the world. . . . Bookkeeper is the only word in the English language that has three consecutive sets of double letters.

HISTORY—
On this date in 1986 the Chernobyl nuclear power plant exploded.

GRAFFITI
We need to be surrounded by more open minds and fewer open mouths.

Quiz Answer: A: JFK; B: W.C. Fields; C: Ronald Reagan

APRIL

TODAY'S THOUGHT:
"Stay humble. Always answer the phone - no matter who else is in the car." —Jack Lemmon

BIRTHDAYS—
Samuel Morse, 1791; Ulysses S. Grant, 1822; Jack Klugman, 1922; Coretta Scott King, 1927; Casey Kasem, 1932; Anouk Aimee, 1934; Sandy Dennis, 1937; Sheena Easton, 1959

NEW WORD—
negus - noun: a drink made of hot water, wine, sugar, lemon and nutmeg

QUIZ—
Is the tomato a fruit or a vegetable?

TRIVIA
A popular breakfast of Ulysses Grant's was a cucumber soaked in vinegar. . . . Samuel Morse actually made his living as a portrait painter. . . . The message keyed on the first telegraph line in the United States was, "What hath God wrought?"

HISTORY—
On this date in 1897 U.S. Grant made a posthumous move to his permanent residence in Grant's Tomb, New York City.

GRAFFITI
Cookbooks are full of stirring passages.

Quiz Answer: It is a case of you say "tomato" and I say "tomahto". Botanists classify the tomato as a fruit but the United States Supreme Court has settled the matter, legally ruling it a vegetable.

A P R I L

TODAY'S THOUGHT:

"The reason there are two senators for every state is so that one can be the designated driver." —Jay Leno

OBSERVANCES/EVENTS—

Sneak up on your significant other and surprise them on Kiss Your Mate Day.

BIRTHDAYS—

James Monroe, 1758; Lionel Barrymore, 1878; Ann-Margret, 1941; Marcia Strassman, 1948; Jay Leno, 1950; Barry Larkin, 1964

NEW WORD—

gulosity - noun: greediness, gluttony

QUIZ—

True or False?
Only African elephants are trained.

TRIVIA

The only animal with four knees is the elephant. . . . The only mammal that can't jump is the elephant. . . . The only animal that can be taught to stand on its head is the elephant.

HISTORY—

On this date in 1789 one of the most famous events in the annals of the sea occurred, the Mutiny on the Bounty. Captain Bligh pulled off one of the most amazing feats of seamanship ever accomplished by sailing 3,600 miles in a small open boat back to civilization. Fletcher Christian took the Bounty to Tahiti to pick up supplies and women, and then went on to lonely Pitcairn Island to live out his days.

GRAFFITI

Tickling the ivories: when elephants floss.

Quiz Answer: False, it is exactly the opposite. Only Indian elephants perform.

A P R I L

TODAY'S THOUGHT:
"Don't be afraid to make a mistake; your readers might like it."
—William Randolph Hearst

BIRTHDAYS—
William Randolph Hearst, 1863; Duke Ellington, 1899; Emperor Hirohito, 1901; Tom Ewell, 1909; Celeste Holm, 1919; Zubin Mehta, 1936; Daniel Day-Lewis, 1957; Michelle Pfeiffer, 1958; Andre Agassi, 1970

NEW WORD—
quadrel - noun: a square tile, stone or brick

QUIZ—
Who is Frank Wills and what small but crucial role did he play in recent American history?

TRIVIA
After denouncing his divinity in 1946, Hirohito became a recognized world authority in marine biology. . . . The world's oldest gloves were found in King Tut's tomb and are over 3,300 years old. . . . The oldest house in America is in Santa Fe, New Mexico and was built of mud.

HISTORY—
On this date in 1553 the practice of using starch on linen was introduced by Mrs. Dingheim, a Flemish woman living in England.

GRAFFITI
Doctor's fees are ill-gotten gains.

Quiz Answer: Wills was the twenty-four-year old security guard who discovered the Watergate break-in, the "third-rate burglary" that eventually toppled the Nixon administration.

A P R I L

TODAY'S THOUGHT:
"A friend that ain't in need is a friend indeed." —Kin Hubbard

OBSERVANCES/EVENTS—
Observe National Honesty Day today.

BIRTHDAYS—
Eve Arden, 1907; Corinne Calvet, 1926; Cloris Leachman, 1930; Willie Nelson, 1933; Gary Collins, 1938; Jill Clayburgh, 1944; Al Toon, 1963

NEW WORD—
avitaminosis - noun: any disease caused by a lack of vitamins

QUIZ—
Which two states have names that come from the Sioux word meaning "friend"?

TRIVIA
Lampoon is a French phrase meaning "Let's drink!" . . . Robot comes from the Czech word for slave. . . . P. T. Barnum coined the phrase "Siamese twins".

HISTORY—
On this date in 1900 John Luther Jones, whose nickname came from his hometown of Cayce, Kentucky died while bravely staying at the controls of the Illinois Central railroad's Cannonball Express as it crashed into the caboose of a freight train, thereby inspiring many a legend and famous folk song.

GRAFFITI
**The real reason a dog is man's best friend
is that they don't understand a word you're saying.**

Quiz Answer: North and South Dakota

M A Y

TODAY'S THOUGHT:
"I came from a poor family. We never had meat at our house. And whenever I would go by a butcher's window I thought there had been a terrible accident." —Jack Paar

OBSERVANCES/EVENTS—
Loyalty Day, Mother Goose Day, Law Day and May Day are all celebrated today.

BIRTHDAYS—
Singer Kate Smith, 1909; Glenn Ford, 1916; Jack Paar, 1918; Joseph Heller, 1923; Judy Collins, 1939; Rita Coolidge, 1945; jockey Steve Cauthen, 1960

NEW WORD—
keek - verb: to look furtively; to peek

QUIZ—
What was the full name of Skipper on "Gilligan's Island"?

TRIVIA
Early film star Mary Pickford, known as "America's sweetheart", was born in Canada. . . . The city of Hollywood was formerly known as Paradise Valley. . . . The first 3-D movie release was 1922's "Power of Love".

HISTORY—
On this date in 1931 the Empire State Building was opened by President Hoover and Governor Smith.

GRAFFITI
A toupee is a top secret.

Quiz Answer: Jonas Grunby

M A Y

TODAY'S THOUGHT:
"There are only two things a child will share willingly — communicable diseases and his mother's age." —Dr. Benjamin Spock

BIRTHDAYS—
Artist Mary Cassatt, 1844; Lorenz Hart, 1895; Dr. Benjamin Spock, 1903; Bing Crosby, 1904; Theodore Bikel, 1924; Leslie Gore, 1946; Larry Gatlin, 1949

NEW WORD—
panopticon - noun: a prison arranged so all points of the interior are visible from a single point

QUIZ—
From the College of Trivial Knowledge: On what campus would you find the "Animal House"?

TRIVIA
Australia is the only continent without an active volcano. . . . Nine-tenths of the ice in the world can be found in Antarctica. . . . If you discount the "North" and "South" in the Americas, each of the world's continents begin and end with the same letter (e.g., EuropE, AmericA, AsiA).

HISTORY—
On this date in 1885 the first issue of "Good Housekeeping" cleaned up at the newsstands.

GRAFFITI
Kids go to college so they can graduate and join the work farce.

Quiz Answer: Faber College

M A Y

TODAY'S THOUGHT:
"For the parents of a Little Leaguer, a baseball game is simply a nervous breakdown into innings." —Earl Wilson

BIRTHDAYS—
Mary Astor, 1906; Earl Wilson, 1907; Pete Seegar, 1919; James Brown, 1934; Gerry Dorsey (Englebert Humperdinck), 1936; Frankie Valli, 1937; Doug Henning, 1947

NEW WORD—
eloign - verb: to remove oneself to a distance

QUIZ—
Can you guess the famous names of the following folks?
- A: Ellis McDaniel
- B: Krekor Ohanian
- C: Edward Bridge Danson III
- D: Shelton Lee
- E: Sarah Ophelia Colley Cannon

TRIVIA
The white shark has a perpetual appetite. No matter how much it eats, it is always hungry. . . . A jellyfish that has been dead for months can still sting you if you walk on it in bare feet. . . . The lobster always burrows tail first.

HISTORY—
On this date in 1973 Chicago's Sears Tower, the world's tallest building, opened for business.

GRAFFITI
Overcoats only last one season because they are designed to be worn out.

Quiz Answer: A - Bo Diddley; B - Mike Connors; C - Ted Danson; D - Spike Lee; E - Minnie Pearl

M A Y

TODAY'S THOUGHT:
"The temperature in any room is room temperature." —Steven Wright

BIRTHDAYS—
Horace Mann, 1796; Howard Da Silva, 1909; Audrey Hepburn, 1929; Roberta Peters, 1930; George F. Will, 1941; Tammy Wynette, 1942; Randy Travis, 1959

NEW WORD—
remiped - adjective: having feet adapted for use as oars

QUIZ—
Who was brought in to dub Lauren Bacall's singing in "To Have and Have Not"?

TRIVIA
It is impossible to sneeze and keep your eyes open at the same time. . . . The jawbone is the hardest bone in the body. . . . The face has the dirtiest skin of the body.

HISTORY—
On this date in 1961 Commander Alan B. Shepard Jr. sat atop a Redstone booster at Cape Canaveral and became the first American in space with his brief suborbital flight.

GRAFFITI
A bad musician should keep his dissonance.

Quiz Answer: A very young Andy Williams provided her with those velvety tones.

M A Y

TODAY'S THOUGHT:
"I once wanted to become an atheist, but I gave up - they have no holidays." —Henny Youngman

OBSERVANCES/EVENTS—
Children's Day is observed in Japan on this fifth day of the fifth month.

BIRTHDAYS—
Karl Marx, 1818; Nelly Bly, 1867; Tyrone Power, 1914; Alice Faye, 1915; Pat Carroll, 1927; Roger Rees, 1944

NEW WORD—
nuncupative - adjective: oral; not written

QUIZ—
Which of the following celebrities was *not* born in the city indicated?
   A: Henny Youngman - Liverpool, England
   B: Audrey Meadows - Wu Chang, China
   C: Sid Caesar - Mexico City, Mexico
   D: John Charles Daly - Johannesburg, South Africa

TRIVIA
A golf ball can not weigh more than 1.62 ounces or be smaller than 1.68 inches in diameter. . . . Bowling pins are made out of maple. . . . A bowling ball outweighs a ping pong ball 2800 to 1.

HISTORY—
On this date in 1904 Cy Young pitched baseball's first perfect game as the Boston Americans beat Philadelphia 3-0.

GRAFFITI
What do you say when God sneezes?

Quiz Answer: C - Sid Caesar was born in far-off, exotic Yonkers, New York.

M A Y

TODAY'S THOUGHT:
"George Washington said to his father, 'If I never tell a lie, how can I get to be president?'" —Red Buttons

BIRTHDAYS—
John Penn, 1740; explorer Robert E. Peary, 1856; Rudolph Valentino, 1895; Stewart Granger, 1913; Willie Mays, 1931; Bob Seger, 1945

NEW WORD—
buccal - adjective: of or pertaining to the cheek

QUIZ—
Which of the following amazing facts is bogus?
- A: During World War I sheep were employed to mow the grass at the White House.
- B: Clark Gable had webbed feet.
- C: Conductors live longer than average because of their regular upper body workouts.
- D: Walter Cronkite once hosted a game show.

TRIVIA
The average adult in the United States reads just 24 minutes a day. . . . The typical American reads 36 magazines a year. . . . One out of 10 Americans reads the Bible every day.

HISTORY—
On this date in 1626 Peter Minuit bought Manhattan Island for $24.
In 1937 the Hindenburg, pride of the Third Reich, exploded and burned as it approached the mooring mast in Lakehurst, New Jersey. Reporter Herb Morrison uttered the now famous phrase, "Oh, the humanity!"

GRAFFITI
A hangover is the wrath of grapes.

Quiz Answer: B is for bogus. The King had normal tootsies. The name of that Walter Cronkite game show was "It's News to Me", 1951-54 on CBS.

M A Y

TODAY'S THOUGHT:
"What a good thing Adam had — when he said a good thing, he knew nobody had said it before." —Mark Twain

BIRTHDAYS—
Poet Robert Browning, 1812; Johannes Brahms, 1833; Archibald MacLeish, 1892; Gary Cooper, 1901; inventor Edwin Land, 1909; Darren McGavin, 1922; Theresa Brewer, 1931

NEW WORD—
hotchpotch - noun: a thick stew of vegetables or meat, often thickened with barley

QUIZ—
Who was Chester Carlson and why did he and the Haloid Company make history?

TRIVIA
The last battleship built in the United States was the U.S.S. Missouri. . . . "The third time's a charm": In 1871 the George F. Whitney was launched. The schooner went on the rocks during its maiden voyage. It was rebuilt and wrecked again on its second voyage. Rebuilt again, it sailed off over the horizon of Lake Michigan and was never seen again. . . . The motto of the FBI is "Fidelity, Bravery, Integrity".

HISTORY—
On this date in 1915 the Lusitania went to the bottom after being torpedoed by a German U-boat, hastening American involvement in World War I.

GRAFFITI
Noise is an earitation.

Quiz Answer: Carlson was an inventor with a new idea, the first xerographic copy, who was turned down by every major corporation including RCA and IBM. He finally sold his patents to the small Haloid Company which soon changed its name to Xerox.

M A Y

TODAY'S THOUGHT:
"I have found the best way to give advice to your children is to find out what they want and then advise them to do it." —Harry S Truman

OBSERVANCES/EVENTS—
It is No Socks Day. According to its organizers, this is a day to cut back on the laundry and help the environment.

BIRTHDAYS—
Harry S Truman, 1884; naturalist David Attenborough, 1926; Don Rickles, 1926; Peter Benchley, 1940; Ricky Nelson, 1940; Toni Tennille, 1943; Melissa Gilbert, 1964

NEW WORD—
larrikin - adjective: disorderly; rowdy

QUIZ—
What does the S in Harry S Truman stand for?

TRIVIA
A died-in-the-wool Democrat, Harry Truman refused to have anything to do with Dumbo the Elephant on a 1957 visit to Disneyland. . . . President Roosevelt nicknamed his political advisors the Tennis Cabinet. . . . The president and vice-president of the United States are not allowed to travel together.

HISTORY—
On this date in 1886 Dr. John Pemberton of Atlanta, Georgia invented Coca Cola.

GRAFFITI
Kids make parents want to jump for joy . . . off very tall buildings.

Quiz Answer: The S was not an initial; it did not stand for anything.

M A Y

TODAY'S THOUGHT:
"My uncle's funeral cost five thousand dollars so far. We buried him in a rented tuxedo." —Dave Madden

BIRTHDAYS—
Abolitionist John Brown, 1800; author James Barrie, 1860; Mike Wallace, 1918; Candice Bergen, 1946; Billy Joel, 1949; Tony Gwynn, 1960

NEW WORD—
girandole - noun: a rotating firework

QUIZ—
What was the shortest month on record?

TRIVIA
Umbrellas have a life span of two and a half years. . . . Early watches had only one hand which indicated the hour. . . . Candice Bergen, television's "Murphy Brown", was once offered a slot on "60 Minutes".

HISTORY—
On this date in 1783 the first Purple Hearts were awarded to Sergeants Daniel Bissell, William Brown and Elijah Churchill.

GRAFFITI
Fish get chicken pox on a small scale.

Quiz Answer: September, 1752 - During the switch from the Gregorian to the Julian calendar, eleven days were dropped from the month. That means absolutely nothing happened between September 3 and September 13 of that year. That would also make 1752 the shortest *year* on record.

M A Y

TODAY'S THOUGHT:
"The hardest job kids face today is learning good manners without seeing any." —Fred Astaire

BIRTHDAYS—
Composer Dimitri Tiomkin, 1894; Fred Astaire, 1899; David O. Selznick, 1902; pediatrician T. Berry Brazleton, 1918; Nancy Walker, 1922; Ara Parseghian, 1923; Gary Owens, 1936; Rony Seikaly, 1965

NEW WORD—
vertiginous - adjective: whirling; spinning

QUIZ—
Walt Disney received one big Oscar and seven small Oscars at the 1938 Academy Awards. What were they for?

TRIVIA
Fred Astaire was allergic to feathers. . . . Ivory soap babies who went on to big things include Brooke Shields and musician Dr. John. . . . Josephine Esther Mentzer underwent a cosmetic name-change to Estee Lauder.

HISTORY—
On this date in 1869 the Golden Spike was driven in Promontory, Utah to complete the first transcontinental railroad.

GRAFFITI
**Never race a train across the tracks . . .
if you end up in a tie, you lose.**

Quiz Answer: "Snow White and the Seven Dwarfs"

M A Y

TODAY'S THOUGHT:
"Liberals feel unworthy of their possessions. Conservatives feel they deserve everything they've stolen." —Mort Sahl

BIRTHDAYS—
Irving Berlin, 1888; Martha Graham, 1894; Salvador Dali, 1904; Phil Silvers, 1912; Denver Pyle, 1920; Mort Sahl, 1927; Doug McClure, 1935; Randy Quaid, 1950

NEW WORD—
calvaria - noun: the dome of the skull

QUIZ—
What is the only team in American pro sports to be named after an insect?

TRIVIA
It takes about a yard of sugar cane to make one sugar cube. . . . The record for spitting a watermelon seed is 65 feet, 4 inches. . . . Spinach loses fifty percent of its vitamin C content within 24 hours after being picked.

HISTORY—
On this date in 1752 the first United States fire insurance policy was issued.

GRAFFITI
You get indigestion when a square meal doesn't fit in a round stomach.

Quiz Answer: The NBA's Charlotte Hornets - The name, selected in a 1988 contest, refers to a letter British General Charles Cornwallis sent to the king of England from the Carolinas during the Revolutionary War. In it he wrote, "This place is like fighting in a hornet's nest."

M A Y

TODAY'S THOUGHT:
"You can observe a lot just by watching." —Yogi Berra

OBSERVANCES/EVENTS—
It is Limerick Day, in honor of author Edward Lear.

BIRTHDAYS—
Florence Nightingale, 1820; Yogi Berra, 1925; Burt Bacharach, 1929; Tom Snyder, 1936; George Carlin, 1937; Steve Winwood, 1948; Bruce Boxleitner, 1951; Emilio Estevez, 1962

NEW WORD—
tussah - noun: a tan silk from India

QUIZ—
What vegetable do you discard the outside, cook the inside, eat the outside and chuck the inside?

TRIVIA
Florence Nightingale kept her pet owl in her pocket at all times. . . . There is a separate silk strand for each kernel on an ear of corn. . . . On a single ear of corn, there is almost always an even number of rows.

HISTORY—
On this date in 1896 the New York City Department of Health passed a law prohibiting spitting.

GRAFFITI
Stay young - eat right, exercise and lie about your age.

Quiz Answer: Corn on the cob

M A Y

TODAY'S THOUGHT:
"Have you ever noticed that mice don't have shoulders?" —George Carlin

BIRTHDAYS—
Composer Sir Arthur Sullivan, 1842; Joe Louis, 1914; Beatrice Arthur, 1926; Mary Wells, 1943; Peter Gabriel, 1950; Stevie Wonder, 1951; Dennis "Worm" Rodman, 1961

NEW WORD—
jundy - verb: to shove; push; jostle

QUIZ—
In which mid-sixties movie did Stevie Wonder make his film debut?

TRIVIA
In 1915 the average annual American family income was $687. . . . Female canaries do not sing. . . . "The Ballad of Davy Crockett" was dashed off when frantic producers discovered their show was going to run a few minutes short. It went on to sell over ten million records.

HISTORY—
On this date in 1950 the first Diner's Club credit card was issued.

———— GRAFFITI ————
Musicians always strive to be noteworthy.

Quiz Answer: "Little" Stevie Wonder was in "Muscle Beach Party" with Frankie Avalon and Annette Funicello. He was such a hit they brought him back for "Bikini Beach".

M A Y

TODAY'S THOUGHT:
"Gossip is the art of saying nothing in a way that leaves practically nothing unsaid." —Walter Winchell

OBSERVANCES/EVENTS—
It is Underground America day, designed to consider the advantages of building structures underground.

BIRTHDAYS—
Gabriel Fahrenheit, 1686; Thomas Gainsborough, 1727; George Lucas, 1944; Jose Martinez, 1955; Mike Quick, 1959; Walter Berry, 1964

NEW WORD—
yirr - verb: to growl or snarl

QUIZ—
Can you identify these behind the scenes voices?
- A: Charlie from "Charlie's Angels"
- B: The voice of God in the 1966 film, "The Bible"
- C: The narrator of television's "Untouchables"

TRIVIA
100 million Americans drink three cups of coffee daily. . . . Rice is eaten by one half of all the people in the world every day. . . . Over 100 million Americans are on a diet on any given day.

HISTORY—
On this date in 1853 Gail Borden applied for a U.S. patent for his process for making condensed milk. His process turned out to be a cash cow as it was eventually marketed by a company - no coincidence here - called Borden.

GRAFFITI
Nurses are panhandlers.

Quiz Answer: A-John Forsythe; B-John Huston, who also directed; C - Walter Winchell

M A Y

TODAY'S THOUGHT:
"If your wife wants to learn to drive, don't stand in her way."
—Sam Levenson

OBSERVANCES/EVENTS—
Today is Police Officers Memorial Day.

BIRTHDAYS—
L. Frank Baum, 1856; James Mason, 1909; Eddy Arnold, 1918; photographer Richard Avedon, 1923; Anna Marie Alberghetti, 1936; Trini Lopez, 1937; George Brett, 1953; Joey Browner, 1960

NEW WORD—
mackle - noun: a blur in printing

QUIZ—
Where did author L. Frank Baum get the name for Oz, his magical land over the rainbow?

TRIVIA
The higher a plane flies, the less fuel it uses as the atmosphere is thinner and the vehicle meets less resistance. . . . The wingspan of a Boeing 747 is greater than the entire flying distance of the Wright Brothers famous first foray into the wild blue yonder. . . . Just in case you weren't sure, of the Wright brothers, it was Orville who made the first airplane flight, at 10:35 a.m. on December 17, 1903.

HISTORY—
On this date in 1930 Ellen Church, the first "air hostess", greeted passengers aboard a United Airlines flight between California and Wyoming.

GRAFFITI
**Astronomers and press agents both
make their living off the stars.**

Quiz Answer: Baum got it from a filing cabinet drawer, O-Z.

M A Y

TODAY'S THOUGHT:
"You know that bank I used to cry all the way to? I bought it." —Liberace

OBSERVANCES/EVENTS—
Biographers Day commemorates the meeting in 1763 of James Boswell and Samuel Johnson. To celebrate, begin reading or writing a biography today.

BIRTHDAYS—
Henry Fonda, 1905; author Studs Terkel, 1912; Liberace, 1919; Billy Martin, 1928; gymnast Olga Korbut, 1955; Jack Morris, 1955; Debra Winger, 1955; Janet Jackson, 1966

NEW WORD—
atroceruleous - noun: a deep blue-black color

QUIZ—
Who was Margaret Herrick and what unique place does she hold in the history of the Academy Awards?

TRIVIA
King Camp Gillette created the safety razor with throwaway blades in 1895. . . . The electric razor was invented by Jacob Schick in 1928. . . . The average American spends about 3,500 hours shaving in his lifetime.

HISTORY—
On this date in 1929 the first Oscars were given out.

GRAFFITI
Custer was Siouxed.

Quiz Answer: She was a secretary who happened to remark that the new statuette looked like her Uncle Oscar, and the name stuck. Years later she became executive director of the academy.

M A Y

TODAY'S THOUGHT:

"Outside of a dog, a book is a man's best friend. Inside of a dog, it's too dark to read." —Groucho Marx

BIRTHDAYS—

Physician Edward Jenner, 1749; Maureen O'Sullivan, 1911; Dennis Hopper, 1936; Sugar Ray Leonard, 1956

NEW WORD—

zaptiah - noun: a Turkish policeman

QUIZ—

What was the distinction of the 1969 bestseller "Naked Came the Stranger"?

TRIVIA

Cold-blooded animals do not dream. . . . Cows eat seven times more than sheep. . . . Reindeer are superb swimmers.

HISTORY—

On this date in 1620 the first merry-go-round was introduced at a Turkish fair.
In 1875 the first Kentucky Derby was run at Churchill Downs.

GRAFFITI
Evolution is nature's way of trying to cover its mistakes.

Quiz Answer: The book, which sold almost 100,000 hardcover and 2,000,000 paperback, was a gag. A group of 25 writers of "Newsday" slapped it together over one weekend, each working on a separate chapter. The book was credited to Penelope Ashe, supposedly a Long Island housewife.

M A Y

TODAY'S THOUGHT:
"I'd rather hit than have sex." —Reggie Jackson

OBSERVANCES/EVENTS—
It is Visit Your Relatives Day as well as International Museum Day. So why not take your relatives to the museum?

BIRTHDAYS—
Ezio Pinza, 1892; Frank Capra, 1897; Meredith Wilson, 1902; Perry Como, 1912; Margot Fonteyn, 1919; Pernell Roberts, 1928; Reggie Jackson, 1946

NEW WORD—
fisc - noun: a royal or state treasury

QUIZ—
Who is the only player in major league baseball history to legally run the bases backwards after hitting a home run?

TRIVIA
In 1993 Ireland's Eamonn Coghlan ran the mile in 3 minutes, 58.15 seconds, becoming the first man over 40 to run a mile in less than four minutes. . . . Half of all females and 30 percent of boys ages 6 to 12 cannot run a mile in less than 10 minutes. . . . A jogger's heel strikes the ground 1,500 times a mile.

HISTORY—
On this date in 1917 the Selective Service, better known to those eligible for the military as the "draft board", was created.

GRAFFITI
Fencing Motto - In God We Thrust.

Quiz Answer: Jimmy Piersall - While playing for the 1963 New York Mets, he did it to celebrate his 100th career homer. The next day the big league rulebook was changed to make this illegal.

M A Y

TODAY'S THOUGHT:
"I have enough money to last me the rest of my life - unless I buy something." —Jackie Mason

BIRTHDAYS—
Malcolm X, 1925; David Hartman, 1937; astronaut Francis Scobee, 1939; Nora Ephron, 1941; Grace Jones, 1952; Rick Cerone, 1954; Bill Laimbeer Jr., 1957

NEW WORD—
xylotomous - adjective: cutting or boring into wood, as with certain insects

QUIZ—
Are there more than a million millionaires in the United States?

TRIVIA
Just like fingerprints, no two lip prints are alike. . . . In the United States a car is stolen every thirty seconds. . . . The busiest phone number in New York City is 911 with about 18,000 calls pouring in per day at a rate of 800 an hour.

HISTORY—
On this date in 1911 the long arm of the law first used fingerprints to get a conviction.

GRAFFITI
Cold cash is never in your pocket long enough to get warm.

Quiz Answer: Yes - There are approximately 2,500,000 or one out of every hundred people.

The Bathroom Trivia Almanac

M A Y

TODAY'S THOUGHT:
"If it wasn't for electricity we'd all be watching television by candlelight."
—George Gobel

OBSERVANCES/EVENTS—
Today is Weights and Measures Day.

BIRTHDAYS—
Dolly Madison, 1768; philosopher John Stuart Mill, 1806; James Stewart, 1908; George Gobel, 1920; Peggy Lee, 1920; Joe Cocker, 1944; Cher, 1946

NEW WORD—
dwine - verb: to fade, to waste away

QUIZ—
True or False?
The camel drinks up to thirty gallons of water at a time, which it stores in its hump.

TRIVIA
A rat can go longer without water than a camel. . . . Rats can't vomit. . . . Quick — which travels farther on a bike, the front wheel or back wheel? It's the front wheel, which moves back and forth as the bike is steered while the back wheel travels in a straight path.

HISTORY—
On this date in 1927 "Lucky Lindy", Charles Augustus Lindbergh, began his successful solo flight across the Atlantic.
In 1932 Amelia Earhart completed her transatlantic solo flight.

GRAFFITI
The metric system doesn't measure up.

Quiz Answer: True *and* false - It *can* drink up to thirty gallons of water but it isn't stored in the hump. Rather, it remains in pockets which line its stomach.

M A Y

TODAY'S THOUGHT:
"According to statistics, a man eats a prune every twenty seconds. I don't know who this fellow is, but I know where to find him."
—Morey Amsterdam

BIRTHDAYS—
Poet Alexander Pope, 1688; Fats Waller, 1904; Harold Robbins, 1916; Raymond Burr, 1917; Peggy Cass, 1924; Leo Sayer, 1948; Mr. T, 1952

NEW WORD—
ormolu - noun: an alloy of copper and zinc used to imitate gold

QUIZ—
How many teeth does a typical dog have?

TRIVIA
Your skin weighs twice as much as your brain. . . . The human tooth has approximately fifty miles of canals in it. . . . Your heel is the body part least sensitive to pain.

HISTORY—
On this date in 1881 Clara Barton founded the American Red Cross in Washington, D.C.

GRAFFITI
Old Siamese twins never die - they just join the dear departed.

Quiz Answer: 42 - 20 on top and 22 on the lower jaw

M A Y

TODAY'S THOUGHT:
"Be kind to your mother-in-law, and if necessary pay for her board at some good hotel." —Josh Billings

OBSERVANCES/EVENTS—
Today is National Maritime Day.

BIRTHDAYS—
Sir Arthur Conan Doyle, 1859; Sir Laurence Olivier, 1907; critic Judith Crist, 1922; Charles Aznavour, 1924; Richard Benjamin, 1938; Susan Strasberg, 1938; Tommy John, 1943

NEW WORD—
scombroid - adjective: resembling the mackerel

QUIZ—
Bathroom Brain Teaser:
Charles Chaplin's chaplain chided Charlie constantly concerning Chaplin's cow-like chewing. How many C's are there in all?

TRIVIA
Christmas is celebrated with fireworks in Brazil. . . . Terlingua, Texas is a ghost town that hosts the annual International Chili Society's cook off. . . . Last Chance Gulch, the 1860's mining camp, later changed its name to Helena and is now the capital of Montana.

HISTORY—
On this date in 1992 it was "Therrrrrre Goes Johnny!" After a reign that spanned the Cuban Missile Crisis, Woodstock, Watergate, disco, Reagan and the Gulf War, Johnny Carson retired from "The Tonight Show".

GRAFFITI
Coffee is break fluid.

Quiz Answer: There are no C's in "all".

M A Y

TODAY'S THOUGHT:
"Mary had a little lamb. The doctor fainted." —Anonymous

BIRTHDAYS—
Douglas Fairbanks, 1883; Artie Shaw, 1910; John Payne, 1912; Rosemary Clooney, 1928; Joan Collins, 1933; Marvin Hagler, 1952

NEW WORD—
wrick - verb: to wrench; strain

QUIZ—
Can you identify the cities bearing the following nicknames?
- A: Rubber capital of the world
- B: Pretzel city
- C: Peanut city
- D: Magic city
- E: The world's playground

TRIVIA
Caves have been found in every state except Rhode Island. . . . It would take twenty states the size of New Hampshire to fill up the state of Texas. . . . Florida's state song is "Old Folks at Home".

HISTORY—
On this date in 1785 Ben Franklin was old enough to need bifocals, so he invented them.
In 1934 Bonnie and Clyde's crime spree came to an abrupt end in a hail of bullets in Louisiana.

GRAFFITI
Most born executives had a parent who started the business.

Quiz Answer: A-Akron, Ohio; B-Reading, Pennsylvania; C-Suffolk, Virginia; D-Birmingham, Alabama; E-Atlantic City, New Jersey

M A Y

TODAY'S THOUGHT:
"The two biggest sellers in any bookstore are the cookbooks and the diet books. The cookbooks tell you how to prepare the food, and the diet books tell you how not to eat any of it." —Andy Rooney

BIRTHDAYS—
Wilbur Mills, 1909; Lilli Palmer, 1914; "Radar" Gary Burghoff, 1934; Bob Dylan, 1941; "Muppeteer" Frank Oz, 1944; Priscilla Presley, 1946; Jeffrey Kreismer, 1986

NEW WORD—
importunate - adjective: urgent or persistent in solicitation

QUIZ—
Which of these is a butterfly?
- A: Swallowtail   C: Fish tail
- B: Fantail   D: None of the above

TRIVIA
The Gap clothing store chain opened in 1969 in San Francisco and was named by its owners, Donald and Doris Fisher, after the "generation gap". . . . IBM was originally called the Computing-Tabulating-Recording Company. . . . And Nike was originally named Blue Ribbon Sports. The athletic shoemakers changed the name in 1968 to Nike after the Greek goddess of victory.

HISTORY—
On this date in 1935 baseball fans saw the light as the first major league baseball game was played at night at Crosley Field in Cincinnati.

GRAFFITI
Recall Ralph Nader.

Quiz Answer: A - (This reminds us of the one about the two caterpillars who were talking to one another when a butterfly flew past. One caterpillar says to the other, "You'll never get me up in one of those things.")

M A Y

TODAY'S THOUGHT:
"What can you say about a society that says that God is dead and Elvis is alive?" —Irv Kupcinet

OBSERVANCES/EVENTS—
Today is National Tap Dance Day, observed annually on the birthday of Bill "Bojangles" Robinson.

BIRTHDAYS—
Ralph Waldo Emerson, 1803; aeronautical engineer Igor Sikorsky, 1889; Bennett Cerf, 1898; Claude Akins, 1918; Miles Davis, 1926; Tom T. Hall, 1936; Dixie Carter, 1939; Leslie Uggams, 1943; Karen Valentine, 1947; Connie Selleca, 1955

NEW WORD—
quebrada - noun: a ravine

QUIZ—
Beverly Hills, 90210 might be the country's most famous postal code but which New York City landmarks bear the zip codes 10047 and 10048?

TRIVIA
The Custer Battlefield Monument in Montana has the world's first solar-powered toilet. . . . The Washington Monument sinks an average of six inches a year. . . . The presidential mansion in South Korea is known as the Blue House.

HISTORY—
On this date in 1968 the Gateway Arch in St. Louis formally opened. In 1986 six million Americans linked hands in "Hands Across America".

GRAFFITI
The world keeps shrinking, but postal rates keep rising.

Quiz Answer: Each of the World Trade Towers in lower Manhattan has its own zip code.

M A Y

TODAY'S THOUGHT:
"The four stages of man are infancy, childhood, adolescence and obsolescence." —Art Linkletter

BIRTHDAYS—
Al Jolson, 1886; John Wayne, 1907; James Arness, 1923; Jim Frey, 1931; Brent Musburger, 1939; Darrell Evans, 1947; Stevie Nicks, 1948; Hank Williams Jr., 1949; Sally Ride, 1951; Wesley Walker, 1955

NEW WORD—
hypocorism - noun: a pet name

QUIZ—
True or False?
In the typical American household, the television is on about four hours a day.

TRIVIA
500,000 trees are used to supply Americans with their Sunday newspapers every week. . . . Americans get almost 2 million tons of junk mail annually, using approximately 100 million trees. . . . The oldest tree ever was a bristlecone pine found in eastern Nevada. When it was cut down, it was estimated to be 5,100 years old.

HISTORY—
On this date in 1978 Atlantic City became the first city outside Nevada to offer legalized casino gambling.

GRAFFITI
**Put your best foot forward -
just watch where you step.**

Quiz Answer: False - not even close. The TV is on almost 7½ hours a day!

M A Y

TODAY'S THOUGHT:
"The nice thing about being a celebrity is that when you bore people, they think it's their fault." —Henry Kissinger

BIRTHDAYS—
Isadora Duncan, 1878; scientist Rachel Carson, 1907; Hubert Humphrey, 1911; Vincent Price, 1911; Herman Wouk, 1915; Henry Kissinger, 1923; Lee Meriwether, 1935; Lou Gossett Jr., 1936; Christopher Dodd, 1944; Pat Cash, 1965

NEW WORD—
rabot - noun: a block of hardwood used for rubbing marble prior to polishing

QUIZ—
Which person on today's birthday list was named an honorary Harlem Globetrotter?

TRIVIA
Dr. Kissinger's real name is Heinz, not Henry. . . . A tuna can swim a hundred miles in one day. . . . Approximately 98% of all coupons go unused.

HISTORY—
On this date in 1937 the Golden Gate Bridge in San Francisco opened.

——— GRAFFITI ———
There'd be more elephant hunters if the decoys weren't so heavy.

Quiz Answer: Given the choice, it wasn't THAT hard, was it? Of all the people on the list, Henry Kissinger has done the most "globetrotting" by far.

M A Y

TODAY'S THOUGHT:
"Having children is like having a bowling alley installed in your brain."
—Martin Mull

BIRTHDAYS—
Athlete Jim Thorpe, 1888; Caroll Baker, 1931; Rudolph Guiliani, 1944; Gladys Knight, 1944; Sondra Locke, 1947; Kirk Gibson, 1957

NEW WORD—
ouananiche - noun: a landlocked salmon in Quebec province

QUIZ—
What three animals move their front and hind legs on one side and then their front and hind legs on the other side when they walk?

TRIVIA
A hippopotamus can outrun a man. . . . It takes a skunk three weeks to crank out one ounce of foul odor. . . . A 25 pound turkey has about 4,000 feathers.

HISTORY—
On this date in 1934 an international sensation began with the birth of quintuplets Cecile, Marie, Emile, Yvonne and Annette Dionne in Ontario, Canada.

GRAFFITI
**Early to bed, early to rise . . .
probably means there's a baby in the house**

Quiz Answer: A cat, a camel and a giraffe

M A Y

TODAY'S THOUGHT:
"You know you are getting old when the candles cost more than the cake." —Bob Hope

BIRTHDAYS—
Patrick Henry, 1736; Bob Hope, 1903; John F. Kennedy, 1917; Fay Vincent, 1938; Al Unser, 1939; Tony Geary, 1948

NEW WORD—
umbrose - adjective: shady

QUIZ—
Bathroom Brain Teaser:
A man arrived home late one night. When he opened the door he heard the clock chime once. A half hour later it chimed once. The same thing happened a half hour later. And a half hour after that, the clock chimed only once. If the clock chimes the number of times to indicate the hour, and then once on the half-hour, what time did the the man arrive home?

TRIVIA
Some more silly statutes: You can be fined for playing dominoes in Alabama on Sunday. . . . It is illegal to hunt camels in Arizona. . . . Every citizen of Kentucky is required by law to take a bath once a year.

HISTORY—
On this date in 1953 Sir Edmund Hillary and Tenzing Norkay became the first men to reach the summit of Mount Everest.

GRAFFITI
Lambs get more sheepish with age.

Quiz Answer: Midnight — He heard the last chime at twelve, one at 12:30, another at 1:00 A.M. and one more at 1:30.

M A Y

TODAY'S THOUGHT:

"When a man has to make a speech, the first thing he has to decide is what to say." —Gerald Ford

BIRTHDAYS—

Mel Blanc, 1908; Benny Goodman, 1909; Clint Walker, 1927; Michael J. Pollard, 1939; Gale Sayers, 1940

NEW WORD—

gulgul - noun: a combination of pulverized seashells and oil used on the wooden hull of a sailing ship to deter boring worms

QUIZ—

True or False? Saudi Arabia imports camels and sand.

TRIVIA

Birds are even more warm-blooded than mammals. A body temperature of 108 degrees is not uncommon. . . . Emperor penguins have square pupils. . . . The city of Los Angeles employs a professional skunk hunter.

HISTORY—

On this date in 1911 the first Indy 500 was held. Ray Harroun took first place with the blistering speed of 75 miles per hour.

GRAFFITI

**If the chicken had used his noodle,
he wouldn't be in the soup.**

Quiz Answer: True - The desert sand is not suitable for building so river sand from Scotland is imported. Camels are getting scarce and must be imported from North Africa.

M A Y

TODAY'S THOUGHT:
"I like long walks, especially when they are taken by people who annoy me." —Fred Allen

BIRTHDAYS—
Walt Whitman, 1819; Fred Allen, 1894; Norman Vincent Peale, 1898; Clint Eastwood, 1930; Peter Yarrow, 1938; Terry Waite, 1939; Johnny Paycheck, 1941; Sharon Gless, 1943; Joe Namath, 1943; Tom Berenger, 1950; Gregory Harrison, 1950; Brooke Shields, 1965

NEW WORD—
foison - noun: plenty; abundance

QUIZ—
Who is the only swimmer to win five individual medals in a single Olympics?

TRIVIA
Black sheep have a keener sense of smell than white sheep. . . . The breed of dog with the best eyesight is the greyhound. . . . Bulls don't necessarily attack when they see a red cape; they are colorblind.

HISTORY—
On this date in 1965 Jim Clark cracked the 150 mph barrier to win auto racing's Indianapolis 500.

GRAFFITI
Dogs are tough . . .
they can lick everyone in the family.

Quiz Answer: If you guessed Mark Spitz, you're wrong. Australian schoolgirl Shane Gould won three golds, a silver and a bronze in the 1972 Olympics in Munich. For the record, Spitz won seven gold medals in the '72 Games but three of them were in relay events.

J U N E

TODAY'S THOUGHT:
"I've been on a calendar, but never on time." —Marilyn Monroe

OBSERVANCES/EVENTS—
Hurricane season begins today in the Atlantic, Caribbean, Gulf of Mexico and Central Pacific.

BIRTHDAYS—
Brigham Young, 1801; Andy Griffith, 1926; Marilyn Monroe, 1926; Pat Boone, 1934; Morgan Freeman, 1937; Cleavon Little, 1939; Lisa Hartman, 1956

NEW WORD—
lignicolous - adjective: growing on or in wood

QUIZ—
Columbus, Ohio's Mary Campbell is the only person to win what title for two consecutive years?

TRIVIA
Birthday girl Marilyn Monroe was born Norma Jean Baker. . . . The first "Playboy" covergirl was Marilyn Monroe. . . . Marilyn Monroe claimed the only thing she wore to bed was Chanel Number 5.

HISTORY—
On this date in 1925 Lou Gehrig began his major league career and played in the first of his 2,130 consecutive baseball games.

GRAFFITI
Make money hand over fist - become a boxer.

Quiz Answer: Miss America, in 1922 and 1923

J U N E

TODAY'S THOUGHT:
"A diplomat is a man who always remembers a woman's birthday but never remembers her age." —Robert Frost

BIRTHDAYS—
Martha Washington, 1732; Marquis de Sade, 1740; Sally Kellerman, 1936; Marvin Hamlisch, 1944; Jerry Mathers, 1948; Diana Canova, 1953

NEW WORD—
wanigan - noun: a lumberjack's trunk

QUIZ—
What is the longest running prime time network TV program?

TRIVIA
In the wintertime squirrels lose about half of their nuts because they forget where they stored them. . . . Meteorologically speaking, partly cloudy and partly sunny mean the same thing. . . . CHOICE COD - Hold this upside-down in front of a mirror and you'll see that the first two words of this item read the same.

HISTORY—
On this date in 1953 Elizabeth II was crowned in Westminster Abbey.

GRAFFITI
Stucco - What you get when you sit on gummo.

Quiz Answer: On the air since 1968, it's "60 Minutes", still ticking away after all these years.

J U N E

TODAY'S THOUGHT:
"Television is an invention that permits you to be entertained in your living room by people you wouldn't have in your home." —David Frost

OBSERVANCES/EVENTS—
Chimborazo Day is held to publicize the fact that Ecuador's Equatorial mountain, Chimborazo, sticks further out in space than any other point on Earth.

BIRTHDAYS—
Jefferson Davis, 1808; Maurice Evans, 1901; Colleen Dewhurst, 1924; Tony Curtis, 1925; poet Allen Ginsberg, 1926; Chuck Barris, 1929; Deniece Williams, 1951

NEW WORD—
balaustine - adjective: of or pertaining to the pomegranate

QUIZ—
You have ten seconds . . . The name of which talk show host, spelled backwards, is one of the Marx brothers?

TRIVIA
In New Brunswick, Canada there is a waterfall that sometimes flows upwards, called the Reversing Falls of St. John. . . . Canada has more lakes than the rest of the world put together. . . . The Sahara Desert is expanding south at the rate of about a half mile a year.

HISTORY—
On this date in 1888 Ernest L. Thayer's "Casey at the Bat" first appeared in the "San Francisco Examiner".

GRAFFITI
**If experience is such a great teacher,
how come you never get to graduate?**

Quiz Answer: Time's up! The answer is . . . Oprah.

J U N E

TODAY'S THOUGHT:
"A hair in the head is worth two in the brush." —Oliver Herford

BIRTHDAYS—
George III, 1738; Rosalind Russell, 1912; Robert Merrill, 1919; Gene Barry, 1921; Dennis Weaver, 1924; Bruce Dern, 1936; El DeBarge, 1961; Xavier Maurice McDaniel, 1963; Andrea Jaeger, 1965

NEW WORD—
skink - verb: to serve a beverage

QUIZ—
A few decades ago, George DeMaestral took a walk in the woods. Afterwards, the cockleburs he noticed sticking to his clothing became his inspiration for what invention?

TRIVIA
The average person's bones weigh forty pounds. . . . An adult's hair can stretch 25 percent of its length without breaking. . . . According to "Harper's Index", 80 percent of Americans believe in miracles. (The other 20 percent have been audited.)

HISTORY—
On this date in 1896 Henry Ford drove the Quadricycle, his very first automobile, onto the streets of Detroit where he made it several blocks before breaking down.

GRAFFITI
Inventors can make everything . . . except a living.

Quiz Answer: Velcro

J U N E

TODAY'S THOUGHT:
"Never eat anything you can't pronounce." —Erma Bombeck

OBSERVANCES/EVENTS—
International Mother's Peace Day, first celebrated in 1872 by Julia Ward Howe, is observed today.
Today is United Nations World Environment Day.

BIRTHDAYS—
Economist Adam Smith, 1723; William "Hopalong Cassidy" Boyd, 1898; Robert Lansing, 1929; director Jacques Demy, 1931; Bill Moyers, 1934

NEW WORD—
puling - adjective: whining, whimpering

QUIZ—
What music legend's favorite meal was a sandwich of peanut butter and bananas grilled in butter?

TRIVIA
Frank Lloyd Wright wore elevator shoes. . . . The odds against flipping a coin head's up ten times in a row are 1,023 to 1. . . . The reason you haven't seen any cashews in a shell is because they don't have any. A cashew is a seed, not a nut.

HISTORY—
On this date in 1783 man achieved sustained flight for the first time as the Montgolfier brothers of France launched their hot air balloon which rose 1,500 feet and drifted about a mile and a half before landing ten minutes later.

GRAFFITI
If you love your kid, belt him.

Quiz Answer: Elvis Presley

J U N E

TODAY'S THOUGHT:
"Ants can carry twenty times their own body weight, which is useful information if you're moving out and you need help getting a potato chip across town." —Ron Darian

OBSERVANCES/EVENTS—
National Patriot's Month begins today and runs through July 4. All citizens are encouraged to wear red, white and blue each day, to fly the U.S. flag each day, to buy American products and to decorate their homes.

BIRTHDAYS—
Nathan Hale, 1755; Thomas Mann, 1875; Bill Dickey, 1907; Gary U.S. Bonds, 1939; Bjorn Borg, 1956; Ruben Mayes, 1963

NEW WORD—
asthenia - noun: loss of strength

QUIZ—
What sporting disk had its beginnings as the Pluto Platter in the fifties?

TRIVIA
Tug-of-war began as a sport in ancient China. . . . There has been only one Triple Crown winner that sired another Triple Crown winner. Gallant Fox was the father, Omaha the offspring. . . . J. Paul Getty was once a sparring partner for heavyweight champion Jack Dempsey.

HISTORY—
On this date in 1944 Allied troops stormed ashore at Normandy Beach for D-Day, Operation Overload.

GRAFFITI
How do taxi drivers get to work?

Quiz Answer: When inventor Fred Morrison first invented them, he called them "Morrison's Flying Saucers". Wham-O rechristened them "Pluto Platters" but changed their name once more to "Frisbee" in 1958.

J U N E

TODAY'S THOUGHT:
"Never hire anybody whose resume rhymes." —Anonymous

OBSERVANCES/EVENTS—
It is Boone Day in Kentucky, the date that Daniel Boone first discovered the state.

BIRTHDAYS—
Beau Brummel, 1778; Paul Gauguin, 1848; Jessica Tandy, 1909; poet Gwendolyn Brooke, 1917; Tom Jones, 1940; Prince, 1958

NEW WORD—
mib - noun: a playing marble not used as a shooter

QUIZ—
What's next in this sequence: L, C, CC, CD, ____?

TRIVIA
Maine is the only state surrounded on three sides by another country. . . . At Four Corners you can walk in Utah, Colorado, Arizona and New Mexico within a few seconds. . . . There are 132 islands that make up Hawaii, spread out over 1,500 square miles.

HISTORY—
On this date in 1892 the practice of using pinch hitters in baseball began.

GRAFFITI
The world went from being flat to round to crooked.

Quiz Answer: DCCC - The letters are Roman numerals. L = 50; C=100; CC = 200; CD = 400; DCCC = 800

JUNE

TODAY'S THOUGHT:
"When you are eight years old, nothing is any of your business."
—Lenny Bruce

BIRTHDAYS—
Frank Lloyd Wright, 1867; Alexis Smith, 1921; Barbara Bush, 1925; Jerry Stiller, 1929; James Darren, 1936; Joan Rivers, 1937; Nancy Sinatra, 1940; Don Grady, 1944; author Sara Paretsky, 1947

NEW WORD—
edacious - adjective: devouring, consuming

QUIZ—
Which grows faster, your fingernails or toenails?

TRIVIA
Shrapnel shells were invented way back in 1784 by Great Britain's Henry Shrapnel. . . . Louis Pasteur was so obsessive about germs that he refused to shake hands with people. . . . In the Philippine jungles the yo-yo was first used as a weapon.

HISTORY—
On this date in 1869 the housekeeper's friend, I. W. McGaffey, received his patent for the first vacuum cleaner.

GRAFFITI
**Life is like basketball:
some people score points while others just dribble.**

Quiz Answer: Thumbs up for your fingernails. They grow about an inch a year, four times faster than your toenails.

J U N E

TODAY'S THOUGHT:
"What's another word for thesaurus?" —Steven Wright

OBSERVANCES/EVENTS—
Today is Donald Duck's birthday, born June 9, 1934.

BIRTHDAYS—
Cole Porter, 1893; Fred Waring, 1900; Robert McNamara, 1916; Les Paul, 1916; Marvin Kalb, 1930; Jackie Mason, 1934; David Gene Parker, 1951; Michael J. Fox, 1961; Wayman Tisdale, 1964

NEW WORD—
volition - noun: the act or power of flying

QUIZ—
Take a look at the birthday roster and pick out the celebrity who was also an inventor.

TRIVIA
Donald Duck's nephews, Huey, Dewey and Louie, have no father. . . . Ruth G. Wakefield invented the chocolate chip cookie in 1930. . . . Caesar salad has nothing to do with the rulers of Rome. It was first made in a Tijuana bar in the twenties.

HISTORY—
On this date in 1869 Philadelphia drugstore owner, Charles Hires, peddled the first root beer.

GRAFFITI
Ballet keeps you on your toes.

Quiz Answer: Band leader Fred Waring also dabbled in tinkering and, in fact, invented the Waring Blender.

JUNE

TODAY'S THOUGHT:
"I've never looked through a keyhole without finding someone was looking back." —Judy Garland

BIRTHDAYS—
Hattie McDaniel, 1889; Prince Philip, 1921; Judy Garland, 1922; Maurice Sendak, 1928; F. Lee Bailey, 1933; author Jeff Greenfield, 1943

NEW WORD—
ineluctable - adjective: inescapable, incapable of being evaded

QUIZ—
In which appropriately named section of New York City was the first "Please don't squeeze the Charmin" commercial filmed?

TRIVIA
The second most popular Father's Day gift is shaving lotion. We think you know what's first. . . . The average American has a 10,000 word vocabulary. . . . A chicken is the only animal that's eaten before it is born and after it is dead.

HISTORY—
On this date in 1935 Alcoholics Anonymous was founded in New York City by "Doctor Bob" Smith and William G. Wilson.

GRAFFITI
Betty Crocker eats TV dinners.

Quiz Answer: In Flushing, of course - Mr. Whipple, one of the longest running commercial characters on television, was played by Dick Wilson.

J U N E

TODAY'S THOUGHT:
"Remember, if you save nothing, you can't take it with you."
—Stan Laurel

BIRTHDAYS—
Poet Ben Jonson, 1572; composer Richard Strauss, 1864; Jeannette Rankin, 1880; author William Styron, 1925; Chad Everett, 1936; Jackie Stewart, 1939; Gene Wilder, 1939; Adrienne Barbeau, 1945; Joe Montana, 1956

NEW WORD—
quaternian - noun: a group or set of four persons or things

QUIZ—
A pop science quiz:
- A: For what does the term "quasar" stand?
- B: What does the term "geosyncronous orbit" mean?
- C: If H is hydrogen, I is iodine, O is oxygen and Ag is silver, how do you pronounce HIOAg?

TRIVIA
A snake can hear with its tongue. . . . During the Korean War, baseball's Cincinnati Reds changed their name to the Redlegs for political reasons. . . . The "Hollywood" sign in California was originally "Hollywoodland" but the last four letters fell down during World War II.

HISTORY—
On this date in 1770 explorer Captain Cook discovered the Great Barrier Reef off the coast of Australia - by crashing into it!

GRAFFITI
Amphibians tell lies.

Quiz Answer: A - Quasi-stellar radio source; B - It means that a satellite in that orbit stays over the very same spot on the Earth's surface . . .about 23,000 miles up; C - You don't really need any knowledge of chemistry . . . it's "Hi-O Silver!"

JUNE

TODAY'S THOUGHT:
"Grey hair is God's graffiti." —Bill Cosby

BIRTHDAYS—
Anthony Eden, 1897; David Rockefeller, 1915; George Bush, 1924; Vic Damone, 1928; Jim Nabors, 1932; musician Chick Corea, 1941; Marv Albert, 1943

NEW WORD—
xyster - noun: a surgical instrument for scraping bones

QUIZ—
What is the plural of graffiti?

TRIVIA
Trumpeter Herb Alpert played taps for military funerals. . . . George Bush, at eighteen, was the youngest navy pilot of WWII. . . . Football historians claim the quarterback's exclamation of "hut" for the snap stems from Army drills where the drill sergeant would count off "Hut-2-3-4".

HISTORY—
On this date in 1939 the National Baseball Hall of Fame was dedicated in Cooperstown, New York.

GRAFFITI
**Paying taxes to the government
is feeding the hand that bites you.**

Quiz Answer: Graffiti *is* plural. Graffito is singular.

J U N E

TODAY'S THOUGHT:

"The other day I bought a wastebasket and carried it home in a paper bag. And when I got home, I put the paper bag in the wastebasket!"
—Lily Tomlin

BIRTHDAYS—

William Butler Yeats, 1865; Basil Rathbone, 1892; Red Grange, 1904; Paul Lynde, 1926; artist Christo, 1935; Richard Thomas, 1951; Ally Sheedy, 1962; Saurnas Marciulionis, 1964

NEW WORD—

noetic - adjective: of or pertaining to the mind

QUIZ—

From the cutting edge: Who invented the bowie knife?

TRIVIA

Casanova was a novel lover who ended his life as a librarian. . . . Booker T. Washington was nicknamed "Booker" because of his love for books. . . . Winnie-the-Pooh creator A. A. Milne's initials stand for Alan Alexander.

HISTORY—

On this date in 1927 the all time greatest amount of tickertape was released above Charles Lindbergh's head as New York City showered him with affection after his history-making transatlantic solo flight. In 1962 another air traveler, John Glenn, had the second biggest ticker-tape turnout.

GRAFFITI

It is all right for your mind to go blank, as long as you turn off the sound.

Quiz Answer: If you said Jim Bowie, you deserve credit for taking a stab at it. In fact, the inventor was Jim's brother, Rezin Pleasant Bowie.

J U N E

TODAY'S THOUGHT:
"If a cluttered desk is an indication of a cluttered mind, what is indicated by an empty desk?" —Anonymous

OBSERVANCES/EVENTS—
Rally 'round the flag, it's Stars and Stripes forever. Three cheers for the red, white and blue and a snappy salute to Old Glory - it's Flag Day, first celebrated in Philadelphia in 1893.

BIRTHDAYS—
Harriet Beecher Stowe, 1811; Alois Alzheimer, 1864; Burl Ives, 1909; Dorothy McGuire, 1918; Eddie Mekka, 1952; Eric Heiden, 1958; Boy George, 1961; Steffi Graf, 1969

NEW WORD—
tourbillion - noun: a whirlwind

QUIZ—
What do Cary Middlecoff, Paul Revere, Zane Grey, Casey Stengel and Edgar Buchanan have in common?

TRIVIA
Burl Ives' full name is Burl Icle Ivanhoe Ives. . . . John Greenwood was the dentist who made George Washington's false teeth. . . . The Alaskan flag was designed by a thirteen-year-old student who won an American Legion contest.

HISTORY—
On this date in 1951 Univac, the world's first commercial computer, was demonstrated in Philadelphia, Pennsylvania.

GRAFFITI
Dentures are little white lies.

Quiz Answer: All their careers, at one time or another, were looking down in the mouth; they were dentists.

JUNE

TODAY'S THOUGHT:
"You campaign in poetry. You govern in prose." —Mario Cuomo

OBSERVANCES/EVENTS—
It is Magna Carta Day, sealed by King John in 1215. Four original copies still survive.

BIRTHDAYS—
Edvard Grieg, 1843; Mario Cuomo, 1932; Waylon Jennings, 1937; Jim Belushi, 1954; Wade Boggs, 1958; Helen Hunt, 1963

NEW WORD—
chuffy - adjective: surly, churlish

QUIZ—
What famous thoroughfare started out as Bloomingdale Road?

TRIVIA
The longest street in the United States is Figueroa Street in Los Angeles. It runs for thirty miles throughout the city. . . . The longest place name in the United States is also the longest name of a lake in the world - Lake Chargogagogmanchaugagogchaubunagamaug. . . . The longest kiss in movie history occurred in the 1940 release of "You're in the Army Now" when Regis Toomey and Jane Wyman (former wife of Ronald Reagan) puckered up for three minutes and five seconds.

HISTORY—
On this date in 1752 Ben Franklin flew a kite in a thunderstorm and discovered that lightning is electricity.

GRAFFITI
Politicians are skilled at mending fences with hedging.

Quiz Answer: Had it not been changed, George M. Cohan might have written "Give My Regards to Bloomingdale Road". . . . It's Broadway!

JUNE

TODAY'S THOUGHT:
"People with honorary awards are looked upon with disfavor. Would you let an honorary mechanic fix your brand-new Mercedes?" —Neil Simon

BIRTHDAYS—
Stan Laurel, 1890; Katherine Graham, 1917; photographer Irving Penn, 1917; John Howard Griffin, 1920; Erich Segal, 1937; Joyce Carol Oates, 1938; Billy "Crash" Craddock, 1939; Joan Van Ark, 1943; Wayne Rollins, 1955

NEW WORD—
yakka - noun: hard work

QUIZ—
Name two television crime fighters whose first names were never revealed.

TRIVIA
There's no lead in a lead pencil. It's filled with graphite. . . . A prairie dog isn't a dog. It's a rodent. . . . The Red Sea is not red. It's a bluish-green.

HISTORY—
On this date in 1963 Valentina Tereshkova of the Soviet Union became the first female astronaut in space.

GRAFFITI
When you wish upon a star
it takes two hundred million light years to receive the request.

Quiz Answer: Lt. Columbo and Quincy, although viewers once got a peek at Quincy's first initial - R

J U N E

TODAY'S THOUGHT:
"Nothing is more responsible for the good old days than a bad memory."
—Robert Benchley

BIRTHDAYS—
Igor Stravinsky, 1882; Ralph Bellamy, 1904; author John Hersey, 1917; Dean Martin, 1917; Barry Manilow, 1946; Joe Piscopo, 1951; Mark Linn-Baker, 1953

NEW WORD—
jannock - adjective: straightforward, honest

QUIZ—
Identify the states associated with the following nicknames:
- A: The Gopher State
- B: The Pelican State
- C: The Empire State of the South
- D: The Coyote State
- E: The Palmetto State

TRIVIA
The oldest city in the United States is St. Augustine, Florida founded by Menendez de Aviles in September, 1565. . . . In 1950 the town of Hot Springs, New Mexico renamed itself Truth or Consequences in honor of the game show. . . . The most common first name among U.S. presidents is James (6).

HISTORY—
On this date in 1972 the Watergate burglars broke into the offices of the Democratic National Committee.

GRAFFITI
Give a dandelion an inch and it takes over a yard.

Quiz Answer: A: Minnesota; B: Louisiana; C: Georgia; D: South Dakota; E: South Carolina

JUNE

TODAY'S THOUGHT:
"Why pay a dollar for a bookmark? Why not just use the dollar as a bookmark?" —Fred Stoller

BIRTHDAYS—
Bandleader Kay Kyser, 1906; Sammy Cahn, 1913; Sylvia Porter, 1913; E G. Marshall, 1910; journalist Tom Wicker, 1926; Roger Ebert, 1942; Paul McCartney, 1942; Carol Kane, 1952; Isabella Rossellini, 1952

NEW WORD—
equipoise - noun: an equal distribution of weight

QUIZ—
What two teams in major league baseball were once known as the Washington Senators?

TRIVIA
The newspaper in Popeye's hometown of Sweethaven is called the "Sweethaven Daily Poop". . . . Howdy Doody's sister was named Heidi Doody. . . .Dave Thomas, the founder of Wendy's, named the fast food restaurant after his daughter.

HISTORY—
On this date in 1815 the British defeated the French in the Battle of Waterloo. You might say Napoleon had a beef with Wellington and wound up in the water "loo".

——— GRAFFITI ———
Kindred is the fear that your relatives are coming.

Quiz Answer: The Minnesota Twins and the Texas Rangers - The Twins moved to Minnesota from Washington, D.C. in 1961. The newly created Washington Senators left town in 1972 and moved to Arlington, Texas.

J U N E

TODAY'S THOUGHT:

"They say the dog is man's best friend. I don't believe that. How many of your friends have you neutered?" —Larry Reeb

BIRTHDAYS—

Mathematician Blaise Pascal, 1623; Lou Gehrig, 1903; Alan Cranston, 1914; Abe Fortas, 1919; Gena Rowlands, 1936; Salmon Rushdie, 1947; Phylicia Rashad, 1948; Kathleen Turner, 1954; Paula Abdul, 1962

NEW WORD—

ustulation - noun: the act of burning or scorching

QUIZ—

What comic strip character made his first appearance on June 19, 1978?

TRIVIA

On June 19, 1978 "Bud" was the first tropical storm to be named after a male. . . . The average winter temperature in Iceland is warmer than in Chicago. . . . The energy it takes to melt a small iceberg could power a ship across the Atlantic about one hundred times.

HISTORY—

On this date in 1910, inspired by YMCA worker Mrs. John Dodd, the United States celebrated the first Father's Day, three years after Mother's Day was first celebrated.

GRAFFITI
Wall Street is the capital of capital.

Quiz Answer: Jim Davis' "Garfield" purred his way into our hearts.

JUNE

TODAY'S THOUGHT:
"My problem lies in reconciling my gross habits with my net income."
—Errol Flynn

BIRTHDAYS—
Errol Flynn, 1909; Chet Atkins, 1924; Audie Murphy, 1924; Danny Aiello, 1933; Brian Wilson, 1942; Anne Murray, 1945; Lionel Richie, 1949; John Goodman, 1952

NEW WORD—
kolacky - noun: a sweet bun filled with jam

QUIZ—
Who's the only person to appear on "TV Guide's" cover three weeks in a row?

TRIVIA
Ida May Fuller of Vermont was the first person to receive a Social Security check. She got it in 1940 and lived to be over 100, eventually collecting more than $20,000. . . . Princess Margaret's divorce from Lord Snowdon in May of 1978 took all of 53 seconds to finalize and cost a total of $29. . . . Judy Rankin was the first professional female golfer to earn more than $100,000 in a single season.

HISTORY—
On this date in 1863 the National Bank of Philadelphia was the first bank chartered by Congress.
In 1895 Caroline Baldwin became the first woman to earn a doctor of science degree, at Cornell University in Ithaca, New York.

GRAFFITI
Moonlighting is the sun's other job.

Quiz Answer: Michael Landon, 1991

JUNE

TODAY'S THOUGHT:

"The perils of duck hunting are great, especially for the duck."
—Walter Cronkite

BIRTHDAYS—

Martha Washington, 1731; painter Rockwell Kent, 1882; Jean-Paul Sartre, 1905; Jane Russell, 1921; Judy Holliday, 1922; Maureen Stapleton, 1925; Bernie Kopell, 1933; Mariette Hartley, 1941; Meredith Baxter-Birney, 1947; Michael Gross, 1947; Prince William, 1982

NEW WORD—

zymurgy - noun: the branch of chemistry related to fermentation

QUIZ—

What is Bell's Phenomenon?
- A: a ringing in one's ear
- B: the mystery behind the cracked Liberty Bell
- C: the breakup of Ma Bell into separate Baby Bell telephone systems
- D: none of the above

TRIVIA

Liberace started out by giving concerts at high schools under the name of Walter Busterkeys. . . . The last act at Woodstock was Jimi Hendrix. . . . The national anthem of China is "March On, March On".

HISTORY—

On this date in 1964 Jim Bunning pitched a perfect baseball game for the Philadelphia Phillies against the New York Mets.

GRAFFITI
Free advice is usually not worth it.

Quiz Answer: D - When eye muscles relax and the eyes roll back above their usual position, such as when we're asleep, that tendency is known as Bell's Phenomenon.

J U N E

TODAY'S THOUGHT:
"As for butter versus margarine, I trust cows more than chemists."
—Joan Gussow

BIRTHDAYS—
Anne Morrow Lindbergh, 1907; Joseph Papp, 1921; Bill Blass, 1922; Kris Kristofferson, 1936; Ed Bradley, 1941; Meryl Streep, 1949; Lindsay Wagner, 1949; Freddie Prinze, 1954; Clyde Drexler, 1962

NEW WORD—
pandect - noun: a complete code of laws

QUIZ—
Scare an elephant and . . .
- A: it'll charge you
- B: it'll rear up on its hind legs
- C: its ears will stand straight up
- D: you'll wish you hadn't

TRIVIA
Goldie was Smokey the Bear's mate. She bore him Smokey the Bear II. . . . The only dog that sweats is the Mexican hairless. . . . The early bird may catch the worm but the poorwill catches a snooze. It is the only bird that hibernates.

HISTORY—
On this date in 1938 Joe Louis got his revenge on Max Schmeling, the only boxer who had ever beaten him. It took exactly 124 seconds for Louis to drop Schmeling.

GRAFFITI
Almost anything is easier to get into than out of.

Quiz Answer: C — The elephant's ears will stand straight up.

J U N E

TODAY'S THOUGHT:

"It was a lucky thing for all of us when Alexander Graham Bell made his first telephone call, the line was not busy." —Anonymous

BIRTHDAYS—

Irvin Cobb, 1876; Bob Fosse, 1927; June Carter Cash, 1929; Wilma Rudolph, 1940; Ted Shackleford, 1946; Clarence Thomas, 1948

NEW WORD—

gleek - noun: a trick, a joke, a jest

QUIZ—

Who was the first non-American golfer to win the Masters?

TRIVIA

Weatherman Willard Scott was the original Ronald McDonald. . . . Cajun chef Paul Prudhomme weighed 500 pounds at the age of fifteen. . . . Michael Gross and Meredith Baxter, who co-starred as the TV comedy couple on the long-running "Family Ties", were, in real life, both born on the exact same day - June 21, 1947.

HISTORY—

On this date in 1980 "Late Night With David Letterman" premiered on NBC.

GRAFFITI

Old psychiatrists never die - they just shrink away.

Quiz Answer: South African Gary Player first won the Masters in 1961 and followed up in 1974 and 1978.

J U N E

TODAY'S THOUGHT:
"If law school is so hard to get through, how come there are so many lawyers?" —Calvin Trillin

BIRTHDAYS—
Henry Ward Beecher, 1813; Jack Dempsey, 1895; poet John Ciardi, 1916; Mick Fleetwood, 1942; Michelle Lee, 1942; Phyllis George, 1949; Nancy Allen, 1950

NEW WORD—
riant - adjective: cheerful, smiling, laughing

QUIZ—
History Mystery: Who was Thomas Wilson and why was he pretty well known in the early part of the twentieth century?

TRIVIA
Forty percent of M&Ms are brown. . . . Eat a raw cashew and you may "cash-ew" in your chips. A cashew contains a poisonous oil and needs to be roasted before it is safe for eating. . . . The twin Popsicle was created during the Depression so that two children could share a single treat.

HISTORY—
On this date in 1947 the term "flying saucer" was first used to describe a UFO sighting by Kenneth Arnold of Boise, Idaho. He reported seeing nine flying saucers in formation over Mount Rainier, Washington.

GRAFFITI
Man is the only creature that can reason because he is the only one who needs the excuses.

Quiz Answer: He happened to be President of the United States for eight years between 1913 and 1921. He preferred to go by his middle name, Woodrow.

J U N E

TODAY'S THOUGHT:
"All animals are equal, but some animals are more equal than others."
—George Orwell

BIRTHDAYS—
George Abbott, 1887; George Orwell, 1903; director Sidney Lumet, 1924; June Lockhart, 1925; Carly Simon, 1945; Jimmie Walker, 1948; George Michael, 1963

NEW WORD—
logogriph - noun: an anagram

QUIZ—
True or False? There has never been a bachelor president in the United States.

TRIVIA
According to the "New England Journal of Medicine", if your left thumbnail is wider and squarer at the base than the right one, you're a southpaw (and vice-versa). . . . Dogs can understand about a two hundred word human vocabulary while a cat comprehends only about fifty words. . . . The most popular hobby in the world is stamp collecting.

HISTORY—
On this date in 1876 the Battle of Little Big Horn took place. The only member of the Seventh Cavalry to survive the battle was Comanche, a horse who became a national celebrity.

GRAFFITI
Custer wore an Arrow shirt.

Quiz Answer: False - James Buchanan, the fifteenth president, was unhitched.

JUNE

TODAY'S THOUGHT:
"Big sisters are the crab grass in the lawn of life." —Charles Schulz

BIRTHDAYS—
Abner Doubleday, 1819; Pearl Buck, 1892; Peter Lorre, 1904; Eleanor Parker, 1922; Charles Robb, 1939; Greg LeMond, 1961; Jerome Kersey, 1962

NEW WORD—
formir - adjective: of or pertaining to ants

QUIZ—
Can you name the first man-made object which traveled faster than the speed of sound?

TRIVIA
Big Bird from "Sesame Street" has a teddy bear named Radar. . . . Mr. (Fred) Rogers is color blind. So are Paul Newman, Hugh Downs and Jack Nicklaus. . . . About the $24 Peter Minuet paid to the American Indians for Manhattan — invested at 8% compounded daily, that money would be worth more than 30 trillion dollars today.

HISTORY—
On this date in 1819 the patent was issued for the bicycle.
In 1945 the United Nations charter was signed by fifty nations in San Francisco.

GRAFFITI
**When in deep water,
the best thing to do is shut your mouth.**

Quiz Answer: If you're thinking Concorde, you're still up in the air about this. It's the tip of a whip. The noise at the crack of the whip is caused by the tip breaking the sound barrier.

J U N E

TODAY'S THOUGHT:
"A man with one watch knows what time it is. A man with two is never sure." —John Peers

BIRTHDAYS—
Helen Keller, 1880; Bob "Captain Kangaroo" Keeshan, 1927; H. Ross Perot, 1930; Rico Petrocelli, 1943; Julia Duffy, 1951; Craig Hodges, 1960; Chuck Person, 1964

NEW WORD—
niddering - adjective: cowardly

QUIZ—
Which is the most often sung tune in the world?

TRIVIA
Jackie Gleason wrote the theme song for "The Honeymooners". . . . The original working title of the Beatles hit song "Yesterday" was "Scrambled Eggs". . . . Chuck Berry had but a single number one hit, "My Ding-a-ling" in 1972.

HISTORY—
On this date in 1929 Bell Labs conducted the first transmission of color television. That was when the NBC peacock was still an egg.

GRAFFITI
A female moth is a myth.

Quiz Answer: "Happy Birthday to You" — This song, composed by Kentucky schoolteacher Mildred Hill, was originally written as a song for schoolchildren and titled "Good Morning to You". Sister Patty Hill had written the words in 1893 and in 1924 the now familiar "Happy Birthday" lyrics were added.

J U N E

TODAY'S THOUGHT:
"Tragedy is if I cut my finger.
Comedy is if I walk into an open sewer and die." —Mel Brooks

BIRTHDAYS—
Peter Paul Rubens, 1577; Jean-Jacques Rousseau, 1712; Richard Rodgers, 1902; author Eric Ambler, 1909; Mel Brooks, 1928; Kathy Bates, 1948; Don Baylor, 1949; John Elway, 1960; Danielle Brisebois, 1969

NEW WORD—
whid - noun: a quick noiseless movement

QUIZ—
A brain-teasing thought for the throne:
    How can you make six sixes (666666) equal 67?

TRIVIA
In Tiddlywinks, the art of flipping the winks into a cup is called "Potting". . . . According to "Guinness", the world's hardest tongue twister is this: "The sixth sick sheik's sixth sheep's sick." . . . The president of the United States receives an average of 20,000 letters in the mail every day.

HISTORY—
On this date in 1914 Archduke Francis Ferdinand and his wife were assassinated at Sarajevo, Bosnia touching off the conflict that became World War I.

GRAFFITI
**Into each life some rain must fall . . .
usually on weekends.**

Quiz Answer: 66 $^{66}/_{66}$

J U N E

TODAY'S THOUGHT:
"Blessed are the young, for they shall inherit the national debt."
—Herbert Hoover

BIRTHDAYS—
George Washington Goethals, 1858; surgeon William Mayo, 1861; Slim Pickens, 1919; Elizabeth Dole, 1936; Harmon Killebrew, 1936; Gary Busey, 1944; Fred Grandy, 1948

NEW WORD—
quercine - adjective: of or pertaining to an oak

QUIZ—
What are the only members of the animal kingdom to commonly sleep on their backs?

TRIVIA
Red schoolhouses were painted red because it was the cheapest color paint. . . . An ant's sense of smell is just as good as a dog's. . . . Retlaw Yensid was the writer of the 1966 Disney movie "Lt. Robin Crusoe, U.S.N." Retlaw Yensid is Walter Disney backwards.

HISTORY—
On this date in 1949 the United States withdrew its troops from Korea.

GRAFFITI
Pigs are full of baloney.

Quiz Answer: Those animals are human beings.

J U N E

TODAY'S THOUGHT:
"Did you ever notice that when you blow into a dog's face he gets mad, but when you take him in a car he sticks his head out the window?"
—Steve Bluestein

BIRTHDAYS—
David Wayne, 1916; Lena Horne, 1917; Buddy Rich, 1917; Susan Hayward, 1919; Mitch Richmond, 1965; Mike Tyson, 1966

NEW WORD—
arcuate - adjective: bent or curved like a bow

QUIZ—
What do these sentences have in common?
  Pack my box with five dozen liquor jugs.
  The five boxing wizards jump quickly.
  The quick brown fox jumps over a lazy dog.

TRIVIA
"Chop suey" means "odds and ends". . . . The color red is not generally used in the packaging of ice cream because it reminds people of heat. . . . Nyctophobia is the fear of darkness.

HISTORY—
On this date in 1971 the 26th Amendment was ratified giving the vote to eighteen-year-olds.

GRAFFITI
Humpty Dumpty had a great fall.
It made up for a lousy summer.

Quiz Answer: They are pangrams — a sentence that includes every letter of the alphabet.

JULY

TODAY'S THOUGHT:
"The wonderful world of appliances now makes it possible to cook indoors with charcoal and outdoors with gas." —Bill Vaughan

OBSERVANCES/EVENTS—
July is Read an Almanac Month, so just stay put and continue what you are doing.

BIRTHDAYS—
Novelist George Sand, 1804; Charles Laughton, 1899; William Wyler, 1902; Estee Lauder, 1908; Olivia DeHavilland, 1916; Leslie Caron, 1931; Sidney Pollack, 1934; Jamie Farr, 1936; Twyla Tharp, 1941; Dan Akroyd, 1952; Princess Di, 1961; Carl Lewis, 1961

NEW WORD—
ichthyophagis - noun: one who eats or subsists on fish

QUIZ—
In which city did the first United States zoo open?

TRIVIA
The 1,500 pound leatherback turtle carries a shell that is as big as a king size bed, but a lot harder to find fitted sheets for. . . . An elephant smells through its mouth, not its trunk. . . . The most common albino animal is the Siamese cat.

HISTORY—
On this date in 1862 the Bureau of Internal Revenue was established by an act of Congress.

GRAFFITI
Money talks - usually to say goodbye.

Quiz Answer: On July 1, 1874 the first zoo opened in Philadelphia with 1,000 animals on display. There were 3,000 visitors with admission costing adults 25 cents and children 10 cents.

J U L Y

TODAY'S THOUGHT:
"America is the only country in the world where you can burn the flag but can't tear the tag off the mattress." —Jackie Mason

BIRTHDAYS—
Thurgood Marshall, 1908; Dan Rowan, 1922; Polly Holiday, 1937; Richard Petty, 1937; John Sununu, 1939; Cheryl Ladd, 1952; José Canseco, 1964

NEW WORD—
taboret - noun: a stool, a low seat without a back

QUIZ—
What French word, spelled backwards, gives its English translation - a word which describes how the U.S. is made up?

TRIVIA
Abraham Lincoln was a licensed bartender. . . . The real first name of "Bonanza's" Hoss Cartwright was Eric. . . . The average magazine lies around the house for 29 weeks before someone gets around to throwing it out.

HISTORY—
On this date in 1937 aviatrix Amelia Earhart disappeared over the Pacific.

——— GRAFFITI ———
A digital clock doesn't run clockwise.

Quiz Answer: États

J U L Y

TODAY'S THOUGHT:
"Age is a high price to pay for maturity." —Tom Stoppard

OBSERVANCES/EVENTS—
On Compliment-Your-Mirror Day, you should compliment your mirror on having such a wonderful owner.

BIRTHDAYS—
Musician Pete Fountain, 1930; author Tom Stoppard, 1937; Betty Buckley, 1947; Tom Cruise, 1962

NEW WORD—
buskin - noun: a thick-soled laced boot

QUIZ—
Bathroom Brain Teaser:
Which of the following letter designs does not belong with the other six?
Y   E   N   F   H   A   Z

TRIVIA
Half the world's lemons grow in the United States, mostly in California. . . . An avocado has 370 calories, the greatest number of any fruit. . . . Pineapples are not native to Hawaii. They were first planted there in 1790.

HISTORY—
On this date in 1976 an Israeli commando unit raided the Entebbe airport in Uganda and rescued 103 hostages from a hijacked Air France plane.

GRAFFITI
Landlords aim to lease.

Quiz Answer: The letter E, which is made of four straight lines

JULY

TODAY'S THOUGHT:
"Television has proved that people will look at anything rather than each other." —Ann Landers

OBSERVANCES/EVENTS—
It is Independence Day, commemorating the adoption of the Declaration of Independence by the Continental Congress in 1776.

BIRTHDAYS—
Stephen Foster, 1826; Calvin Coolidge, 1872; Louis Armstrong, 1900; Ann Landers, 1918; Abigail Van Buren, 1918; Leona Helmsley, 1920; Eva Marie Saint, 1924; Neil Simon, 1927; Gina Lollobrigida, 1928; George Steinbrenner, 1930; Geraldo Rivera, 1943; Pam Shriver, 1962; Harvey Grant, 1965

NEW WORD—
dacryagogue - adjective: stimulating the secretion of tears

QUIZ—
Which continually published reference work in the English language has been around the longest?

TRIVIA
An excerpt from the diary of King George III of England stated, "Nothing of importance happened today." It was dated 7/4/1776. . . . Calvin Coolidge was the only president to have been sworn in by his own father. . . . Calvin Coolidge loved to fish but always wore gloves and made sure the Secret Service man handled the worms.

HISTORY—
On this date in 1826 both Thomas Jefferson and John Adams died. In 1831 a third president, James Monroe, also died on July 4.

GRAFFITI
I thought I made a mistake once, but I was wrong.

Quiz Answer: The "Encyclopaedia Brittannica" has been in existence since the mid 1700's. Incidentally, George Washington owned a set of the third edition.

J U L Y

TODAY'S THOUGHT:
"Every crowd has a silver lining." —P. T. Barnum

BIRTHDAYS—
Singapore founder Sir Stamford Raffles, 1781; Phineas T. Barnum, 1810; Katherine Helmond, 1934; Goose Gossage, 1951; James Lofton, 1956

NEW WORD—
yare - adjective: lively, agile

QUIZ—
Can you name the only major sport where you play defense when you *have* the ball?

TRIVIA
The wood used to make Lincoln Logs comes from the forests of Oregon. . . . Harry S Truman's first full day as president was on a Friday the thirteenth. . . . When Oreo cookies were first made, they were mound-shaped. The name comes from the Greek word "oreo" which means "hill".

HISTORY—
On this date in 1841 the first travel agency, Thomas Cook & Sons, was founded in London.

GRAFFITI
Only Robinson Crusoe could have everything done by Friday.

Quiz Answer: Baseball

JULY

TODAY'S THOUGHT:
"No matter how thin you slice it, it's still baloney." —Alfred E. Smith

BIRTHDAYS—
Beatrix Potter, 1866; John Paul Jones, 1747; Nancy Reagan, 1921; Merv Griffin, 1925; Janet Leigh, 1927; Ned Beatty, 1937; Sylvester Stallone, 1946

NEW WORD—
jackstraw - noun: a scarecrow or an insignificant person

QUIZ—
What city is located on two continents?

TRIVIA
"1812 Overture" composer Tchaikovsky suffered from nervous disorders and hallucinations and had a morbid fear that his head would roll off his shoulders while conducting the orchestra. . . . "Double hemisphere action" is the term used for the ability to write, simultaneously, something completely different with both your left and right hands. . . . Thomas Edison was 32 when he invented the light bulb.

HISTORY—
On this date in 1933 the first All-Star game was played with the American League winning 4-2.

GRAFFITI
**The probability of someone watching you
is directly proportional to the stupidity of your actions.**

Quiz Answer: Istanbul, Turkey is in both Asia and Europe.

The Bathroom Trivia Almanac

J U L Y

TODAY'S THOUGHT:
"I was stopped once for going 53 in a 35 mph zone, but I told them I had dyslexia." —Spanky McFarland

OBSERVANCES/EVENTS—
July is National Baked Bean Month and Sauerkraut, Salad and Sandwich season.
Fortunately, it is also National Outdoor Recreation and Parks Month.

BIRTHDAYS—
Gustav Mahler, 1860; George Cukor, 1899; composer Gian Carlo Menotti, 1911; William Kunstler, 1919; Pierre Cardin, 1922; Doc Severinsen, 1927; Ringo Starr, 1940; Jessica Hahn, 1959

NEW WORD—
cabotage - noun: navigation or trade along the coast

QUIZ—
Let's play "Jeopardy!" He was the show's first host, appearing on 1,858 shows between 1964 and 1979. And the question is . . .?

TRIVIA
Peter Graves is the younger brother of James Arness. . . . The Lone Ranger's sidekick was Tonto who was played by Jay Silverheels who was born Harold J. Smith. . . . Before making a name for herself as an opera star, Beverly Sills was known as Belle "Bubbles" Silverman.

HISTORY—
On this date in 1891 the patent was issued for traveler's checks.

GRAFFITI
If people go on vacations for peace and quiet, why do they dress so loud?

Quiz Answer: Who is Art Fleming?

JULY

TODAY'S THOUGHT:
"There are three periods in life: youth, middle age and 'how well you look.' " —Nelson Rockefeller

BIRTHDAYS—
Nelson Rockefeller, 1908; drama critic Walter Kerr, 1913; Roone Arledge, 1931; Steve Lawrence, 1935; ballerina Cynthia Gregory, 1946; Angelica Huston, 1951

NEW WORD—
sabulous - adjective: sandy, gritty

QUIZ—
Which state has the most miles of highway and the most vehicles per square mile?

TRIVIA
The Rolls Royce Corporation was founded in 1904 by two Englishmen, Rolls and Royce. . . . The largest production car ever made was the 1927 Golden Bugatti. It measured 27 feet from bumper to bumper. Only six of these were ever made and some are still around. . . . The first person to be arrested for speeding was a New York City cab driver. On May 20, 1899 Jacob German was arrested for doing a breakneck 12 mph.

HISTORY—
On this date in 1835 the Liberty Bell cracked - again - while tolling the death of the first Chief Justice, John Marshall.

GRAFFITI
Most of us wouldn't mind the rat race so much if we only could get a little more cheese.

Quiz Answer: The Garden State, New Jersey

J U L Y

TODAY'S THOUGHT:

"Fear of losing is what makes competitors so great. Show me a gracious loser and I'll show you a perennial loser." —O. J. Simpson

BIRTHDAYS—

Novelist Ann Ward Radcliffe, 1764; Elias Howe, 1819; James Hampton, 1936; Brian Dennehy, 1938; O. J. Simpson, 1947; Tom Hanks, 1956; Jimmy Smits, 1958

NEW WORD—

harmatten - noun: a dry parching land breeze in West Africa, charged with dust

QUIZ—

Sixties Flashback:

A: What comedian ran for President in 1968?

B: What was U Thant's first name?

C: What pitcher had the dubious distinction of serving up Roger Maris' record breaking 61st?

D: What cigarette advertised the slogan "LS/MFT"?

TRIVIA

The K in K-Mart stands for Kresge, from Sebastian S. Kresge who founded the store in Detroit in 1897. . . . Avon, the cosmetics giant, got its name because the founder was fond of Shakespeare, so the company was named after Stratford-on-Avon. . . . Elephants can get flat feet.

HISTORY—

On this date in 1872 the patent was issued for the doughnut cutter (although the inventor went in a hole).

GRAFFITI

There is a big difference between looking cool and not so hot.

Quiz Answer: A-Pat Paulsen; B-He had none. "U" is a Burmese honorific; C - Tracy Stallard of the Red Sox; D - Lucky Strike Means Fine Tobacco

JULY

TODAY'S THOUGHT:
"I think God invented rain to give dead people something to complain about." —David Brenner

BIRTHDAYS—
Painter James Whistler, 1834; Marcel Proust, 1871; Saul Bellow, 1915; David Brinkley, 1920; Fred Gwynne, 1926; Jerry Herman, 1933; Arthur Ashe, 1943; Arlo Guthrie, 1947; Andre Dawson, 1954; Roger Craig, 1960

NEW WORD—
unco - adjective: remarkable, extraordinary

QUIZ—
Which Ohio town doesn't belong and why? (Hint: "A man a plan a canal, Panama!")

    A: Ada   C: Anna
    B: Akron D: Ava

TRIVIA
Ketchup was originally a Chinese medicine. . . . 2.8 million pieces of airline luggage are misrouted every year. . . . The average American laughs fifteen times a day.

HISTORY—
On this date in 1942 the Allies invaded Sicily.
In 1958 the world's heaviest man, Robert Earl Hughes of Monticello, Illinois passed away. Weighing approximately a half ton, he was buried in a piano case.

———— GRAFFITI ————
Weatherman have their heads in the clouds.

Quiz Answer: B - The other towns are all palindromes (words that read the same backward and forward). Wow!

J U L Y

TODAY'S THOUGHT:
"When I am dead and buried, on my tombstone I would like to have it written, 'I have arrived.' Because when you feel that you have arrived, you are dead." —Yul Brynner

OBSERVANCES/EVENTS—
United Nations: World Population Day tries to focus public attention on the urgency and importance of population issues.

BIRTHDAYS—
John Quincy Adams, 1767; Thomas Mitchell, 1892; Yul Brynner, 1920; Tab Hunter, 1931; Debbie Harry, 1945; Bonnie Pointer, 1951; Leon Spinks, 1953

NEW WORD—
egregious - adjective: remarkable in a bad way

QUIZ—
Which is taller, St. Louis' Gateway Arch or the Washington Monument in Washington, D.C.?

TRIVIA
Your nose and ears never stop growing. . . . Dr. Seuss coined the term "nerd". . . . Greer Garson delivered the longest acceptance speech ever in the history of the Academy Awards when she won the Oscar for Best Actress in "Mrs. Miniver". Her speech lasted thirty minutes.

HISTORY—
On this date in 1804 Alexander Hamilton and Vice President Aaron Burr held their duel. Hamilton missed . . . Burr didn't.

GRAFFITI
Some celebrities think they're photogenic, when they're just overexposed.

Quiz Answer: The Gateway Arch, at 630 feet, is 75 feet taller than the Washington Monument.

J U L Y

TODAY'S THOUGHT:
"I never found the companion that was so companionable as solitude."
—Henry David Thoreau

BIRTHDAYS—
Pottery designer Josiah Wedgewood, 1730; Henry David Thoreau, 1817; Oscar Hammerstein, 1895; Milton Berle, 1908; Andrew Wyeth, 1917; Mark Hatfield, 1922; Van Cliburn, 1934; Bill Cosby, 1938; Richard Simmons, 1948

NEW WORD—
kaolin - noun: fine white clay used for the manufacture of porcelain

QUIZ—
In an average lifetime, an American drinks about:

      A: 2,000 gallons of water
      B: 4,000 gallons of water
      C: 6,000 gallons of water
      D: 11,000 gallons of water
      E: 120,000 gallons of water

TRIVIA
Edgar Allan Poe often wrote his works with his cat seated on his shoulder. . . . U.S. paper currency measures $6\frac{1}{8}$ by $2\frac{9}{16}$ inches. . . . Each of your toes has three bones except for your big toe which has but two.

HISTORY—
On this date in 1862 the Congressional Medal of Honor was created.

GRAFFITI
**Show me someone with a clear conscience
and I'll show you someone with a lousy memory.**

Quiz Answer: D - 11,000 gallons of water

J U L Y

TODAY'S THOUGHT:
"Too often we . . . enjoy the comfort of opinion without the discomfort of thought." —John F. Kennedy

BIRTHDAYS—
Dave Garroway, 1913; author David Storey, 1933; Jack Kemp, 1935; Robert Forster, 1941; Harrison Ford, 1942; Roger McGuinn, 1942; Erno Rubick, 1944; Spud Webb, 1963

NEW WORD—
objurgate - verb: to berate harshly

QUIZ—
You've spent countless hours watching "The Honeymooners", but did you ever happen to catch Alice's maiden name? And what famous comedian did a guest stint as the Kramden's landlord?

TRIVIA
The first female cabinet member was Frances Perkins, appointed by FDR in 1933 as Secretary of Labor. . . . Dogs are more likely to have a nervous breakdown than any other non-human animal. . . . Morris the Cat, originally named Lucky, was the first animal to be featured on "Lifestyles of the Rich and Famous".

HISTORY—
On this date in 1960 the Democratic Party nominated John F. Kennedy for president.

GRAFFITI
They are called sitcoms
because the audience sits and gets comatose.

Quiz Answer: Before she met Ralph and embarked on her life of luxury, Alice's last name was Gibson. Ralph had good reason to call the landlord stingy . . . he was played in one episode by Jack Benny.

JULY

TODAY'S THOUGHT:
"Celibacy is not hereditary." —Guy Goden

OBSERVANCES/EVENTS—
Today is Bastille Day.

BIRTHDAYS—
Terry-Thomas, 1911; Woody Guthrie, 1912; Gerald Ford, 1913; Edward Douglas, 1917; Ingmar Bergman, 1918; Frances Lear, 1923; John Chancellor, 1927; Polly Bergen, 1930; Steve Stone, 1947; Missy Gold, 1970

NEW WORD—
vaticinal - adjective: prophetic

QUIZ—
Did America ever have a King for president?

TRIVIA
Gerald Ford was the only American president to have been a male model. He modeled winter sports clothes for "Look" magazine in 1939. . . . The only president to attend the Indy 500 was Gerald Ford in 1979. . . . Ford was the only president to have been an Eagle Scout.

HISTORY—
On this date in 1881 Sheriff Pat Garrett shot and killed Billy the Kid.

GRAFFITI
Earthquake predictors are faultfinders.

Quiz Answer: Yes, former President Gerald R. Ford was born Leslie King. He has the distinction of being the only nonelected vice president and president in United States history.

J U L Y

TODAY'S THOUGHT:
"Rise early. Work late. Strike oil." —J. Paul Getty

OBSERVANCES/EVENTS—
It is St. Swithin's Day. Not too much is known about the Saint's life but the legend is that whatever the weather is on this day, it will continue for the next forty days.

BIRTHDAYS—
Rembrandt van Rijn, 1605; Clement Moore, 1779; Alex Karras, 1935; Ken Kercheval, 1935; Jan-Michael Vincent, 1944; Linda Ronstadt, 1946; Willie Aames, 1960; model Kim Alexis, 1960

NEW WORD—
malic - adjective: derived from or pertaining to apples

QUIZ—
Name the three states in the U.S. that begin and end with the letter "A".

TRIVIA
The oldest bridegroom in history was Ralph Cambridge who was 105 when he tied the knot with his 70-year-old bride, Adriana Kapp. . . . Turn-of-the-century multimillionaire Russell Sage amassed much of his money by never buying underwear. You could say he saved all his long john silver! . . . The word "karate" means empty hand.

HISTORY—
On this date in 1933 Wiley Post took off from New York in a Lockheed Vega thus beginning the first around-the-world flight.

GRAFFITI
It is easy to find someone to look up to if you're always sitting down.

Quiz Answer: Alabama, Alaska and Arizona

J U L Y

TODAY'S THOUGHT:
"If President Lincoln were alive today, he'd roll over in his grave."
—Gerald R. Ford

BIRTHDAYS—
Mary Baker Eddy, 1821; Roald Amundsen, 1872; Barbara Stanwyck, 1907; Ginger Rogers, 1911; Bernard Hughes, 1915; Bess Myerson, 1924; Margaret Court, 1942; violinist Pinchas Zukerman, 1948; Barry Sanders, 1968

NEW WORD—
borasca - noun: a squall, usually accompanied by lightning and thunder

QUIZ—
The winner of what race wins the Borg-Warner trophy?

TRIVIA
Composer Johann Sebastian Bach had 20 children. . . . Sleepwalking is hereditary. And 2.5% of Americans do it regularly. . . . Lady Randolph Churchill, Winston's mother, invented the Manhattan cocktail in 1874.

HISTORY—
On this date in 1790 legislation was signed by George Washington selecting the District of Columbia as the permanent capital of the United States.
In 1945 scientists exploded the first atomic bomb at Alamagordo, New Mexico.

GRAFFITI
**Kleptomaniacs help themselves
because they can't help themselves.**

Quiz Answer: The Indianapolis 500

J U L Y

TODAY'S THOUGHT:
"Never go to bed mad. Stay up and fight." —Phyllis Diller

OBSERVANCES/EVENTS—
It is Wrong Way Corrigan Day. In one of the biggest goofs ever, Douglas Corrigan took off in his plane from Brooklyn in 1938 intending to land at Los Angeles. A little over 28 hours later, he arrived at Dublin, Ireland and discovered that he had been following the wrong end of his compass needle.

BIRTHDAYS—
Erle Stanley Gardner, 1889; James Cagney, 1899; Phyllis Diller, 1917; Diahann Carroll, 1935; Donald Sutherland, 1935; David Hasselhoff, 1952

NEW WORD—
quondam - adjective: former, that formerly existed

QUIZ—
In honor of Erle Stanley Gardner's birthday, here is a Perry Mason question: What was the major casting shake-up which took place just before the long running series debuted on CBS?

TRIVIA
Dorothy's pet cow in "The Wizard of Oz" was named Imogene. . . . Great Danes come from Germany, not Denmark. . . . Albert Einstein's brain is in a mason jar in a Wichita, Kansas laboratory.

HISTORY—
On this date in 1941 Joe DiMaggio's record 56 game hitting streak came to an end when he went 0-3 against the Cleveland Indians.

GRAFFITI
A diet is a weigh of life.

Quiz Answer: Originally Raymond Burr was to play hapless D. A. Hamilton Burger, but when Erle Stanley Gardner saw him, he insisted Burr was the man to play Perry.

J U L Y

TODAY'S THOUGHT:
"I'm desperately trying to figure out why kamikaze pilots wore helmets."
—Dave Edison

BIRTHDAYS—
S. I. Hayakawa, 1906; Clifford Odets, 1906; Hume Cronyn, 1911; Red Skelton, 1913; Nelson Mandela, 1918; John Glenn, 1921; Dick Button, 1929; Dion DiMucci, 1939; Martha Reeves, 1941; Ricky Skaggs, 1954; Elizabeth McGovern, 1961

NEW WORD—
ramentum - noun: a particle, scraping or shaving

QUIZ—
Bathroom Brain Teaser:
June 21, the first day of summer, is called the longest day of the year. What day is actually longer?

TRIVIA
In the 19th century, nine pins were used in bowling. . . . U.S. presidents U.S. Grant, William Howard Taft, Herbert Hoover and Dwight D. Eisenhower never held any other elective office. . . . Alligator shirts have crocodiles on them.

HISTORY—
On this date in 1969 Edward Kennedy's car plunged off the Chappaquiddick Bridge killing passenger Mary Jo Kopechne.

GRAFFITI
Language is funny. Just when you think you know the meaning of the word 'stupid', someone comes along and redefines it.

Quiz Answer: The day the clocks are turned back to end Daylight Savings Time, which is 25 hours

J U L Y

TODAY'S THOUGHT:

"Never run after your hat - others will be delighted to do it; why spoil their fun?" —Mark Twain

BIRTHDAYS—

George McGovern, 1922; Rosey Grier, 1932; Vicki Carr, 1941; Ilie Nastase, 1946

NEW WORD—

feneration - noun: usury, the lending of money on interest

QUIZ—

Can you name the TV character who was so popular that when she died of a stroke in 1980, "Newsweek" ran a half-page obituary?

TRIVIA

If you think you eat like a bird, think again. Birds eat from one quarter to one half their body weight every day. . . . The Roman Colosseum was formerly called the Flavian Amphitheater. . . . Every single hamster in the U.S. today comes from a single litter captured in Syria in 1930.

HISTORY—

On this date in 1990 baseball great Pete Rose was sentenced to 5 months in prison, 3 months in a halfway house, plus 1,000 hours community service and a $50,000 fine for cheating on his taxes.

GRAFFITI

Old basketball players never die - they just dribble away.

Quiz Answer: Edith Bunker of TV's "All in the Family"

J U L Y

TODAY'S THOUGHT:
"The greater the fool the better the dancer." —Theodore Hook

BIRTHDAYS—
Theda Bara, 1890; Sir Edmund Hillary, 1919; Chuck Daly, 1933; Nelson Doubleday, 1933; Sally Ann Howes, 1934; Diana Rigg, 1938; Kim Carnes, 1946; Carlos Santana, 1947

NEW WORD—
winklehawk - noun: an "L" shaped tear in fabric

QUIZ—
Every telephone area code in the United States has a three digit number with the middle digit always being one of two numbers. Do you know both of them?

TRIVIA
The oldest subway in the world went into service in 1863 in London. . . . Henry Wadsworth Longfellow is the only American whose bust is in Westminster Abbey. . . . It doesn't matter what the birth certificate says in England; all royal birthdays are celebrated in June.

HISTORY—
On this date in 1969 the lunar module from Apollo XI landed on the moon.
In 1976 Viking I landed on Mars.

GRAFFITI
**It took about fifty years
for movies to go from silent to unspeakable.**

Quiz Answer: 0 or 1

JULY

TODAY'S THOUGHT:
"Have you ever wondered if illiterate people get the full effect of alphabet soup?" —John Mendoza

BIRTHDAYS—
Ernest Hemingway, 1899; Marshall McLuhan, 1911; Isaac Stern, 1920; Don Knotts, 1924; Norman Jewison, 1926; Robin Williams, 1952

NEW WORD—
marmoreal - adjective: of or like marble

QUIZ—
Besides deep water, what additional deterrent did medieval moats offer against those invaders who wanted to storm the castle?

TRIVIA
Ernest Hemingway rewrote the last page of "A Farewell to Arms" 39 times. . . . Horatio Alger is a most prolific author with publication of 119 full length novels in 30 years. . . . In the James Bond novels by Ian Fleming, the Bond family's motto was "The World Is Not Enough".

HISTORY—
On this date in 1925 the Monkey Trial ended with John Scopes being fined $100 for teaching the theory of evolution.

GRAFFITI
Bell ringers are always at the end of their rope.

Quiz Answer: The moat also served as a sewer.

J U L Y

TODAY'S THOUGHT:
"If you're hanging around with nothing to do and the zoo is closed, come over to the Senate. You'll get the same kind of feeling and you won't have to pay." —Robert Dole

OBSERVANCES/EVENTS—
It is Rat Catcher's Day commemorating the Pied Piper of Hamelin.

BIRTHDAYS—
Stephen Vincent Benet, 1898; Robert Dole, 1923; Orson Bean, 1928; Oscar De La Renta, 1932; Bobby Sherman, 1945; Albert Brooks, 1947; Danny Glover, 1947; Don Henley, 1947

NEW WORD—
quern - noun: a primitive, hand operated grain grinding mill

QUIZ—
Which one of these famous generals graduated number one in his class at West Point?

    A: Douglas MacArthur   C: William Westmoreland
    B: Dwight Eisenhower   D: George Patton

TRIVIA
Frank Lloyd Wright coined the word "carport".... The largest fruit crop on earth is grapes. . . . Al Capone carried a business card stating that he was "a second hand furniture dealer".

HISTORY—
On this date in 1934 John Dillinger, Public Enemy #1, was gunned down by federal agents in Chicago after being betrayed by the woman in red. Dillinger had gone to the movies to see Myrna Loy in "Manhattan Melodrama".

GRAFFITI
Ban Graffiti.

Quiz Answer: A - All of the others failed to finish within the top 45 of their graduating class.

J U L Y

TODAY'S THOUGHT:
"If you want to know how old a woman is, ask her sister-in-law."
—Ed Howe

BIRTHDAYS—
Raymond Chandler, 1883; Gloria DeHaven, 1925; architect Arata Isozaki, 1931; Bert Convy, 1933; Don Drysdale, 1936; journalist Nicholas Gage, 1939; Belinda Montgomery, 1950; Gary Payton, 1968

NEW WORD—
cothurnus - noun: tragic acting

QUIZ—
What baseball feat was Sal Durante famous for in 1961?

TRIVIA
In 1938 Charles Zibbleman swam the Hudson River from Albany to New York City, traveling 147 miles and setting the record for handicapped swimmers. Zibbleman had no legs. . . . In 1960 Michael Eufemia had the world's longest continuous run in a straight pool match, sinking 625 balls without a miss. . . . A pro golfer whacks the ball at 170 mph or more.

HISTORY—
On this date in 1984 Vanessa Williams became the first Miss America to resign after photographs of her surfaced and scandalized the executives of the pageant.

GRAFFITI
Two wrongs don't make a right, but three lefts will.

Quiz Answer: He is the baseball fan who caught Roger Maris' record breaking 61st home run.

JULY

TODAY'S THOUGHT:
"The problem with cats is that they get the exact same look for a moth or an ax murderer." —Paula Poundstone

BIRTHDAYS—
Simon Bolivar, 1783; Alexandre Dumas, 1802; Amelia Earhart, 1898; Bella Abzug, 1920; cartoonist Pat Oliphant, 1935; Ruth Buzzi, 1936; Robert Hays, 1947; Lynda Carter, 1951; Joe Carroll, 1958; Kevin Butler, 1962; Karl Malone, 1963

NEW WORD—
stilb - noun: unit of luminance equal to one candle per square centimeter

QUIZ—
What group has also been dubbed "The Invisible Empire of the South"?

TRIVIA
The delicious apple was originally called the Hawkeye. . . . The average American eats 1,889 Tootsie Rolls in a lifetime. . . . A watermelon is 92 percent water.

HISTORY—
On this date in 1701 Antoine de la Mothe Cadillac, in the service of Louis XIV of France, landed at the site of Detroit. And, yes, the Cadillac car was named for him.

GRAFFITI
Now that we have digital clocks, we'll never be able to turn back the hands of time.

Quiz Answer: The Ku Klux Klan

J U L Y

TODAY'S THOUGHT:
"Any kid will run any errand for you, if you ask at bedtime." —Red Skelton

BIRTHDAYS—
Walter Brennan, 1894; Estelle Getty, 1924; Nate Thurmond, 1941; Walter Payton, 1954; Douglas Drabeck, 1962; Louise Joy Brown, 1978

NEW WORD—
jurant - noun: a person who takes an oath

QUIZ—
What do the names Chang, Schultz and Smith have in common?

TRIVIA
Do you sleep in your birthday suit? 20% of men and 6% of women say they do. . . . Van Gogh signed his paintings with his first name, Vincent. . . . Life Savers are the best-selling candy in the world.

HISTORY—
On this date in 1866 Ulysses S. Grant was named General of the Army, the first officer in the United States to hold that rank.

GRAFFITI
Fight air pollution — inhale.

Quiz Answer: They are the most common last names in China, Germany and the U.S. respectively. Chang is the most popular name in the world.

JULY

TODAY'S THOUGHT:
"She had lost the art of conversation, but not, unfortunately, the power of speech." —George Bernard Shaw

BIRTHDAYS—
George Bernard Shaw, 1856; Aldous Huxley, 1894; Gracie Allen, 1906; Vivian Vance, 1912; Blake Edwards, 1922; Jason Robards, 1922; Mick Jagger, 1943; Susan George, 1950

NEW WORD—
thig - verb: to beg or solicit

QUIZ—
You've heard of the term "south of the Mason-Dixon line", but exactly where is the Mason-Dixon line?

TRIVIA
The Mason-Dixon line was named for the surveyors Charles Mason and Jeremiah Dixon. . . . Alaska is almost three times the size of Texas. . . . Although Illinois license plates boast "Land of Lincoln", until he was an adult Abe Lincoln had never set foot in Illinois.

HISTORY—
On this date in 1947 the Department of Defense, the National Security Council and the CIA were founded.

———— GRAFFITI ————
In Hollywood people try to put their best face forward.

Quiz Answer: It is a 244 mile long dividing line that marks the southern boundary of Pennsylvania. In actuality, such places as part of New Jersey and Washington D.C. are south of the line.

J U L Y

TODAY'S THOUGHT:
"Baseball is ninety percent mental, and the other half is physical."
—Yogi Berra

BIRTHDAYS—
Leo Durocher, 1905; Keenan Wynn, 1916; Norman Lear, 1922; Bobbie Gentry, 1942; Peggy Fleming, 1948; Betty Thomas, 1948; Maureen McGovern, 1949

NEW WORD—
glyptograph - noun: an engraved design on a gem

QUIZ—
What are the only three words in the English language that begin with "dw"?

TRIVIA
Sir Walter Raleigh is buried with his favorite pipe and a tin of tobacco. . . . Statistics show that Saturday is the most dangerous day to drive an automobile. . . . Benjamin Spock's "Common Sense Book of Baby and Child Care" is the best-selling nonfiction book of all time.

HISTORY—
On this date in 1586 Sir Walter Raleigh proved hazardous to the health of Britain when he introduced Virginian tobacco to England.
In 1940 "Billboard" magazine published its first top selling record chart.

GRAFFITI
A low cholesterol diet is the key to heartening of the arteries.

Quiz Answer: dwarf, dwell and dwindle

J U L Y

TODAY'S THOUGHT:
"The one thing I do not want to be called is First Lady. It sounds like a saddle horse." —Jacqueline Kennedy

BIRTHDAYS—
Rudy Vallee, 1901; Jacques Piccard, 1922; Jackie Kennedy Onassis, 1929; Darryl Hickman, 1931; Bill Bradley, 1943; Linda Kelsey, 1946; Sally Struthers, 1948; Terry Fox, 1958

NEW WORD—
pyriform - adjective: pear-shaped

QUIZ—
What happens to your social security number when you die?

TRIVIA
The Rolling Stones got their name from "Rolling Stone Blues" by Muddy Waters. . . . There are 66 acceptable two-letter words in Scrabble. . . . When you breathe, the speed of your exhaled air is about 15 miles per hour.

HISTORY—
On this date in 1933 the very first singing telegram was delivered, wishing a happy birthday to Rudy Vallee.

——— GRAFFITI ———
Overcharging your credit card is cause for plastic surgery.

Quiz Answer: The numbers are retired, naturally. The nine digit combination gives them about one billion to choose from, so unless we extend benefits to the rest of the world, we have plenty of numbers left.

J U L Y

TODAY'S THOUGHT:
"They say you can't do it, but sometimes it doesn't always work."
—Casey Stengel

BIRTHDAYS—
Booth Tarkington, 1869; Benito Mussolini, 1883; William Powell, 1892; Dag Hammarskjold, 1905; Melvin Belli, 1907; Nancy Kassebaum, 1932; Peter Jennings, 1938; Marilyn Tucker Quayle, 1949; Patty Scialfa, 1956; Michael Spinks, 1956

NEW WORD—
lucent - adjective: shining

QUIZ—
What was the original purpose of the tower on the Empire State Building?

TRIVIA
The Empire State Building has 10 million bricks and 6,400 windows. . . . The 110 story Sears Tower, served by 18 elevators, is the world's tallest building with a total height of 1,707 feet. . . . The Statue of Liberty is approximately 20 times life size.

HISTORY—
On this date in 1958 NASA was founded.
In 1981 Prince Charles and Lady Di were wed.

GRAFFITI
**Life resembles the movies:
you're constantly in the dark, making projections.**

Quiz Answer: It was designed for the docking of dirigibles.

J U L Y

TODAY'S THOUGHT:
"How you lose or keep your hair depends on how wisely you choose your parents." —Edward R. Nida

BIRTHDAYS—
Emily Bronte, 1818; Henry Ford, 1863; Casey Stengel, 1891; Edd Byrnes, 1933; Peter Bogdanovich, 1939; Paul Anka, 1941; Arnold Schwarzenegger, 1947; Anita Hill, 1956; Bill Cartwright, 1957

NEW WORD—
heuristic - adjective: serving to indicate, point out, guide, discover, reveal

QUIZ—
What is the only food that doesn't spoil?

TRIVIA
It was (and maybe still is) illegal to wear roller skates in a Portland, Oregon restroom. . . . Arizona had a statute making it illegal to hunt camels in that state. . . . And in New York it is illegal to shoot at a rabbit from a moving trolley car.

HISTORY—
On this date in 1975 James R. Hoffa was last seen outside a restaurant in Michigan. Seven years and 131 days later, on December 8, 1982 Hoffa was declared legally dead.

GRAFFITI
Mud thrown is ground lost.

Quiz Answer: Honey

J U L Y

TODAY'S THOUGHT:
"Artificial hearts are nothing new. Politicians have had them for years."
—Mac McGinnis

BIRTHDAYS—
Economist Milton Friedman, 1912; Irv Kupcinet, 1912; Curt Gowdy, 1919; Don Murray, 1929; Geraldine Chaplin, 1944; Evonne Goolagong, 1951

NEW WORD—
auscultation - noun: act of listening to sounds with the body

QUIZ—
Which heart beats faster, an elephant's or a canary's?

TRIVIA
The Pieta was the only one of Michaelangelo's sculptures that he signed. . . . Leonardo da Vinci had trouble finishing anything. His interest would always wander to something else and he left a trail of partially completed works across Italy. . . . James Whistler had to buy back his most famous painting, "Whistler's Mother", from a pawnshop after his mother passed away.

HISTORY—
On this date in 1970 Chet Huntley said his last "Goodnight, David" on NBC.
In 1981 MTV made its debut.

GRAFFITI
The good thing about mincing your words is that they are easier to eat later on.

Quiz Answer: The canary's beats at a much heartier rate - 1,000 times a minute compared to the 27 times per minute of an elephant's heart.

AUGUST

TODAY'S THOUGHT:
"An utterly fearless man is a far more dangerous comrade than a coward."
—Herman Melville

OBSERVANCES/EVENTS—
It is International Clown Week.

BIRTHDAYS—
Francis Scott Key, 1779; Herman Melville, 1819; Arthur Hill, 1922; cartoonist Tom Wilson, 1931; Dom DeLuise, 1933; Yves Saint Laurent, 1936; Alfonse D'Amato, 1937; Jerry Garcia, 1942

NEW WORD—
enisle - verb: to make an island of; to isolate

QUIZ—
What fateful contact did the Lincoln family have with the Booth family prior to 1865?

TRIVIA
Each quill of the porcupine has about 1,000 tiny sharp barbs. . . . A full grown circus lion consumes about 30 pounds of horse meat a day. . . . A pig always sleeps on its right side.

HISTORY—
On this date in 1790 the first United States census resulted in a head count of about four million people . . . more than that now work for the government!

GRAFFITI
A politician, generally speaking, speaks generally.

Quiz Answer: In one of the strangest coincidences in history, one day in Jersey City a young Robert Todd Lincoln, Abe's son, fell between railroad cars and was rescued by actor Edwin Booth, brother of John Wilkes Booth.

AUGUST

TODAY'S THOUGHT:
"Children have never been very good at listening to their elders, but they have never failed to imitate them." —James Baldwin

OBSERVANCES/EVENTS—
It is National Catfish month, National Eye Exam Month, National Water Quality Month and Romance Awareness Month.

BIRTHDAYS—
Architect Pierre Charles L'Enfant, 1754; Myrna Loy, 1905; Gary Merrill, 1915; Beatrice Straight, 1918; James Baldwin, 1924; Carroll O'Connor, 1924; Peter O'Toole, 1933; Linda Fratianne, 1960

NEW WORD—
inchoate - adjective: just begun

QUIZ—
What nation used to be the kingdom of Siam?

TRIVIA
Asia is four times the size of Europe. . . . The Sahara Desert is over three times the size of the Mediterranean Sea. . . . Only three percent of Norway is under cultivation — the rest is under ice.

HISTORY—
On this date in 1873 the San Francisco cable car had its first trial run.

GRAFFITI
When you jump to conclusions, there is never a safety net.

Quiz Answer: Thailand used to be Siam, if you please.

AUGUST

TODAY'S THOUGHT:
"If you go long enough without a bath, even the fleas will let you alone."
—Ernie Pyle

BIRTHDAYS—
Ernie Pyle, 1900; John Scopes, 1900; Delores Del Rio, 1905; Leon Uris, 1924; Tony Bennett, 1926; Martin Sheen, 1940

NEW WORD—
nescience - noun: lack of knowledge

QUIZ—
Bathroom Brain Teaser:
A boy borrowed a book from the library with the words "How to Hum" printed on it. When he opened it at home, he discovered it was not about humming at all. What was it?

TRIVIA
Over one million drawings went into the movie production of "Pinocchio". . . . The largest single edition of a newspaper was the "New York Times", dated Sunday, October 10, 1971. There were fifteen sections with a total of 972 pages; each copy weighed over seven pounds. . . . "Esquire" named Tiny Tim 'Bridegroom of the Year' in 1969.

HISTORY—
On this date in 1492 Christopher Columbus set sail from Spain on his way to the New World and the discovery of America. The voyage cost about $7,000 which included his personal salary of $300 a year.

GRAFFITI
Collect books - put something away for a brainy day.

Quiz Answer: Part of an encyclopedia

AUGUST

TODAY'S THOUGHT:
"If there were any justice in the world, people would be able to fly over pigeons for a change." —Anonymous

BIRTHDAYS—
Percy Bysshe Shelley, 1792; Elizabeth, the Queen Mother, 1900; Raoul Wallenberg, 1912; journalist Helen Thomas, 1920; Maurice Richard, 1921; Kristofer Tabori, 1952; Roger Clemens, 1962

NEW WORD—
kibosh - noun: nonsense

QUIZ—
Where are 85 percent of all the plants in the world located?

TRIVIA
Former astronaut John Glenn and baseball great Ted Williams were co-pilots during Korean War bombing missions. . . . It costs the U.S. Mint .77 cents to make a penny. . . . Manhole covers are made round because they can't fall through the manhole itself. Other shapes can.

HISTORY—
On this date in 1693 Dom Perignon invented champagne. Now, if you could find a bottle of *that* vintage, you'd really have something!

GRAFFITI
Summer: the times that fry men's soles.

Quiz Answer: Most plants live in the oceans.

AUGUST

TODAY'S THOUGHT:
"Early to bed, early to rise, and your girl goes out with other guys."
—Bob Collins

OBSERVANCES/EVENTS—
Today is National Mustard Day.

BIRTHDAYS—
Mary Beard, 1876; Aiken Conrad, 1899; John Huston, 1906; Robert Taylor, 1911; Neil Armstrong, 1930; Sammi Smith, 1943; Loni Anderson, 1946; Erika Slezak, 1946; Patrick Ewing, 1962

NEW WORD—
mammock - verb: to break; to tear or shred

QUIZ—
Match the portrait with the U.S. paper currency:

1 - Thomas Jefferson	A: $1,000
2 - James Madison	B: $ 500
3 - Grover Cleveland	C: $5,000
4 - William McKinley	D: $ 2

TRIVIA
A stack of a trillion new one dollar bills would reach 69,000 miles high. . . . If you take a penny and double it, and then keep doubling it every day for thirty days, you will wind up with over five million dollars. . . . Paraguay is the only country that doesn't use coins, only paper money.

HISTORY—
On this date in 1957 Dick Clark began hosting "American Bandstand" on ABC.

GRAFFITI
Most people's financial problems are quite simple - they don't have any money.

Quiz Answer: 1 - D; 2 - C; 3 - A; 4 - B

AUGUST

TODAY'S THOUGHT:
"If God wanted us to be brave, why did he give us legs?" —Marvin Kitman

OBSERVANCES/EVENTS—
Judge Crater Day observes the anniversary of his mysterious disappearance. Let's remember all those things that seemingly have vanished forever, such as the socks that enter the dryer, never to be seen again.

BIRTHDAYS—
Alfred Lord Tennyson, 1809; Alexander Fleming, 1881; sociologist Scott Nearing, 1883; Lucille Ball, 1911; Robert Mitchum, 1917; Freddie Laker, 1922; Peter Bonerz, 1938; Catherine Hicks, 1951; David Robinson, 1965

NEW WORD—
shawm - noun: an early double reed woodwind instrument

QUIZ—
What incredible automobile record was set in 1930 by Charles Creighton and James Hargis?

TRIVIA
Mordecai Brown, one of the greatest pitchers in the history of baseball, had only three fingers on his pitching hand. . . . The longest hole-in-one in golf was recorded in Nebraska in 1965, 440 yards. . . . Roller skates, which originally consisted of four wheels on rubber pads, were invented about 1860.

HISTORY—
On this date in 1926 Gertrude Ederle became the first woman to swim the English Channel.

GRAFFITI
Today you get car sickness when you look at the sticker price.

Quiz Answer: They drove cross country without stopping the engine of their Model A roadster. After arriving in Los Angeles they immediately drove back to New York, completing the 7,180 mile round trip in 42 days - completely in reverse!

A U G U S T

TODAY'S THOUGHT:
"It was luxuries like air conditioning that brought down the Roman Empire. With air conditioning their windows were shut; they couldn't hear the barbarians coming." —Garrison Keillor

BIRTHDAYS—
Ralph Bunche, 1904; Stan Freberg, 1926; Garrison Keillor, 1942; B. J. Thomas, 1942; Lana Cantrell, 1943; Alberto Salazar, 1957

NEW WORD—
frowst - verb: to lounge

QUIZ—
Louis Armstrong had four Top 40 hits appear on "Billboard" charts. How many can you name?

TRIVIA
A violin contains seventy separate pieces of wood. . . . A female rabbit is called a doe; a male is a buck. . . . Studies show that Americans favor pepperoni more than any other pizza topping.

HISTORY—
On this date in 1888 Theophilus Van Kannel of Philadelphia received the patent for the revolving door.

GRAFFITI
Flat feet are arch enemies.

Quiz Answer: Satchmo scored big with "A Theme from the Three Penny Opera", better known as "Mack the Knife" in 1956; "Blueberry Hill", 1956; "Hello Dolly", 1964 and "What a Wonderful World", 1988 although he recorded it in 1967.

AUGUST

TODAY'S THOUGHT:
"Of all my wife's relations I like myself the best." —Joe Cook

OBSERVANCES/EVENTS—
It is Sneak Some Zucchini Onto Your Neighbors' Porch Night. If, in the spring, you planted a little zucchini in your garden, tonight is the time to unload this prolific produce.

BIRTHDAYS—
Dino DeLaurentiis, 1919; Esther Williams, 1923; Mel Tillis, 1932; Dustin Hoffman, 1937; Connie Stevens, 1938; Keith Carradine, 1950

NEW WORD—
liana - noun: a climbing plant or vine

QUIZ—
Where did Henry Heinz get the number "57" for his famous slogan "57 Varieties"?

TRIVIA
When Henry VIII became the king of England in 1509, he was only 17 years old. . . . Smithsonian Institution founder James Smith never set foot in the United States. . . . Writers Art Buchwald and Harold Robbins, both orphans, were raised in various foster homes.

HISTORY—
On this date in 1963 "The Great Train Robbery" netted $7 million for a gang of British crooks.

GRAFFITI
In most corporations the biggest guns
are those who have never been fired.

Quiz Answer: Even back in 1892 when the pickle potentate cooked up the slogan, the company was making far more products than that. He was simply fascinated by the number 57 and felt it was lucky for him. It was, and for dozens of heirs as well. You might say the whole family relishes the number.

AUGUST

TODAY'S THOUGHT:
"Anyone who says he can see through women is missing a lot."
—Groucho Marx

BIRTHDAYS—
Izaac Walton, 1593; Rod Laver, 1938; David Steinberg, 1942; Sam Elliott, 1944; Ken Norton, 1945; Melanie Griffith, 1957; Whitney Houston, 1963; Brett Hull, 1964

NEW WORD—
dvandva - noun: in grammar, a compound word in which neither element is subordinate to the other

QUIZ—
When he started the American Messenger Company in 1907 in Seattle, Jim Casey was 19 years old. By the end of World War I, his tiny messenger service had grown considerably and he changed its name to what current outfit?

TRIVIA
The Union Army lost more men to disease than battle during the Civil War. . . . "Dare to Be Free" was the slogan of the American Revolution. . . . "Yankee Doodle" was composed in England as an anti-American tune.

HISTORY—
On this date in 1930 Betty Boop took her opening bow in the "Dizzy Dishes" cartoon.
In 1974 Richard Nixon took his final bow as he resigned the Presidency.

GRAFFITI
An astronomer is a night watchman.

Quiz Answer: United Parcel Service

AUGUST

TODAY'S THOUGHT:

"I don't think anybody should write his autobiography until after he's dead." —Samuel Goldwyn

BIRTHDAYS—

Herbert Hoover, 1874; Jack Haley, 1899; Rhonda Fleming, 1923; Jimmy Dean, 1928; Eddie Fisher, 1928; fashion designer Betsy Johnson, 1942; Rosanna Arquette, 1959

NEW WORD—

piscator - noun: a fisherman

QUIZ—

Two days a year there are no major professional team sporting events. What are they?

TRIVIA

Herbert Hoover was the first president to have a phone on his desk. . . . Charles Curtis, Herbert Hoover's vice president, was a native American, one-half Kaw, who previously served as a senator from Kansas. . . . Oklahoma, Arizona and New Mexico contain nearly half the entire Native American population of the United States.

HISTORY—

On this date in 1981 Pete Rose to the occasion and broke Stan Musial's National League record of 3,630 hits. Rose would later become baseball's all-time hit leader.

GRAFFITI
Apples look alike when pared.

Quiz Answer: The day before and the day after major league baseball's All-Star game

AUGUST

TODAY'S THOUGHT:
"I would have made a good Pope." —Richard Nixon

OBSERVANCES/EVENTS—
It is Presidential Joke Day, to remember the great gaffes of our chief executives.

BIRTHDAYS—
David Atchison, 1807; composer Carrie Bond, 1862; Lloyd Nolan, 1902; Alex Haley, 1921; Mike Douglas, 1925; Carl Rowan, 1925; Jerry Falwell, 1933; Hulk Hogan, 1953; Joe Jackson, 1955

NEW WORD—
nimiety - noun: overabundance, excess

QUIZ—
Name "Time" magazine's Man of the Year in:
- A: 1938
- B: 1930
- C: 1927

TRIVIA
Mary Phelps Jacobs patented the first brassiere in November of 1914. . . . Back in Pilgrim days, a woman who reached the age of thirty and was unmarried, was called a thornback. . . . In 1901 Annie Taylor was the first woman to go over Niagara Falls in a barrel and survive.

HISTORY—
On this date in 1934 the first prisoners arrived on "The Rock", Alcatraz, San Francisco Bay.

GRAFFITI
When you're the toast of the town
everyone tries to butter you up.

Quiz Answer: A - Adolph Hitler; B - Mahatma Gandhi; C - Charles Lindbergh

AUGUST

TODAY'S THOUGHT:
"The human race is faced with a cruel choice: work or daytime television."
—Anonymous

BIRTHDAYS—
Cecil B. DeMille, 1881; Cantinflas, 1911; Jane Wyatt, 1913; choreographer Michael Kidd, 1919; John Derek, 1926; Mstislav Leopoldovich Rostropovich, 1927; Buck Owens, 1929; Porter Wagoner, 1930; writer William Goldman, 1931; John Poindexter, 1936; George Hamilton, 1939

NEW WORD—
embacle - noun: an accumulation of broken ice in a river

QUIZ—
Bathroom Brain Teaser:
Is there better than a 50-50 chance that the next U.S. Tennis Open champion will have more than the average number of arms?

TRIVIA
A 1973 Macon, Georgia minor league hockey team was named the Macon "Whoopies" after the song "Makin' Whoopie". . . . Chop Suey originated in California. . . . Thomas Edison was hard of hearing and often communicated with his wife in Morse Code.

HISTORY—
On this date in 1977 the prototype space shuttle, Enterprise, made its maiden flight within the earth's atmosphere, launched from a 747.

GRAFFITI
It sure isn't called pop music because your dad likes it.

Quiz Answer: Yes. Since the average number of arms on a human is slightly less than two, anyone with two arms has more than the average.

AUGUST

TODAY'S THOUGHT:
"Give them pleasure - the same pleasure they have when they wake up from a nightmare." —Alfred Hitchcock

BIRTHDAYS—
Annie Oakley, 1860; Alfred Hitchcock, 1899; Ben Hogan, 1912; Rex Humbard, 1919; Fidel Castro, 1927; Pat Harrington Jr., 1929; Don Ho, 1930; Dan Fogelberg, 1951

NEW WORD—
whilom - adjective: former

QUIZ—
What was Alfred Hitchcock's given name?

TRIVIA
Fidel Castro's sister runs a drugstore in Miami. . . . In Japan the most common name to see in the phone book is Minoru Suzukis. . . . Hank Aaron and Babe Ruth were both members of the Braves when they hit home run number 714.

HISTORY—
On this date in 1961 the East German government closed the border between East and West Berlin. The Berlin Wall was built later that week and stood until 1989.

GRAFFITI
When I want your opinion, I'll give it to you.

Quiz Answer: Joseph

AUGUST

TODAY'S THOUGHT:
"If the income tax is the price we have to pay to keep the government on its feet, alimony is the price we have to pay for sweeping a woman off hers." —Groucho Marx

BIRTHDAYS—
Ernest Thayer, 1863; Julia Child, 1912; Russell Baker, 1925; Alice Ghostley, 1926; Buddy Greco, 1926; David Crosby, 1941; jockey Robyn Smith, 1944; Steve Martin, 1945; Susan St. James, 1946; Danielle Steel, 1947; Gary Larson, 1950; Magic Johnson, 1959; Neal Anderson, 1964

NEW WORD—
geoponic - adjective: agricultural

QUIZ—
True or False?
During World War II the National Football League's Philadelphia Eagles and Pittsburgh Steelers merged to form the Steagles.

TRIVIA
Lemonade is the top-selling Kool-Aid flavor. . . . If you're the typical American man, you own 22 ties. . . . You use 72 muscles to speak one word.

HISTORY—
On this date in 1945 VJ Day ended World War II. Millions took to the street in celebration and the postwar era began.

GRAFFITI
A bachelor is footloose and fiancee-free.

Quiz Answer: True (because of the shortage of players due to the war effort)

AUGUST

TODAY'S THOUGHT:
"The difference between divorce and legal separation is that a legal separation gives a husband time to hide his money." —Johnny Carson

OBSERVANCES/EVENTS—
It's National Relaxation Day, a great excuse for goofing off, bumming and in general being unproductive.

BIRTHDAYS—
Napoleon Bonaparte, 1769; Sir Walter Scott, 1771; Ethel Barrymore, 1879; Edna Ferber, 1887; Phyllis Stewart Schlafly, 1924; Mike Connors, 1925; Vernon Jordan Jr., 1935; Linda Ellerbee, 1944

NEW WORD—
trochilus - noun: a hummingbird

QUIZ—
What high-water mark of the flower power generation took place in 1969 on this date?

TRIVIA
Stan Laurel was married eight times; however, he only had four wives. . . . Whoopie Goldberg's real name is Caryn Johnson. . . . Queen Elizabeth I suffered from smallpox and was completely bald by the age of 29.

HISTORY—
On this date in 1935 Will Rogers and Wiley Post perished in an Alaskan plane crash.

GRAFFITI
Orchestra leaders throw tempo tantrums.

Quiz Answer: The Woodstock Music and Art Fair began on this date in Bethel, New York drawing over 400,000 people and featuring 24 bands over three days.

AUGUST

TODAY'S THOUGHT:
"Pro football is like nuclear warfare. There are no winners, only survivors."
—Frank Gifford

OBSERVANCES/EVENTS—
It is Joe Miller Joke Day in memory of the early eighteenth century English comic actor, after whom a celebrated joke book was named in 1739.

BIRTHDAYS—
Menachem Begin, 1913; Fess Parker, 1927; Robert Culp, 1930; Frank Gifford, 1930; Eydie Gorme, 1932; Julie Newmar, 1935; Lesley Ann Warren, 1946; Madonna, 1958; Timothy Hutton, 1960

NEW WORD—
brevicaudate - adjective: having a short tail

QUIZ—
What is the most watched movie film in history?

TRIVIA
Arlington National Cemetery was once the site of Robert E. Lee's home. . . . Scrabble and Monopoly were two of Elvis Presley's favorite games. . . . American Revolutionary War hero John Paul Jones became an admiral in the Russian navy.

HISTORY—
On this date in 1977 came the news from Memphis that the King was dead, but it seems that it didn't take. Ever since he has been spotted at filling stations, 7-11's and Mr. Donut Shops all over the heartland.

GRAFFITI
The man who invented football got a kick out of it.

Quiz Answer: "The Wizard of Oz" (seen by more than a billion people)

AUGUST

TODAY'S THOUGHT:

"When women kiss, it always reminds me of prizefighters shaking hands."
—H. L. Mencken

BIRTHDAYS—

Davy Crockett, 1786; Samuel Goldwyn, 1882; Maureen O'Hara, 1920; artist Larry Rivers, 1923; Francis Gary Powers, 1929; Robert DeNiro, 1943; Guillermo Vilas, 1952; Belinda Carlisle, 1958; Sean Penn, 1960

NEW WORD—

verdurous - adjective: freshly green

QUIZ—

Do you know the only word in the English language which ends in sede?

TRIVIA

A woman can talk with less effort than a man because her vocal chords are shorter. . . . A man's beard grows about an inch in eight weeks. . . . Approximately one out of every six adult male Americans weighs more than 200 pounds.

HISTORY—

On this date in 1807 Robert Fulton's steamboat, the Clermont, sailed up the Hudson River from New York City to Albany.
In 1938 Henry Armstrong, the featherweight and welterweight champion, won the lightweight boxing championship to become the first fighter to hold three titles simultaneously.

GRAFFITI
A friend in need is a friend to dodge.

Quiz Answer: Supersede

AUGUST

TODAY'S THOUGHT:
"No one has ever bet enough on a winning horse." —Richard Sasuly

BIRTHDAYS—
Meriwether Lewis, 1774; Marshall Field, 1834; Casper Weinberger, 1917; Shelley Winters, 1922; Rosalynn Carter, 1927; Roman Polanski, 1933; Robert Redford, 1937; Martin Mull, 1943; Patrick Swayze, 1954; Malcolm Jamal Warner, 1970

NEW WORD—
horologe - noun: any instrument for indicating the time

QUIZ—
What famous first did Virginia Dare accomplish on this date in 1587?

TRIVIA
Babies have over 60 more bones than adults. . . . Blood takes about 23 seconds to make one round trip of your body. . . . 60% of your body weight is water.

HISTORY—
On this date in 1859 French stuntman, the Great Blondin, crossed Niagara Falls on a tightrope while carrying a man on his shoulders. In 1992 basketball great Larry Bird announced his retirement.

GRAFFITI
Butchers make both ends meat.

Quiz Answer: Virginia was born, becoming the first child of English parents born in the New World at Roanoke Island, North Carolina.

AUGUST

TODAY'S THOUGHT:

"To keep your marriage brimming,
With love in the loving cup,
Whenever you're wrong, admit it;
Whenever you're right, shut up." —Ogden Nash

OBSERVANCES/EVENTS—

It is National Aviation Day, celebrating the birth, in 1871, of the world's first airplane pilot, Orville Wright.

BIRTHDAYS—

Ogden Nash, 1902; Ring Lardner, Jr., 1915; Malcolm Forbes, 1919; Gene Roddenberry, 1921; Willie Shoemaker, 1931; Jill St. John, 1940; Morton Anderson, 1960; Ron Darling Jr., 1960; John Stamos, 1963

QUIZ—

What term, in almost every language, begins with an "m" sound?

TRIVIA

There are 140 languages spoken around the world and each is spoken by more than one million people. . . . The word "amen" is spoken in more tongues than any other word. . . . The longest nonscientific word in the dictionary is floccinaucinihilipilification, meaning deciding if something has no value.

HISTORY—

On this date in 1888 the first beauty contest was held at Spa, Belgium.

GRAFFITI

Marriage is a dialogue; divorce - two monologues.

Quiz Answer: Mother

AUGUST

TODAY'S THOUGHT:
"A good rule of thumb is if you've made it to thirty-five and your job still requires you to wear a name tag, you've probably made a serious vocational error." —Dennis Miller

BIRTHDAYS—
Benjamin Harrison, 1833; newspaperman Edgar Guest, 1881; Don King, 1931; Isaac Hayes, 1942; Graig Nettles, 1944; Connie Chung, 1946; Mark Langston, 1960

NEW WORD—
chouse - noun: a swindle

QUIZ—
Seventies Flashback: What was television's top rated show in 1970?

TRIVIA
About one in six people is an habitual fingernail biter. . . . Two-thirds of mankind is right-handed. . . . Over half of all Americans wind up wearing some kind of corrective lenses.

HISTORY—
On this date in 1741 Alaska was discovered by Danish navigator Vitus Bering after whom the Bering Sea was named.
In 1882 Tchaikovsky's "1812 Overture" premiered in Moscow.

GRAFFITI
**TV is still in its infancy;
that's why you have to change it so often.**

Quiz Answer: Robert Young was the Prince of Primetime as "Marcus Welby, M.D."

AUGUST

TODAY'S THOUGHT:
"Happiness is having a large, loving, caring close-knit family in another city." —George Burns

BIRTHDAYS—
Aubrey Beardsley, 1872; Count Basie, 1904; Princess Margaret, 1930; Wilt Chamberlain, 1936; Kenny Rogers, 1938; Clarence Williams III, 1939; Jackie DeShannon, 1944; Jim McMahon, 1959

NEW WORD—
zibeline - adjective: of or pertaining to sable

QUIZ—
If only the female mosquito bites, what does the male mosquito live on?

TRIVIA
A mosquito has 47 teeth. . . . Mosquitoes can drink twice their weight in blood. . . . A mosquito's favorite aroma is aftershave.

HISTORY—
On this date in 1959 the flag got its full complement of stars as Hawaii became the last state to join the union.

GRAFFITI
Fishing is making the best of a bass situation.

Quiz Answer: While the female mosquito's reproductive needs call for blood, the male is a non-aggressive vegetarian who lives on plant nectar.

A U G U S T

TODAY'S THOUGHT:
"There are no liberals behind steering wheels." —Russell Baker

BIRTHDAYS—
Claude Debussy, 1862; Dorothy Parker, 1893; Ray Bradbury, 1920; Norman Schwarzkopf, 1934; Carl Yastrzemski, 1939; Bill Parcells, 1941; Valerie Harper, 1941; Cindy Williams, 1948

NEW WORD—
ruth - noun: pity or compassion

QUIZ—
Name a popular professional sport that requires all metal shoes.

TRIVIA
If you plan on being buried in a standard grave your permanent "living" quarters will be 7'8" long X 3'2" wide and, of course, 6' deep. . . . L.L. Bean's initials stand for Leon Leonwood. . . . Richard Nixon's presidency officially ended while he was flying over Kansas City.

HISTORY—
On this date in 1851 the yacht America defeated fourteen British vessels to win the first America's Cup.
In 1989 Nolan Ryan racked up his record 5,000th strikeout for the Texas Rangers.

GRAFFITI
Bodybuilders throw their weight around.

Quiz Answer: Horse racing

AUGUST

TODAY'S THOUGHT:
"What is it about American fathers as they grow older that makes them dress like flags from other countries?" —Cary Odes

OBSERVANCES/EVENTS—
Celebrate Hug Your Boyfriend or Girlfriend Day by showing how much you appreciate them.

BIRTHDAYS—
Oliver Hazard Perry, 1785; Edgar Lee Masters, 1869; Gene Kelly, 1912; Mark Russell, 1932; Barbara Eden, 1934; Antonia Novello, 1944; Shelley Long, 1949; Rick Springfield, 1949; Mike Boddicker, 1957; River Phoenix, 1970

NEW WORD—
abecedarium - noun: a primer for teaching the alphabet

QUIZ—
True or False?
Chicago is nicknamed the "Windy City" because of its blustery politicians.

TRIVIA
The Russian word "kremlin" means "castle". . . . Songwriter Irving Berlin could not read music and could only play the black keys on a piano. . . . Woodpeckers don't get headaches.

HISTORY—
On this date in 1989 Victoria Brucker of San Pedro, California became the first U.S. girl to play in the Little League World Series.

GRAFFITI
What can you expect from a universe that started out as nothing but hot air?

Quiz Answer: True - It's long-winded politicians were the reason for the nickname. In fact, weatherwise, Chicago's not even in the top ten of America's windiest cities. It ranks sixteenth, with an average wind speed of 10.4 miles per hour.

A U G U S T

TODAY'S THOUGHT:
"Cordless phones are great. If you can find them." —Glenn Foster

BIRTHDAYS—
Max Beerbohm, 1872; Louis Teicher, 1924; Mason Williams, 1839; Gerry Cooney, 1956; Steve Guttenberg, 1958; Cal Ripken, Jr., 1960; Marlee Matlin, 1965; Reggie Miller, 1965

NEW WORD—
fozy - adjective: spongy, loose textured

QUIZ—
If you saw Virginia Katherine McMath and Frederick Austerlitz in a movie what would they most likely be doing?

TRIVIA
Alaska has the most outhouses in the United States. . . . There are 3,070 counties in the United States. . . . Of the 3,000 islands that comprise the Bahamas chain in the Caribbean, only 20 are inhabited.

HISTORY—
On this date in 79 A.D. Mount Vesuvius erupted in southern Italy. The falling lava and ash entombed the cities of Pompeii, Herculaneum and Stabiae.
In 1991 Mikhail Gorbachev resigned as head of the Soviet Union's Communist Party.

GRAFFITI
A school is a classy place.

Quiz Answer: Dancing - they are Ginger Rogers and Fred Astaire.

A U G U S T

TODAY'S THOUGHT:
"We have met the enemy, and he is us." —Walt Kelly

BIRTHDAYS—
Allan Pinkerton, 1819; Bret Harte, 1836; Walt Kelly, 1913; Mel Ferrer, 1917; Monty Hall, 1923; Sean Connery, 1930; Anne Archer, 1947; Elvis Costello, 1954

NEW WORD—
knurly - adjective: having knots; gnarled

QUIZ—
How long do baby kangaroos stay in their mother's pouch after birth?

TRIVIA
When it is overloaded, a yak grunts and is called the grunting oxen. . . . Hogs eat any and all kinds of snakes. . . . A gnu has the feet of an antelope, the mane and body of an ass, the head and humped shoulders of a buffalo and the beard of a goat.

HISTORY—
On this date in 1940 the first couple ever to take the plunge with a parachute wedding tied the knot while pulling the ripcord.

GRAFFITI
Limbo is a place where arms and legs go when they die.

Quiz Answer: It is about eight months more until they hop to it and finally give up womb and board.

AUGUST

TODAY'S THOUGHT:
"I have a microwave fireplace. You can lay down in front of the fire all night in eight minutes." —Stephen Wright

OBSERVANCES/EVENTS—
It is Women's Equality Day, originally sponsored in Congress by Bella Abzug.

BIRTHDAYS—
Inventor Lee DeForest, 1873; author Christopher Isherwood, 1904; Ronny Graham, 1919; Ben Bradlee, 1921; Irving R. Levine, 1922; Geraldine Ferraro, 1935; Branford Marsalis, 1960

NEW WORD—
imbrication - noun: an overlapping of tiles or shingles

QUIZ—
As you look at it, which way does the eagle's head face on the flip side of a quarter?

TRIVIA
Opossums do not play dead. They are actually fainting. . . . One out of every 125 Americans will die in an automobile accident. . . . Sir Winston Churchill was the first honorary citizen of the United States.

HISTORY—
On this date in 1920 the 29th Amendment was enacted, giving women the right to vote.
In 1939 sports widows were created as the first major league baseball game was broadcast on WZXBS-TV in New York.

— GRAFFITI —
Women don't admit their age; men don't act theirs.

Quiz Answer: Left

A U G U S T

TODAY'S THOUGHT:
"A vegetarian is a person who won't eat anything that can have children."
—David Brenner

BIRTHDAYS—
Theodore Dreiser, 1871; Lyndon Baines Johnson, 1908; Mother Teresa, 1910; Martha Raye, 1916; Tommy Sands, 1937; Darryl Dragon, 1942; Tuesday Weld, 1943

NEW WORD—
berm - noun: an edge or shoulder running along a road or canal

QUIZ—
What is the longest running show on television?

TRIVIA
"The Great Society" was not coined by LBJ, but by liberal writer Graham Wallas in 1914. . . . Lyndon Johnson's favorite drink was Fresca. He had special taps installed in the White House to dispense the drink. . . . Johnson always knew what he wanted. The day after meeting Lady Bird he proposed. They were married two months later.

HISTORY—
On this date in 1965 the Fab Four met the King as the Beatles had an audience with Elvis in his Los Angeles digs.

GRAFFITI
You have to listen to so much to find out politicians have so little to say.

Quiz Answer: "Meet the Press" which debuted on November 20, 1947

A U G U S T

TODAY'S THOUGHT:
"Friends may come and go but enemies accumulate." —Thomas Jones

BIRTHDAYS—
Johann Wolfgang von Goethe, 1749; Elizabeth Seton, 1774; Lucy Hayes, 1831; Charles Boyer, 1889; Donald O'Connor, 1925; Ben Gazzara, 1930; David Soul, 1946; Ron Guidry, 1950; Scott Hamilton, 1958; Emma Samms, 1960

NEW WORD—
sidereal - adjective: of or pertaining to the stars

QUIZ—
Who "discovered" the Gulf Stream?

TRIVIA
The owl is a real bird-brain and not wise. Crows are thought to be the smartest birds. . . . The largest shopping mall in the U.S. is the Mall of America in Bloomington, Minnesota. . . . A hurricane, typhoon and cyclone are all the same thing.

HISTORY—
On this date in 1963 Dr. Martin Luther King, Jr. made his "I have a dream . . ." speech in Washington, D.C.

GRAFFITI
The inventor who sold his patent for malted milk got a fair shake.

Quiz Answer: Among his many other accomplishments, Benjamin Franklin proposed and mapped the Gulf Stream as his answer to a long-standing problem of commerce and navigation: why did it take some ships two weeks longer to cross the Atlantic than others with slightly different courses? Serious investigation of the phenomenon began about a century after Franklin figured it out.

A U G U S T

TODAY'S THOUGHT:
"Fishing is a delusion entirely surrounded by liars in old clothes."
—Don Marquis

BIRTHDAYS—
Oliver Wendell Holmes, 1809; Ingrid Bergman, 1915; Richard Attenborough, 1923; Jim Florio, 1937; Elliott Gould, 1938; William Friedkin, 1939; Michael Jackson, 1958; Carl Banks, 1962

NEW WORD—
hebdomad - noun: the number 7; a period of 7 successive days

QUIZ—
On the long running TV whodunit, "Murder, She Wrote", what is the middle name of Angela Lansbury's character?

TRIVIA
Three-fourths of all pencils sold in the U.S. are yellow-painted. . . . Cottage cheese is so-called because, in Europe as far back as the Middle Ages, farmers made the cheese in their own cottages from leftover milk after the cream had been skimmed from it for buttermaking. . . . The French poodle originated in Germany.

HISTORY—
On this date in 1885 Gottlieb Daimler became the first "biker" when he got a patent on the world's original motorcycle.

GRAFFITI
An editor makes a long story short.

Quiz Answer: Her name is Jessica Beatrice Fletcher.

AUGUST

TODAY'S THOUGHT:
"If you don't think too good, don't think too much." —Ted Williams

BIRTHDAYS—
Roy Wilkins, 1901; Fred MacMurray, 1908; Ted Williams, 1918; Kitty Wells, 1919; Elizabeth Ashley, 1941; Jean-Claude Killy, 1943; Timothy Bottoms, 1951

NEW WORD—
thirl - verb: to pierce

QUIZ—
How is "par" on a golf hole determined?

TRIVIA
Lee Trevino, Jerry Heard and Bobby Nichols were all struck by lightning during the same golf tournament in 1975 . . . June 16, 1976 marked the first "rain-in" of a baseball game. The Houston Astros - Pittsburgh Pirates contest was called off because severe flooding made it impossible for fans to get to the Astrodome. . . . The home team provides 24 footballs for an NFL game.

HISTORY—
On this date in 1991 Mike Powell leaped 29 feet, 4½ inches to break the previous long-jump record of 29 feet, 2½ inches held by Bob Beamon.

GRAFFITI
Use tweezers, in a pinch.

Quiz Answer: Par, meaning equal, is ideally the point at which the course and a top notch golfer are evenly matched, but it is determined by the length of the hole and the sex of the golfer. For instance, a man's par 3 hole is anything up to 250 yards. A woman's par 3 is only up to 210 yards.

AUGUST

TODAY'S THOUGHT:
"Few things are harder to put up with than a good example."
—Mark Twain

BIRTHDAYS—
Fredric March, 1897; William Saroyan, 1908; Alan Jay Lerner, 1918; Buddy Hackett, 1924; James Coburn, 1928; Frank Robinson, 1935; Itzhak Perlman, 1945; Richard Gere, 1949; Edwin Moses, 1955; Debbie Gibson, 1970

NEW WORD—
nexus - noun: a connected series or group

QUIZ—
By what name is William Jefferson Blythe IV better known?

TRIVIA
Frank Robinson was the only baseball player to win the MVP award in each league. . . . The 1944 World Series was played by two teams from the same city and in the same park. The St. Louis Browns played the St. Louis Cardinals at Sportsman's Park. . . . Cal Hubbard is the only man inducted into the Baseball and Football Halls of Fame.

HISTORY—
On this date in 1963 Walter Cronkite began his 18 year stint as anchorman on the CBS Evening News.

GRAFFITI
Bakers go on strike for more dough.

Quiz Answer: Bill Clinton - The U.S. president was named after his late father and at age 16 he legally changed his name to that of his stepfather.

SEPTEMBER

TODAY'S THOUGHT:
"We're all in this together - by ourselves." —Lily Tomlin

OBSERVANCES/EVENTS—
It is Emma Nutt Day, in remembrance of the world's first telephone operator who began her career in Boston in 1878.

BIRTHDAYS—
Edgar Rice Burroughs, 1875; Philip Reuther, 1907; Yvonne De Carlo, 1924; Ann Richards, 1933; Conway Twitty, 1933; Lily Tomlin, 1939; Barry Gibb, 1946; Vinnie Johnson, 1956

NEW WORD—
mephitic - adjective: offensive to the smell; noxious

QUIZ—
Bathroom Brain Teaser:
The 22nd and 24th presidents of the U.S. had the same mother and the same father, yet they were not brothers. Why not?

TRIVIA
The first modern traffic light stopped traffic on Euclid Avenue in Cleveland in 1914. . . . Bubble gum first appeared in 1933, but it wasn't until 1947 that Topp's Chewing Gum Company started to produce Bazooka. . . . The first United States medical school was established in Philadelphia in 1765.

HISTORY—
On this date in 1972 the great chess war ended as Bobby Fischer defeated Boris Spassky for the world title.

GRAFFITI
Switchboard operators plug away at their jobs.

Quiz Answer: They were the same man, Grover Cleveland, who served as president from 1885 to 1889 and from 1893 to 1897.

SEPTEMBER

TODAY'S THOUGHT:
"The meek shall inherit the earth. They won't have the nerve to refuse it." —Jackie Vernon

BIRTHDAYS—
Cleveland Amory, 1917; Peter Ueberroth, 1937; Terry Bradshaw, 1948; Christa McAuliffe, 1948; Jimmy Connors, 1952; Linda Purl, 1955

NEW WORD—
gharry - noun: a horse-drawn carriage in India

QUIZ—
Identify the phony fact:
- A: Jim Thorpe's Indian name was "Swift-Running Deer".
- B: Monkeys have no feet.
- C: A typical ant has five noses.
- D: In Australia sanitation engineers are called "Garbos".
- E: Montgomery Ward's first catalog consisted of a single page.

TRIVIA
In the U.S. a baby is born every 8½ seconds. . . . . According to the FDA, two out of five women dye their hair. . . . You have a 1 in 600,000 chance of being struck by lightning sometime during your life.

HISTORY—
On this date in 1944 Navy pilot George Bush was shot down by the Japanese during a World War II bombing run in the Bonin Islands. Bush was rescued but his two crew members died.

GRAFFITI
Wine is grape expectations.

Quiz Answer: A - Thorpe's Indian name was "Bright Path".

SEPTEMBER

TODAY'S THOUGHT:
"One of the advantages bowling has over golf is that you seldom lose a bowling ball." —Don Carter

OBSERVANCES/EVENTS—
September is Baby Safety Month, Cable TV Month, Children's Eye Health & Safety Month, Library Card Sign-Up Month, National Courtesy Month, National Piano Month and Self-Improvement Month.

BIRTHDAYS—
Violin maker Nicolo Amati, 1596; Alan Ladd, 1913; Kitty Carlisle, 1915; Anne Jackson, 1926; Eileen Brennan, 1937; Valerie Perrine, 1943; Charlie Sheen, 1965

NEW WORD—
velodrome - noun: a sports arena equipped with a banked track for cycling

QUIZ—
In a baseball game box score, what word's last letter was selected to indicate a strikeout?

TRIVIA
Irving Berlin was the only person in the history of the Academy of Motion Picture Arts and Sciences ever to present the Oscar to himself. . . . If the wire of a Slinky was laid out flat, it would measure 87 feet. . . . Wilkes-Barre, Pennsylvania is the only city with a hyphen in its name.

HISTORY—
On this date in 1930 the first electric train, one of Thomas Edison's last inventions, began service between Hoboken and Montclair in New Jersey.

GRAFFITI
Do rivers sleep in river beds?

Quiz Answer: Struck

SEPTEMBER

TODAY'S THOUGHT:
"The history of things that didn't happen has never been written."
—Henry Kissinger

OBSERVANCES/EVENTS—
It is Newspaper Carrier Day, commemorating the birthday of the first newsboy in the U.S., Barney Flaherty in 1833.

BIRTHDAYS—
Anton Bruckner, 1824; architect Daniel Burnham, 1846; Alexander Liberman, 1912; Paul Harvey, 1918; Craig Claiborne, 1920; Dick York, 1928; Mitzi Gaynor, 1931; Dawn Fraser, 1937; Tom Watson, 1949

QUIZ—
You may have some "degree" of difficulty with this one. What word in the English language has no vowels (and no y, either)?

TRIVIA
The letters LED on a digital watch stand for "light-emitting diode". . . . Baseball great Jackie Robinson's brother Mack finished second to Jesse Owens in the 200-meter race in the 1936 Olympics. . . . The most popular crossword puzzle subject is the Bible.

HISTORY—
On this date in 1972 swimmer Mark Spitz won a record 7th gold medal in the 400-meter relay at the Olympic Games in Munich, Germany.

GRAFFITI
Vegetables are mailed by parsley post.

Quiz Answer: Nth (as in the Nth degree)

S E P T E M B E R

TODAY'S THOUGHT:

"Realtors are people who did not make it as used-car salesmen."
—Bob Newhart

BIRTHDAYS—

Florence Eldridge, 1901; Darryl F. Zanuck, 1902; Arthur Koestler, 1905; Bob Newhart, 1929; Carol Lawrence, 1935; John Danforth, 1936; William Devane, 1939; Raquel Welch, 1942; Cathy Lee Guisewite, 1950; Willie Gault, 1960

NEW WORD—

reive - verb: to rob; plunder

QUIZ—

Which of the following did *not*, at one time or another, work on a daytime soap?

  A: Robert DeNiro
  B: Kathleen Turner
  C: Wilford Brimley
  D: Alec Baldwin
  E: Larry Hagman

TRIVIA

Soap operas were so named because most of the sponsors were soap companies. . . . Bob Newhart's real first name is George. . . . Dr. Martin Luther King's first name was Michael.

HISTORY—

On this date in 1698 Russian men had a close shave with higher taxes as the government placed a levy on beards.

GRAFFITI
Radiologists expose you for what you are.

Quiz Answer: C, and for those who can't believe DeNiro did a soap, just talk with any longtime "Search For Tomorrow" fan.

SEPTEMBER

TODAY'S THOUGHT:
"Never invest your money in anything that eats or needs repairing."
—Billy Rose

BIRTHDAYS—
John Dalton, 1766; Jane Addams, 1860; Billy Rose, 1899; Jo Anne Worley, 1937; Swoozie Kurtz, 1944; Jane Curtin, 1947

NEW WORD—
impone - verb: to wager, stake

QUIZ—
What is the daily consumption of mouthwash in the U.S.?

- A: 700 gallons
- B: 7,000 gallons
- C: 70,000 gallons
- D: 700,000 gallons

TRIVIA
Home plate in baseball was square until 1900 when it was made five-sided to help umpires in calling balls and strikes. . . . Liberace owned a $200,000 tea set that once belonged to Napoleon. . . . Early American colonists made gray paint for their homes by boiling blueberries in milk.

HISTORY—
On this date in 1620 the Mayflower set sail from Plymouth, England carrying 103 Pilgrims. She landed with 103, but not the same ones. During the voyage, two died but two were born.

GRAFFITI
Years teach more than books.

Quiz Answer: C - There's a whole lot of gargling going on as Americans chase away bad breath with about 70,000 gallons daily.

S E P T E M B E R

TODAY'S THOUGHT:
"Guys are like dogs. They keep comin' back. Ladies are like cats. Yell at a cat one time, they're gone." —Lenny Bruce

BIRTHDAYS—
Queen Elizabeth I, 1533; Grandma Moses, 1860; Taylor Caldwell, 1900; Michael DeBakey, 1908; Elia Kazan, 1909; Arthur Ferrante, 1921; Buddy Holly, 1936; John Philip Law, 1937; Richard Roundtree, 1942; Julie Kavner, 1951; Corbin Bernsen, 1954; Michael Feinstein, 1956

NEW WORD—
obumbrate - verb: to darken, overshadow

QUIZ—
Bathroom Brain Teaser:
If a man was born in 50 B.C., in what year would he celebrate his 100th birthday?

TRIVIA
Wonder Bread introduced sliced bread in 1930. . . . In 1931 Cleveland Indians catcher Joe Sprinz caught a baseball dropped 800 feet from a balloon. The impact created such a jolt through his body that he broke his jaw. . . . Just how fast is a snail's pace? About 25 feet per hour for most species.

HISTORY—
On this date in 1921 16-year old Margaret Gorman of Washington, D.C. won the first Miss America Pageant.

GRAFFITI
Historians are a thing of the past.

Quiz Answer: 51 A.D.

SEPTEMBER

TODAY'S THOUGHT:
"When you are courting a nice girl an hour seems like a second. When you sit on a red-hot cinder a second seems like an hour. That's relativity." —Albert Einstein

BIRTHDAYS—
Claude Pepper, 1900; Sid Caesar, 1922; Peter Sellers, 1925; Patsy Cline, 1932; Sam Nunn, 1938; Rogie Vachon, 1945; Maurice Cheeks, 1956; Heather Thomas, 1957

NEW WORD—
zwitterion - noun: an ion with both a positive and negative charge

QUIZ—
What is the world's northernmost capital?

TRIVIA
A soap bubble's wall is but a few millionths of an inch thick. . . . Electric fans actually increase the temperature of the air. . . . One pound of nickel can be stretched into a fine wire eighty miles long.

HISTORY—
On this date in 1974 an unconditional pardon to Richard Nixon was granted by President Gerald Ford for all federal crimes that he "committed or may have committed" while president.

GRAFFITI
When you know the right answers, no one asks you the right questions.

Quiz Answer: Reykjavik, Iceland

SEPTEMBER

TODAY'S THOUGHT:

"There is something supremely reassuring about television: the worst is always yet to come." —Jack Gould

BIRTHDAYS—

Colonel Sanders, 1890; Jimmy "the Greek" Snyder, 1923; Cliff Robertson, 1925; Otis Redding, 1941; Billy Preston, 1946; Joe Theisman, 1949; Michael Keaton, 1951; Kristy McNichol, 1962; B. J. Armstrong, 1967

NEW WORD—

aurify - verb: to cause to appear golden

QUIZ—

What distinction does radio station WHB in Kansas City hold?

TRIVIA

Tiny earthworms have five hearts. . . . A humpback whale can travel up to 4,000 miles in a year. . . . The hippopotamus has skin two inches thick in some places.

HISTORY—

On this date in 1956 Elvis Presley sprang upon a largely unsuspecting public on the "Ed Sullivan Show".

GRAFFITI
Absence makes the heart go wander.

Quiz Answer: WHB was the first radio station to go to an all rock 'n' roll format.

 **SEPTEMBER**

TODAY'S THOUGHT:
"Thanks to the interstate highway system, it is now possible to travel across the country from coast to coast without seeing anything."
—Charles Kuralt

OBSERVANCES/EVENTS—
Swap Ideas Day encourages people to work for the benefit of humanity through an exchange of ideas.

BIRTHDAYS—
Robert Wise, 1914; Arnold Palmer, 1929; Charles Kuralt, 1934; Jose Feliciano, 1945; Amy Irving, 1953; Cap Boso, 1963

NEW WORD—
helminth - noun: a parasitic worm

QUIZ—
Leapin' Lizards! What did Gary Stewart of Ohio do 177,737 times to set a record in California on May 25-26, 1992?

TRIVIA
A football is made of cowhide, not pigskin. . . . There are 170,000,000,000,000,000,000,000,000,000 ways to play the ten opening moves in a chess game. . . . San Francisco has the largest Chinese population outside the Orient.

HISTORY—
On this date in 1846 the world was soon to be in stitches as Elias Howe received a patent on his sewing machine.

GRAFFITI
Don't be so hard on your relatives; they had no choice in the matter either.

Quiz Answer: He bounced on a pogo stick; that's the land record, of course. Fans of underwater pogo hopping were jumping up and down over Ashrita Furman who made 3,309 jumps in $8\frac{1}{2}$ feet of water, breathing only on the rebound.

S E P T E M B E R

TODAY'S THOUGHT:
"I consider exercise vulgar. It makes people smell."
— Alec Yuill Thornton

BIRTHDAYS—
O. Henry, 1862; D. H. Lawrence, 1885; Hedy Lamarr, 1915; Tom Landry, 1924; Alfred Slote, 1926; Bob Packwood, 1932; Brian DePalma, 1940; Lola Falana, 1943

NEW WORD—
potamic - adjective: of or pertaining to rivers

QUIZ—
Look at the birthday list and see if you can guess which one of those folks once designed a torpedo guidance system for the U.S. Navy.

TRIVIA
Michigan has the longest shoreline in the continental U.S. . . . Reno, Nevada is located further west than Los Angeles. . . . There are five counties in Texas that are larger than the state of Rhode Island.

HISTORY—
On this date in 1847 Stephen Foster sold the rights to "Oh, Susanna" to a bartender for a bottle of whiskey so he could celebrate the song's first public performance.

GRAFFITI
A good conversationalist lets others do the talking.

Quiz Answer: Believe it or not, it was screen actress Hedy Lamarr.

SEPTEMBER

TODAY'S THOUGHT:
"Why is it that men who can go through severe accidents, air raids, and any other major crisis always seem to think they are at death's door when they have a simple head cold?" —Shirley Booth

BIRTHDAYS—
H. L. Mencken, 1880; Jesse Owens, 1913; George Jones, 1931; Linda Gray, 1941; Peter Scolari, 1954; Deron Cherry, 1959; Timothy Hardaway, 1966

NEW WORD—
bistoury - noun: a small narrow surgical knife

QUIZ—
Name the only X-rated movie to win a Best Picture Oscar.

TRIVIA
The highest sand dunes in the world are in the Sahara. They build up to a height of 1,410 feet. . . . The world's longest bridge has a span of 23.8 miles. It is the causeway over Lake Pontchartrain in Louisiana. . . . The geographic center of the U.S. is located near Castle Rock, South Dakota.

HISTORY—
On this date in 1976 53-year old Minnie Minoso of the Chicago White Sox became the oldest player in major league baseball history to get a hit in a game.

GRAFFITI
A person has to work hard to make an easy living.

Quiz Answer: "Midnight Cowboy", starring Dustin Hoffman and Jon Voight

S E P T E M B E R

TODAY'S THOUGHT:

"Bargain: something you can't use at a price you can't resist."
—Franklin P. Jonas

BIRTHDAYS—

Walter Reed, 1851; John Pershing, 1860; Claudette Colbert, 1905; Mel Torme, 1925; Ernest Boyer, 1928; artist Robert Indiana, 1928; Fred Silverman, 1937; Judith "Miss Manners" Martin, 1938; Jacqueline Bisset, 1944; Nell Carter, 1948

NEW WORD—

tristichous - adjective: arranged in three rows

QUIZ—

What do the British call tic-tac-toe?

TRIVIA

Coca Cola was banned from India in 1977 for refusing to disclose its secret formula.. . . Men are eight times more likely to be colorblind than women. . . . Of every 100 people in the world, 21 live in China. Five out of 100 live in the U.S.

HISTORY—

On this date in 1971 a 30-year old U.S. Marine captain, Wayne Rollings, stationed in Hawaii, did 17,000 sit-ups in 7 hours, 27 minutes.

GRAFFITI

Some who are not paid what they are worth ought to be glad.

Quiz Answer: Noughts and crosses

 **SEPTEMBER**

TODAY'S THOUGHT:
"I enjoy convalescence. It is the part that makes the illness worthwhile."
—George Bernard Shaw

BIRTHDAYS—
Margaret Sanger, 1879; Jack Hawkins, 1910; Clayton Moore, 1914; author Allan Bloom, 1930; Zoe Caldwell, 1933, Kate Millett, 1934; Joey Heatherton, 1944; Mary Crosby, 1959

NEW WORD—
naos - noun: a temple

QUIZ—
If you add up all those between beat rests that your heart takes in the course of a lifetime, you will find that your heart stands still for:
- A: about 9 months
- B: 2¼ years
- C: 5 years
- D: 8 years
- E: 20 years

TRIVIA
The leading untreated illness in the U.S. is mental depression. . . . American consumers spend a billion dollars a year on cold relief medicines, and that's nothing to sneeze at. . . . Heart attacks claim the fewest men on Fridays.

HISTORY—
On this date in 1814 Francis Scott Key wrote the words to the national anthem. The melody of "The Star-Spangled Banner" comes from an old English drinking song, "Anachreon in Heaven".

GRAFFITI
An onion a day keeps everybody away.

Quiz Answer: E - for twenty years

S E P T E M B E R

TODAY'S THOUGHT:
"An archaeologist is the best husband any woman can have: The older she gets, the more interested he is in her." —Agatha Christie

BIRTHDAYS—
James Fenimoore Cooper, 1789; William Howard Taft, 1857; Agatha Christie, 1890; Roy Acuff, 1903; Jackie Cooper, 1922; Bobby Short, 1926; Norm Crosby, 1927; Gaylord Perry, 1938; Merlin Olsen, 1940; Tommy Lee Jones, 1946; Oliver Stone, 1946; Joe Morris, 1960; Dan Marino, 1961; Prince Harry of Wales, 1984

NEW WORD—
septentrional - adjective: northern

QUIZ—
True or False?
Chewing gum was initially intended to be a rubber substitute.

TRIVIA
Mary Westmacott was the pen name of Agatha Christie when she was writing romantic novels. . . . The famous Orient Express ran from Paris to Istanbul, Turkey. . . . The novel "Les Miserables" contains one of the longest sentences in the French language - 823 words without a period.

HISTORY—
On this date in 1971 the environmental organization, Greenpeace, was founded in Vancouver, British Columbia.

GRAFFITI
Nothing gives you indigestion like eating your own words.

Quiz Answer: True - Santa Ana tried to sell chicle to the U.S. as a rubber substitute but Thomas Adams got the idea to sell it as chewing gum. Later he added some licorice flavoring and Blackjack gum was born.

 **SEPTEMBER**

TODAY'S THOUGHT:
"Baseball players are smarter than football players. How often do you see a baseball team penalized for too many men on the field?"
—Jim Bouton

BIRTHDAYS—
Francis Parkman, 1823; Allen Funt, 1914; inventor Marvin Middlemark, 1919; Janis Paige, 1923; Lauren Bacall, 1924; B. B. King, 1925; John Knowles, 1926; Peter Falk, 1927; Ed Begley Jr., 1949; Robin Yount, 1955; David Copperfield, 1956; Orel Hershiser, 1958; Tim Raines, 1959

NEW WORD—
jauk - verb: to dawdle, dally

QUIZ—
When John Kennedy was president of the United States in the early 1960's, there was another John Kennedy who was a Senator in Washington and who, coincidentally, had the same birthday as JFK, May 29. Do you remember him?

TRIVIA
The most common black surname in the U.S. is Johnson. . . . Teflon was called "fluon" when it was first discovered in 1938. . . . Rats can swim half a mile and tread water for three days.

HISTORY—
On this date in 1630 the little town of Shawmut, Massachusetts decided to change its name to Boston, and it's "bean" that ever since.
In 1908 General Motors was founded by William Durant of Flint, Michigan.

GRAFFITI
Opinion is the substitute we use for thought.

Quiz Answer: John Kennedy was a third baseman for the Washington Senators baseball club.

SEPTEMBER

TODAY'S THOUGHT:
"How many of those dead animals you see on the highway are suicides?" —Dennis Miller

OBSERVANCES/EVENTS—
It is Citizenship Day, so stand tall and proud.

BIRTHDAYS—
Roddy McDowall, 1928; Anne Bancroft, 1931; Dorothy Loudon, 1933; Ken Kesey, 1935; David Souter, 1939; Phil Jackson, 1945; cartoonist Jeff MacNelly, 1947; John Ritter, 1948; Cassandra "Elvira" Peterson, 1951; Anthony Carter, 1960

NEW WORD—
funambulist - noun: a tightrope walker

QUIZ—
Can you name the two dogs who have stars on Hollywood's Walk of Fame?

TRIVIA
Mickey Mouse has four fingers on each hand. . . . Olive Oyl's measurements are 19-19-19. . . . Of Pluto the planet and Pluto the canine, the Disney dog was named first.

HISTORY—
On this date in 1911 C. P. Rogers began the first transcontinental airplane flight from New York to Pasadena. It wasn't exactly a non-stop express; it took over 82 hours.

GRAFFITI
Immigration is the sincerest form of flattery.

Quiz Answer: Lassie and Rin Tin Tin

The Bathroom Trivia Almanac

 SEPTEMBER

TODAY'S THOUGHT:
"At 50, everyone has the face he deserves." —George Orwell

BIRTHDAYS—
Samuel Johnson, 1709; Eddie "Rochester" Anderson, 1905; Greta Garbo, 1905; Rossano Brazzi, 1916, Jack Warden, 1920; Robert Blake, 1938; Frankie Avalon, 1940; Ryne Sandberg, 1959

NEW WORD—
lungi - noun: a cloth used as a turban or scarf

QUIZ—
How did the following fashions come into being?
A: The blazer   B: The cardigan   C: Panama hats

TRIVIA
The Federal Government forbids the portrait of any living person to appear on a U.S. postage stamp. . . . The diameter of a basketball hoop is 18 inches. . . . Albert Einstein was 26 when he published his theory of relativity.

HISTORY—
On this date in 1947 the United States Air Force took off into the wild blue yonder as it became a separate military service.

GRAFFITI
You're never too busy to talk about how busy you are.

Quiz Answer: A - The captain of the HMS Blazer grew tired of seeing his crew shabbily attired so he had blue jackets made for all of them. The fashion caught on and was named after the vessel. B - This was named for the Earl of Cardigan who led the Charge of the Light Brigade and sometimes wore similar sweaters. C - They come from Ecuador but, since they were shipped from ports in Panama, became known as Panama hats.

S E P T E M B E R

TODAY'S THOUGHT:
"Never tell a woman that you didn't realize she was pregnant until you're certain that she *is*." —Dave Barry

BIRTHDAYS—
Joe Pasternack, 1901; William Golding, 1911; journalist Clifton Daniel, 1912; Frances Farmer, 1913; Adam West, 1928; Paul Williams, 1940; Randolph Mantooth, 1945; Jeremy Irons, 1948; Leslie "Twiggy" Hornby, 1949; Joan Lunden, 1951; Jim Abbott, 1967

NEW WORD—
divulsion - noun: a violent separating or tearing apart

QUIZ—
Bathroom Brain Teaser:
In what order are the numbers below?
8   5   4   9   1   7   6   3   2   0

TRIVIA
When he signed the statehood bills for North and South Dakota on the same day, President Benjamin Harrison wouldn't tell which one he signed first, so no one knows which is the 39th or 40th state. . . . Los Angeles is the second most populous Mexican city. . . . The most popular color in the U.S. is blue but the most popular car and house color is white.

HISTORY—
On this date in 1928 the first sound cartoon, "Steamboat Willie", debuted at New York's Colony Theater and launched the career of Mickey Mouse.

GRAFFITI
Marriage is the chief reason for divorce.

Quiz Answer: Alphabetical order

 # SEPTEMBER

TODAY'S THOUGHT:
"A woman's dress should be like a barbed-wire fence: serving its purpose without obstructing the view." —Sophia Loren

BIRTHDAYS—
Upton Sinclair, 1878; Jellyroll Morton, 1885; Red Auerbach, 1917; Anne Meara, 1924; author Donald Hall, 1928; Sophia Loren, 1934; Guy LaFleur, 1951

NEW WORD—
arsis - noun: the upbeat stroke in conducting

QUIZ—
What is the best selling children's book in history?

TRIVIA
For her fortieth birthday Sophia Loren's husband presented her with a 14-carat gold toilet seat. . . . There were no toilets of any kind in the Louvre or in the Palace of Versailles. Members of the court were expected to take care of business before they entered. . . . Every time Joan Crawford got a divorce she changed toilet seats.

HISTORY—
On this date in 1873 the New York Stock Exchange was forced to close for the first time in its history due to the great Panic of '73. In 1973 Bobby Riggs was forced to close his mouth after Billie Jean King whipped him in three straight sets in the great Battle of the Sexes tennis match.

GRAFFITI
When opportunity knocks, chances are you'll be in the shower.

Quiz Answer: "The Tale of Peter Rabbit", by Beatrix Potter

SEPTEMBER

TODAY'S THOUGHT:
"Advertising is legalized lying." —H. G. Wells

BIRTHDAYS—
Margaret Taylor, 1788; H. G. Wells, 1866; Larry Hagman, 1931; Henry Gibson, 1935; Stephen King, 1947; Artis Gilmore, 1949; Bill Murray, 1950; Sidney Montcrief, 1957; Rob Morrow, 1962; Cecil Fielder, 1963

NEW WORD—
risible - adjective: having the ability, disposition or readiness to laugh

QUIZ—
What First Lady of the United States carried a loaded revolver in her purse?
- A: Rachel Jackson
- B: Eleanor Roosevelt
- C: Jackie Kennedy
- D: Nancy Reagan

TRIVIA
According to Hoyle, poker is the national card game of the U.S. . . . Bela Lugosi is buried in his black Dracula cape. . . . Those little white particles on the bottom half of English muffins are farina, which not only adds to the taste, but also prevents the dough from sticking to the oven plate during cooking.

HISTORY—
On this date in 1989 Hurricane Hugo slammed into the southeast coast of the U.S., causing billions of dollars of lost profits for insurance companies.

GRAFFITI
Termites never die. They live happily ever rafter.

Quiz Answer: B - After receiving numerous death threats, the Secret Service advised her to carry a gun.

 **SEPTEMBER**

TODAY'S THOUGHT:
"They have Dial-a-Prayer for atheists now. You can call up and it rings and rings and nobody answers." —Tommy Blaze

OBSERVANCES/EVENTS—
To recognize the important contributions American working women have made, American Business Women's Day is observed today.

BIRTHDAYS—
Michael Faraday, 1791; Paul Muni, 1895; John Houseman, 1902; Tommy Lasorda, 1927; Shari Belafonte-Harper, 1954; Debbie Boone, 1956; Wally Backman, 1959; Scott Baio, 1961; Catherine Oxenberg, 1961

NEW WORD—
dendrophilous - adjective: living in or on trees

QUIZ—
Name the five U.S. presidents who had beards.

TRIVIA
One of Thomas Jefferson's many inventions was the swivel chair. . . . Andrew Jackson's pet parrot was in attendance at the former president's burial service but had to be removed for screeching profanities. . . . John Tyler was the father of fifteen children - so why did they call George Washington the "Father of Our Country"?

HISTORY—
On this date in 1776 Nathan Hale was executed as a spy by the British. In 1789 the United States Post Office was established.

GRAFFITI
Would two apples a day keep two doctors away?

Quiz Answer: The five are Abraham Lincoln, Ulysses Grant, Rutherford B. Hayes, James Garfield and Benjamin Harrison.

S E P T E M B E R

TODAY'S THOUGHT:
"You always pass failure on the way to success." —Mickey Rooney

BIRTHDAYS—
Walter Lippman, 1889; Walter Pidgeon, 1898; Mickey Rooney, 1920; Ray Charles, 1930; Julio Iglesias, 1943; Mary Kay Place, 1947; Bruce Springsteen, 1949; Tony Mandarich, 1966

NEW WORD—
lorimer - noun: a craftsman who makes hardware for harnesses and riding habits

QUIZ—
President Clinton has Socks, the cat, but most chief executives have had dogs, possibly because dogs stay loyal no matter what your standing at the polls. Can you remember the names of the presidential pooches that went with the following administrations?

 A: Lyndon Johnson B: George Bush C: Franklin Roosevelt
    D: Dwight Eisenhower E: Ronald Reagan

TRIVIA
The greyhound is the fastest dog in the world, clocked at 41.7 miles per hour. . . . In eight years a male greyhound in London sired 2,414 registered puppies as well as 600 others that weren't registered. . . . According to an intelligence test of 79 dog breeds, the smartest is the border collie.

HISTORY—
On this date in 1952 Richard Nixon made his famous "Checkers" speech, in which he vowed not to return his beloved cocker spaniel which had been a gift to his daughters from some political supporters.

GRAFFITI
If dogs are so dumb, how come they stay at home sleeping while their masters go to work?

Quiz Answer: A - He and She; B - Millie; C - Fala; D - Heidi; E - Rex and Lucky

SEPTEMBER

TODAY'S THOUGHT:
"Last night I dreamt I had insomnia. When I woke up, I was completely exhausted but too well rested to go back to sleep." —Bob Nickman

BIRTHDAYS—
John Marshall, 1755; F. Scott Fitzgerald, 1896; Jim McKay, 1921; Sheila MacRae, 1923; Anthony Newley, 1931; Jim Henson, 1936; Linda McCartney, 1942; Rafael Palmeiro, 1964

NEW WORD—
wase - noun: a wisp, bundle, pad of straw

QUIZ—
According to the British Parliament back in 1770, what could a man do if he found out his wife was wearing artificial teeth, wigs or any other phony body parts?

TRIVIA
Approximately 75 percent of all ulcer patients are men. . . . In humans, the right lung weighs more than the left . . . The most common noncontagious disease is tooth decay.

HISTORY—
On this date in 1934 Babe Ruth played his last game for the Yankees and bid farewell to his fans at Yankee Stadium.

GRAFFITI
The weaker the argument, the stronger the words.

Quiz Answer: He could declare their marriage null and void since he was deceived by sham and trickery. Even high heels were considered a deception.

S E P T E M B E R

TODAY'S THOUGHT:
"You know you're getting old when you stoop to tie your shoes and wonder what else you can do while you're down there."
—George Burns

BIRTHDAYS—
Red Smith, 1905; Dmitri Shostakovich, 1906; Phil Rizzuto, 1918; Aldo Ray, 1926; Barbara Walters, 1931; Juliet Prowse, 1936; Robert Walden, 1943; Michael Douglas, 1944; Mark Hamill, 1951; Christopher Reeve, 1952; Heather Locklear, 1961; Scottie Pippen, 1965

NEW WORD—
exonarthex - noun: a covered walk, a vestibule

QUIZ—
They say "break a leg" in show biz, but Jack Palance, Edward G. Robinson, Ann-Margret, Montgomery Clift and Jason Robards Jr. have something else in common. Do you know what it is?

TRIVIA
NFL coaching legend Vince Lombardi coined the phrase "game plan". . . . Attorneys and lawyers are not necessarily the same. Anyone can act on your behalf and be called your attorney but to be called a lawyer he must be a graduate of law school. . . . A cat's sense of smell is ten times better than a human's.

HISTORY—
On this date in 1981 Sandra Day O'Connor was sworn in as the first female Justice of the Supreme Court.

GRAFFITI
The best advice - don't give it.

Quiz Answer: They have all been in serious accidents that required facial reconstructive surgery.

SEPTEMBER

TODAY'S THOUGHT:
"Marriage is a wonderful institution. But who would want to live in an institution?" —H. L. Mencken

BIRTHDAYS—
Johnny Appleseed, 1774; T. S. Eliot, 1888; George Gershwin, 1898; Marty Robbins, 1925; Julie London, 1926; Patrick O'Neal, 1927; Lynn Anderson, 1947; Olivia Newton-John, 1948; Melissa Sue Anderson, 1962; Shamu, 1985

NEW WORD—
globose - adjective: globelike

QUIZ—
Olivia Newton-John wasn't the first in her family to be famous. Who was her illustrious ancestor?

TRIVIA
Olivia Newton-John got her start in show business when she won a Hayley Mills lookalike contest. . . . T. S. Eliot's favorite gift to critics was exploding cigars. . . . Listen up! About that ear that van Gogh cut off - it was his left one.

HISTORY—
On this date in 1969 the Beatles thirteenth and final album, "Abbey Road", was released.

GRAFFITI
Boys will be boys - for much longer than is necessary.

Quiz Answer: Her grandfather was one of the greatest scientists of the century, Nobel Prize winner Max Born.

SEPTEMBER

TODAY'S THOUGHT:
"If you die in an elevator, be sure to press the UP button."
—Sam Levenson

BIRTHDAYS—
Samuel Adams, 1722; Thomas Nast, 1840; William Conrad, 1920; director Arthur Penn, 1922; Sada Thompson, 1929; Wilford Brimley, 1934; Greg Morris, 1934; Marvin Lee "Meatloaf" Aday, 1947; Mike Schmidt, 1949; Shaun Cassidy, 1959

NEW WORD—
cyaneous - adjective: deep blue, azure

QUIZ—
Match the sport with the location of its Hall of Fame:
1) Bowling   A) Newport, RI
2) Horse Racing B) St. Louis, MO
3) Tennis   C) Pinehurst, NC
4) Golf   D) Saratoga Springs, NY

TRIVIA
The first bathroom to be installed in a U.S. residence was in the Vanderbilt home in New York in 1855. . . . Benjamin Franklin owned the first bathtub in the colonies. Good thing he didn't try the lightning experiment there. . . . Cary Grant was expelled from school at age fourteen for sneaking into the girls' bathroom.

HISTORY—
On this date in 1964 the Warren Commission issued its endlessly debated report that Lee Harvey Oswald acted alone in the assassination of President Kennedy.

GRAFFITI
A backseat driver never runs out of gas.

Quiz Answer: 1 - B; 2 - D; 3 - A; 4 - C

SEPTEMBER

TODAY'S THOUGHT:
"People always say 'He died penniless', as if it's a terrible thing. Sounds like good timing to me." —Al Cleathen

BIRTHDAYS—
Confucius, 551 B.C.; Kate Douglass Wiggin, 1856; Al Capp, 1909; Peter Finch, 1916; William Windom, 1923; Marcello Mastroianni, 1924; Jerry Clower, 1926; Brigitte Bardot, 1934; Ben E. King, 1938; Steve Largent, 1954; Johnny Dawkins Jr., 1963

NEW WORD—
precocial - adjective: active and able to move about freely when hatched

QUIZ—
Try "Taxi"ing your brain and name the cab company in the television series "Taxi".

TRIVIA
Confucius was not always a famous philosopher; at age seventeen he was a corn inspector at the markets. . . . Kim Basinger, Raquel Welch, Dyan Cannon, Carly Simon and Steve Martin were all cheerleaders. . . . Before getting into acting and directing, Sidney Poitier trained as a physiotherapist in a mental hospital.

HISTORY—
On this date in 1941 Boston Red Sox baseball great Ted Williams became the last big leaguer to hit over .400 as he wound up the season with a .406 average.
And on this same date in 1960 Williams wound up his career by hitting a home run, his 521st, in his very last at-bat.

GRAFFITI
Confucius say - He who carries tale makes monkey of self.

Quiz Answer: The Sunshine Taxi Company

SEPTEMBER

TODAY'S THOUGHT:
"If there is a God, give me a sign! . . . See, I told you that the knlupt smflrt glpptnrr . . ." —Steve Martin

OBSERVANCES/EVENTS—
Today is Goose Day.

BIRTHDAYS—
Horatio Nelson, 1758; Enrico Fermi, 1901; Gene Autry, 1907; Anita Ekberg, 1931; Jerry Lee Lewis, 1935; Larry Linville, 1939; Madeline Kahn, 1942; Bryant Gumbel, 1948; John Paxson, 1960; Hersey Hawkins Jr., 1965

NEW WORD—
frangible - adjective: breakable

QUIZ—
How many millions are in a trillion?

TRIVIA
Only 4% of comic book collectors are female. . . . The only state to have developed a distinct breed of dog is Maryland with its Chesapeake Bay retriever. . . . The goldfish has a life span of 25 years.

HISTORY—
On this date in 1983 "A Chorus Line" staged its 3,389th performance, thus becoming the longest running show in Broadway history.

GRAFFITI
Nothing goes to sleep as easily as one's conscience.

Quiz Answer: One million (A thousand millions make a billion and one thousand billions make a trillion.)

SEPTEMBER

TODAY'S THOUGHT:
"If life was fair, Elvis would be alive and all the impersonators would be dead." —Johnny Carson

BIRTHDAYS—
Lester Maddox, 1915; Deborah Kerr, 1921; Truman Capote, 1924; Angie Dickinson, 1931; Johnny Mathis, 1935; Marilyn McCoo, 1943; Deborah Allen, 1953

NEW WORD—
sectile - adjective: capable of being cut smoothly with a knife

QUIZ—
Bathroom Brain Teaser:
If you drive a bus from New York to Philadelphia with 40 people on board, and drop off 4 people at six different stops and pick up 5 people at each of these stops, when you get to Philadelphia three hours later, what is the driver's name?

TRIVIA
In sky writing the average letter is nearly two miles high. . . . 62 out of 100 Americans say that the worst day of the week is - you guessed it - Monday. . . . The second man to walk on the lunar surface was Buzz Aldrin. His mother's maiden name is Moon.

HISTORY—
On this date in 1911 Lt. H. H. Arnold became the first stuntman while performing dangerous feats for the film "The Military Air Scout".
In 1935 the classic Gershwin musical "Porgy and Bess" opened at the Colonial Theater in Boston to very mixed reviews.

GRAFFITI
Taxidermists know their stuff.

Quiz Answer: Your Name

OCTOBER

TODAY'S THOUGHT:
"Be nice to your children, for they will choose your rest home."
—Phyllis Diller

OBSERVANCES/EVENTS—
This is Computer Learning Month, Family History Month, National Dental Hygiene Month, National Pasta Month, National Youth Against Tobacco Month and Pizza Festival Month.

BIRTHDAYS—
Vladimir Horowitz, 1904; Walter Matthau, 1920; Jimmy Carter, 1924; William Rehnquist, 1924; Tom Bosley, 1927; George Peppard, 1928; Julie Andrews, 1935; Grete Waitz, 1953

NEW WORD—
dandiprat - noun: a silver coin of 16th century England approximately equal to a twopence

QUIZ—
What's the only state in the U.S. that ends in "k"?

TRIVIA
The first president born in a hospital was Jimmy Carter. . . . Hartford, Connecticut's "Courant", published since 1764, is the oldest newspaper in the U.S. . . . According to a Gallup poll, the most hated food in America is liver.

HISTORY—
On this date in 1903 the first World Series began.
In 1971 Disney World opened in Orlando, Florida.

GRAFFITI
It's easy the night before to get up early the next morning.

Quiz Answer: New York

 # O C T O B E R

TODAY'S THOUGHT:
"Politics is the art of looking for trouble, finding it everywhere, diagnosing it incorrectly and applying the wrong remedies."
—Groucho Marx

OBSERVANCES/EVENTS—
Today is Phileas Fogg's Wager Day from Jules Verne's "Around the World in Eighty Days".

BIRTHDAYS—
Groucho Marx, 1890; Mahatma Gandhi, 1869; Spanky McFarland, 1928; Rex Reed, 1940; Don McLean, 1945; Sting, 1951

NEW WORD—
ratiocinate - verb: to reason

QUIZ—
Which came first, Coke or Pepsi?

TRIVIA
Because his son-in-law was late with the carriage, Thomas Jefferson had to walk to his own inauguration. . . . Most trips taken in the U.S. by car are under five miles. . . . President Ulysses S. Grant was arrested for exceeding the speed limit while driving a team of wild horses through the streets of Washington.

HISTORY—
On this date in 1950 "Peanuts" premiered. It is now in 2,400 newspapers and translated into 26 languages in 68 countries.
In 1959 Rod Serling first beckoned Americans into the "Twilight Zone".

GRAFFITI
A dead flower is a late bloomer.

Quiz Answer: Coca Cola was introduced in 1896. Pepsi Cola followed ten years later.

O C T O B E R

TODAY'S THOUGHT:
"I wish people who have trouble communicating would just shut up."
—Tom Lehrer

OBSERVANCES/EVENTS—
It is a big day for the over 12,000 members of "The Andy Griffith Show" Rerun Watchers Club as they celebrate the anniversary of the first telecast of their all-time favorite series.

BIRTHDAYS—
George Bancroft, 1800; Gertrude Berg, 1899; Gore Vidal, 1925; Madlyn Rhue, 1934; Chubby Checker, 1941; Lindsey Buckingham, 1947; Dave Winfield, 1951; Dennis Eckersley, 1954

NEW WORD—
higgle - verb: to bargain

QUIZ—
Who did Johnny and the Moondogs eventually become?

TRIVIA
The average person loses 50-100 strands of hair every day. . . . Stainless steel can be rolled into strips thinner than a human hair. . . . Tiny hairs on the feet of flies act like tastebuds as they stroll over your food.

HISTORY—
On this date in 1955 Annette slapped on her first pair of giant ears as "The Mickey Mouse Club" hit the airwaves. Remember Roy on that show? Besides appearing on camera he also wrote the theme song.

GRAFFITI
Temper improves when you don't use it.

Quiz Answer: They went on to become the Foreverly Brothers and the Moonshiners, The Quarrymen Skiffle Group and finally, the Beatles.

OCTOBER

TODAY'S THOUGHT:
"It costs a lot of money to look this cheap." —Dolly Parton

OBSERVANCES/EVENTS—
It's Ten-Four Day, observed as a day of recognition for radio operators everywhere for whom "10-4" signals an affirmative reply as in, "That's a big 10-4, good buddy!"

BIRTHDAYS—
Rutherford B. Hayes, 1822; Damon Runyan, 1884; Jan Murray, 1917; Charlton Heston, 1922; Patti LaBelle, 1944; Clifton Davis, 1945; Susan Sarandon, 1946

NEW WORD—
bidarka - noun: a sealskin boat of the Alaskan Eskimo

QUIZ—
Can you guess the celebrities who go with these given names?
- A: Aaron Chwatt
- B: Nathan Birnbaum
- C: Nicholas Coppola
- D: John Elroy Sanford
- E: Paul Reubenfeld

TRIVIA
75% of optometrists wear eyeglasses. . . . Marietta, Ohio is named for Marie Antoinette. . . . Olympic gold is really silver. There are 92.6 grams of silver in each Olympic gold medal and only 6 grams of gold.

HISTORY—
On this date in 1957 Wally and the Beav first shuffled into America's living rooms as "Leave It to Beaver" debuted on TV.

GRAFFITI
Grocery shopping carts go faster than $55/hour.

Quiz Answer: A - Red Buttons; B - George Burns; C - Nicholas Cage (and yes, he is related); D - Redd Foxx; E - Pee Wee Herman

OCTOBER

TODAY'S THOUGHT:

"Van Gogh became a painter because he had no ear for music."
—Nikki Harris

BIRTHDAYS—

Chester A. Arthur, 1829; Robert Goddard, 1882; Ray Kroc, 1902; Donald Pleasence, 1919; Glynnis Johns, 1923; Bill Dana, 1924; Steve Miller, 1943; Bob Geldof, 1951

NEW WORD—

limnetic - adjective: pertaining to or living in the open water of a fresh-water pond or lake

QUIZ—

Are forts your forte? Match the following with their location.

1:	Ft. Ticonderoga	A:	Pittsburgh, PA
2:	Ft. Sumter	B:	Wyoming
3:	Ft. Laramie	C:	New York State
4:	Ft. Duquesne	D:	Charleston, SC

TRIVIA

During a game of jai alai, the speed of the ball can reach 160 miles per hour. . . . In 1976 twenty invited guests witnessed an official marriage ceremony between a Los Angeles secretary and a fifty-pound rock. . . . An elephant grows six sets of teeth during a lifetime.

HISTORY—

On this date in 1921 Graham McNamee took to the radio airwaves to broadcast the first play-by-play coverage of a World Series game on station WJZ in Newark, New Jersey.

GRAFFITI
Oceanography is a study in depth.

Quiz Answer: 1 - C; 2 - D; 3 - B; 4 - A

O C T O B E R

TODAY'S THOUGHT:
"We must believe in luck. For how else can we explain the success of those we don't like?" —Jean Cocteau

OBSERVANCES/EVENTS—
It's German-American Day, a day to honor those of German extraction and thank them for all those Oktoberfest parties that keep things interesting this time of year.

BIRTHDAYS—
Jenny Lind, 1820; George Westinghouse, 1846; Carole Lombard, 1908; Thor Heyerdahl, 1914; Shana Alexander, 1925; Britt Ekland, 1942; Fred Travalena, 1942; Stephanie Zimbalist, 1956

NEW WORD—
whigmaleerie - noun: a whim, notion

QUIZ—
What is the official language of Greenland?

TRIVIA
The Ouija board's name comes from combining the French and German words for "yes". . . . The average American generates three pounds of garbage a day. . . . Smokey the Bear is the only one in America with his own zip code - 20252.

HISTORY—
On this date in 1863 the first Turkish bath opened in Brooklyn, operated by Dr. C. H. Sheperd. You could take a bath there for $1, considerably cheaper than taking a bath on Wall Street.
In 1991 Elizabeth Taylor tied the knot for the 8th time, marrying construction worker Larry Fortensky.

GRAFFITI
In order to lead the band, you must face the music.

Quiz Answer: Danish

O C T O B E R

TODAY'S THOUGHT:

"The reason grandparents and grandchildren get along so well is that they have a common enemy." —Sam Levenson

BIRTHDAYS—

James Whitcomb Riley, 1853; June Allyson, 1917; Bishop Desmond Tutu, 1931; Oliver North, 1943; John Cougar Mellencamp, 1951

NEW WORD—

maduro - adjective: strong and dark, a term for cigars

QUIZ—

Which is the only one of the Seven Wonders of the Ancient World still in existence?

TRIVIA

Not to rain on your parade, but there are over one quadrillion ants living on the planet. . . . Ants will not cross a white chalk line. . . . The reaction time of a cockroach is $^{54}/_{1000}$ of a second so you best not get into a gunfight.

HISTORY—

On this date in 1916 the greatest rout ever to take place on the gridiron was played as Georgia Tech whipped Cumberland University 222-0.

In 1968 the film rating system was established, thereby guaranteeing that teenagers, who might not realize that a film might contain sex, would see an "R" rating and immediately go out of their way to see it.

——— GRAFFITI ———
Blowing your top doesn't make you a dynamic person.

Quiz Answer: The Sphinx

OCTOBER

TODAY'S THOUGHT:
"Never look down on anybody unless you're helping him up."
—Jesse Jackson

BIRTHDAYS—
Eddie Rickenbacker, 1890; Juan Peron, 1895; Rona Barrett, 1936; David Carradine, 1940; Jesse Jackson, 1941; Chevy Chase, 1943; Sarah Purcell, 1948; Sigourney Weaver, 1949

NEW WORD—
nocuous - adjective: likely to cause damage or injury

QUIZ—
Which president is credited with making Thanksgiving an official holiday?

TRIVIA
Eddie Rickenbacker raced in the first five Indy 500 races before becoming a WWI flying ace. . . . The Marines have the highest desertion rate of any of the armed services. . . . An Associated Press correspondent died with General Custer at the Battle of the Little Big Horn.

HISTORY—
On this date in 1871 Mrs. O'Leary's cow turned the tables on would-be barbecuers as it began the Great Chicago Fire which virtually destroyed the city.
In 1896 Dow Jones began reporting the average of industrial stocks.

GRAFFITI
Seconds count - especially when dieting.

Quiz Answer: Abe Lincoln proclaimed the last Thursday in November be celebrated back in 1863.

O C T O B E R

TODAY'S THOUGHT:
"Will the people in the cheaper seats clap your hands? All the rest of you, if you'll just rattle your jewelry." —John Lennon

BIRTHDAYS—
Cartoonist Russell Myers, 1938; John Lennon, 1940; Joe Pepitone, 1940; Jackson Browne, 1950; Mike Singletary, 1958

NEW WORD—
euryphagous - adjective: able to subsist on a wide variety of foods

QUIZ—
True or False?
Pittsburgh, Pennsylvania is farther east than Miami, Florida.

TRIVIA
Playing the piano can use up more calories than doing light exercise. . . . The original title of the Beatles' hit "Yesterday" was "Scrambled Eggs". . . . When NBC plays three musical notes with its logo on TV, those notes are "G - E - C" for the General Electric Corporation which owns the network.

HISTORY—
On this date in 1888 the Washington Monument opened.

GRAFFITI
Two halves make a hole, and the fullback goes through.

Quiz Answer: True

O C T O B E R

TODAY'S THOUGHT:
"Somewhere on this globe, every ten seconds there is a woman giving birth to a child. She must be found and stopped." —Sam Levenson

OBSERVANCES/EVENTS—
It's Double 10th Day, for obvious reasons.

BIRTHDAYS—
Painter Benjamin West, 1738; Guiseppe Verdi, 1813; John M. Studebaker, 1833; Helen Hayes, 1900; Dorothy Lamour, 1914; Harold Painter, 1930; Ben Vereen, 1946; Martina Navratilova, 1956; Tanya Tucker, 1958

NEW WORD—
pleach - verb: to interweave branches or vines for a hedge or arbor

QUIZ—
Where is the only place the United States flag is flown at full staff 24 hours a day, 365 days a year without ever being raised, lowered or saluted?

TRIVIA
Last names in China are always one syllable. . . . Pepto Bismol, when introduced in 1901, was called Mixture Cholera Infantum. . . . A grasshopper's blood is white.

HISTORY—
On this date in 1886 Griswold Lorillard showed up at the Autumn Ball at the Tuxedo Park Country Club, New York positively resplendent, decked out in the first formal dinner jacket. He was the talk of the town and the name tuxedo stuck.

GRAFFITI
Death is nature's way of saying "Howdy".

Quiz Answer: The moon

O C T O B E R

TODAY'S THOUGHT:

"I have nothing to say and I am saying it." —John Cage

OBSERVANCES/EVENTS—

Today is General Pulaski Memorial Day.

BIRTHDAYS—

Eleanor Roosevelt, 1884; journalist Joseph Alsop, 1910; Jerome Robbins, 1918; Dottie West, 1932; Roy Scheider, 1935; Darryl Hall, 1948

NEW WORD—

guddle - verb: to grope with hands for fish under rocks

QUIZ—

Bathroom Brain Teaser:

This is a true fact about a man who went to a builder with plans to put an addition on his house. They had never met before but the builder said he'd be happy to build the extension at no charge. Why?

TRIVIA

Eleanor Roosevelt's maiden name was Roosevelt. . . . For 186 days a year, the sun is not seen at the North Pole. . . . Kodak camera inventor George Eastman hated to have his picture taken.

HISTORY—

On this date in 1950 the FCC granted CBS permission to start broadcasting selected TV shows in color.

In 1984 Dr. Kathryn Sullivan became the first woman astronaut to walk in space.

GRAFFITI
God Bless America - and please hurry.

Quiz Answer: The man was Picasso and the builder figured that by getting the plans for the house he'd have a Picasso original which would be worth much more than the construction cost.

 # O C T O B E R

TODAY'S THOUGHT:
"If you come to a fork in the road, take it." —Yogi Berra

OBSERVANCES/EVENTS—
To observe International Moment of Frustration Scream Day reach deep inside your tortured psyche and dredge up a good primal scream to vent your frustration. Go outside at twelve hundred hours Greenwich time and howl for thirty seconds.

BIRTHDAYS—
Jonathan Trumbull, 1710; Joe Cronin, 1906; Jean Nidetch, 1923; Dick Gregory, 1932; Luciano Pavarotti, 1935; Tony Kubek, 1936; Susan Anton, 1950; astronaut Ronald McNair, 1950; Adam Rich, 1968; Kirk Cameron, 1970

NEW WORD—
tump - noun: a small mound or hill

QUIZ—
During the Civil War, were there any slave states that remained part of the Union?

TRIVIA
The banana is considered the most ancient fruit on the earth. . . . Lettuce is the world's most popular green. . . . Onions can be stored for longer periods of time than any other vegetable.

HISTORY—
On this date in 1792 the first celebration of Columbus took place, on the 300th anniversary of Columbus' expedition.

GRAFFITI
People believe anything if you whisper it.

Quiz Answer: Yes, they were Delaware, Maryland, Kentucky and Missouri.

O C T O B E R

TODAY'S THOUGHT:

"People want to know why I do this, why I write such gross stuff. I like to tell them I have the heart of a small boy and I keep it in a jar on my desk." —Stephen King

BIRTHDAYS—

Molly Pitcher, 1754; Nipsey Russell, 1924; Margaret Thatcher, 1925; Eddie Mathews, 1931; Paul Simon, 1941; Reggie Theus, 1957; Marie Osmond, 1959; Glenn Anton "Doc" Rivers, 1961; Jerry Lee Rice, 1962

NEW WORD—

afebrile - adjective: feverless

QUIZ—

What famous sixties musical act was known in the fifties as Tom and Jerry?

TRIVIA

Big Ben is not the clock or the tower but the bell that rings out each hour. . . . Henry VIII had Sir Nicholas Carew beheaded because he bested him in a bowling match. . . . The "London Times" printed one of the smallest newspapers ever to commemorate the Queen's Doll House at the Empire Exhibition in 1924.

HISTORY—

On this date in 1792 the cornerstone of the White House was laid.

GRAFFITI

A chef is a man for all seasonings.

Quiz Answer: Tom and Jerry later became somewhat more famous as Simon and Garfunkel.

O C T O B E R

TODAY'S THOUGHT:
"I'm not bald - I'm just taller than my hair." —Thom Sharpe

OBSERVANCES/EVENTS—
It is Be Bald and Be Free Day, a day for baldheaded men to shine!

BIRTHDAYS—
William Penn, 1644; Dwight David Eisenhower, 1890; e e cummings, 1894; Lillian Gish, 1896; C. Everett Koop, 1916; Roger Moore, 1928; John Dean, 1938; Ralph Lauren, 1939; Greg Evigan, 1953

NEW WORD—
moiety - noun: a half; an indefinite portion

QUIZ—
True or False?
The term "meatless Mondays" referred to Catholicism's abstinence from meat until 1960 when Pope John XXIII changed the day to "fish Fridays".

TRIVIA
Eisenhower was known as an inveterate cat hater and ordered any cat found on his property shot on sight. . . . Stogies get their name from the drivers of Conestoga wagons who often chomped on stubby cigars. . . . West Point originated class rings.

HISTORY—
On this date in 1917 France executed one Margaretha Zelle for her activities on behalf of Germany. History knows her as Mata Hari.

GRAFFITI
**You know you're getting old
when your little brother starts going bald.**

Quiz Answer: False - "Meatless Mondays" originated during World War I when Herbert Hoover, then director of the Food Administration, urged Americans not to eat meat on that day in order to conserve food for the war.

O C T O B E R

TODAY'S THOUGHT:
"I don't want any yes-men around me. I want everyone to tell me the truth even if it costs them their jobs." —Samuel Goldwyn

OBSERVANCES/EVENTS—
It is National Grouch Day, a time to honor those who are forever letting their pet peeves off the leash, but never clean up after them.

BIRTHDAYS—
Virgil, 70 A.D.; John L. Sullivan, 1858; John Kenneth Galbraith, 1908; John Schlesinger Jr., 1917; Mario Puzo, 1920; Lee Iacocca, 1924; Linda Lavin, 1939; Penny Marshall, 1942; Jim Palmer, 1945; Roscoe Tanner, 1951; Trace Armstrong, 1965

NEW WORD—
uxorious - adjective: doting upon, foolishly fond of

QUIZ—
What two geographical records are held by Inyo County, California?

TRIVIA
Jacksonville, Florida has the largest total area of any U.S. city, covering 460 square miles, almost twice the area of Los Angeles. . . . The U.S. would fit into the African continent three times. . . . Boston was the first city in the U.S. with a subway.

HISTORY—
On this date in 1951 "I Love Lucy" debuted on CBS.

GRAFFITI
The future isn't what is used to be.

Quiz Answer: Both the highest and lowest spots in the continental United States are found within that county and only 86 miles apart. Mount Whitney is 14,495 feet above sea level while Death Valley is 276 feet below sea level.

OCTOBER

TODAY'S THOUGHT:
"A form of ugliness so intolerable that we have to alter it every six months." —Oscar Wilde, on fashion

OBSERVANCES/EVENTS—
It's National Boss Day so why not take the boss to lunch? It's a great excuse to take one of those loooooong lunches like he does everyday . . .

BIRTHDAYS—
Noah Webster, 1758; Oscar Wilde, 1854; David Ben-Gurion, 1886; Eugene O'Neill, 1888; photographer Paul Strand, 1890; Angela Lansbury, 1925; Suzanne Somers, 1946; Melissa Belote, 1956; Manute Bol, 1962

NEW WORD—
scunner - noun: an irrational dislike

QUIZ—
In the poem "Casey at the Bat", who was Mudville's opponent and what was the final score of the game?

TRIVIA
Oscar Wilde's last words were, "This wallpaper is killing me; one of us has to go." . . . Rodin's "The Thinker" was actually supposed to be the poet, Dante. . . . Writer William Saroyan and David Seville of Chipmunk fame were cousins.

HISTORY—
On this date in 1793 Marie "Let them eat cake" Antoinette was beheaded.

GRAFFITI
Small talk comes out of big mouths.

Quiz Answer: The Mudville Nine lost to an anonymous team, 4-2.

O C T O B E R

TODAY'S THOUGHT:

"I never worry about diets. The only carrots that interest me are the number you get in a diamond." —Mae West

BIRTHDAYS—

Spring Byington, 1893; Arthur Miller, 1915; Rita Hayworth, 1918; Beverly Garland, 1926; Jimmy Breslin, 1930; Steve Douglas McMichael, 1937; Evel Knievel, 1938; Bob Seagren, 1946; Margot Kidder, 1948; George Wendt, 1948

NEW WORD—

craunch - verb: to crunch

QUIZ—

If you are dining in England and order broccoli, what will you get?

TRIVIA

At birth a hippopotamus weighs about 100 pounds. . . . Not long ago, a Bulgarian woman was allowed only one bath in her lifetime - and that was on the day before her wedding. . . . Buckingham Palace is the former site of a brothel.

HISTORY—

On this date in 1989 the World Series was delayed by an earthquake measuring 7.1 on the Richter Scale as it rocked Candlestick Park and the San Francisco Bay area.

GRAFFITI
Crash the houseboat party - barge in.

Quiz Answer: Cauliflower

OCTOBER

TODAY'S THOUGHT:

"All pro athletes are bilingual. They speak English and profanity."
—Gordie Howe

BIRTHDAYS—

A. J. Liebling, 1904; Pierre Trudeau, 1919; Jesse Helms, 1921; Melina Mercouri, 1925; Chuck Berry, 1926; George C. Scott, 1927; Mike Ditka, 1939; Wendy Wasserstein, 1950; Pam Dawber, 1951; Tommy Hearns, 1958; Erin Moran, 1961

NEW WORD—

insalubrious - adjective: unfavorable to health

QUIZ—

In a standard deck of playing cards, which one of the four kings is shown in profile?

TRIVIA

Johnny Unitas threw at least one touchdown pass in 47 consecutive games. . . . A tennis court (singles) is 36 feet wide and 78 feet long. . . . Former baseball player Carlos May is the only big leaguer to have worn his birthday on his back. His number was 18 and his last name, which appeared above the number, read the same as the month in which he was born.

HISTORY—

On this date in 1869 "Seward's Folly" was consummated as the United States took possession of Alaska from the Russians.

GRAFFITI
Recycling: the return trip of a bike race.

Quiz Answer: The king of diamonds

O C T O B E R

TODAY'S THOUGHT:
"There is no shortage of lawyers in Washington, D.C. In fact, there may be more lawyers than people." —Sandra Day O'Connor

OBSERVANCES/EVENTS—
It is Evaluate Your Life Day, a day to look back and reflect.

BIRTHDAYS—
Mordecai Brown, 1876; Fannie Hurst, 1889; Jack Anderson, 1922; John LeCarre, 1931; Peter Max, 1937; John Lithgow, 1945; Jeannie C. Riley, 1945; Bradley Lee Daugherty, 1965; Amy Carter, 1967

NEW WORD—
ferity - noun: a wild, untamed or uncultivated state

QUIZ—
Backward thinking is required for this one. What do the words uncomplimentary, unnoticeably and subcontinental have in common?

TRIVIA
Cleopatra was a direct descendant of four generations of inbred marriages. She married two of her brothers before she killed them. . . . Statisticians say if the government job sector continues growing at the rate it has for the past decade, by the year 2049 everyone will be working for the government. . . . J. Edgar Hoover would not allow anyone to walk on his shadow.

HISTORY—
On this date in 1781 Cornwallis surrendered to Washington at Yorktown, effectively ending the Revolutionary War.

———— GRAFFITI ————
At least George Washington didn't blame his troubles on the previous administration.

Quiz Answer: They all have the vowels a-e-i-o-u in reverse order.

OCTOBER

TODAY'S THOUGHT:

"The older I get, the less important the comma becomes. Let the reader catch his own breath." —Elizabeth Clarkson Zwart

BIRTHDAYS—

Sir Christopher Wren, 1632; John Dewey, 1859; Charles Ives, 1874; Arlene Francis, 1908; Art Buchwald, 1925; Dr. Joyce Brothers, 1928; Mickey Mantle, 1931; Keith Hernandez, 1953

NEW WORD—

pech - noun: a short breath or gasp

QUIZ—

What 492 foot long memorial did Yale student Maya Ying Lin design?

TRIVIA—

Cows don't like spinach. . . . Wall Street's name stems from colonial times when a wall was built around Lower Manhattan to protect cattle from Indian raids. . . . Albert Einstein was four years old before he could talk.

HISTORY—

On this date in 1944 General Douglas MacArthur proved to be a man of his word as he and thousands of his troops returned to the Philippines.

GRAFFITI
We have seen the future - and it is expensive.

Quiz Answer: The Vietnam Veterans Memorial in Washington, D.C.

OCTOBER

TODAY'S THOUGHT:

"To my embarrassment, I was born in bed with a lady."

—Wilson Mizner

BIRTHDAYS—

Samuel Taylor Coleridge, 1772; conductor Sir Georg Solti, 1912; Dizzy Gillespie, 1917; composer Sir Malcolm Arnold, 1921; Whitey Ford, 1928; Elvin Bishop, 1942; Carrie Fisher, 1956; George Bell, 1959

NEW WORD—

vispine - adjective: of or pertaining to a wasp

QUIZ—

Which dam is on the Colorado River between Nevada and Arizona, the Hoover Dam or the Boulder Dam?

TRIVIA

The average American adult male is 5 feet 9.1 inches tall. The average woman is 5 feet 3.7 inches tall. . . . The 1990 graduating class of the U.S. Navy's top school received diplomas stating they'd graduated from the Navel Academy. . . . If you're cynophobic, you have a fear of dogs.

HISTORY—

On this date in 1879 Edison's brightest idea came to light as he invented the first practical incandescent electric light bulb.

GRAFFITI
Exercise to exorcise the extra size.

Quiz Answer: They are the same dam thing. Erected from 1931-1936, the Hoover (or Boulder) Dam is over 700 feet high and 1,200 feet long.

O C T O B E R

TODAY'S THOUGHT:
"A baby boomer is a man who hires someone to cut the grass so he can play golf for exercise." —Anonymous

OBSERVANCES/EVENTS—
It is World's End Day, the anniversary celebration of William Miller's prediction of the end of the world in 1844. Don't worry; you didn't miss it; we still have it to look forward to.

BIRTHDAYS—
Franz Liszt, 1811; Jimmie Foxx, 1907; Joan Fontaine, 1917; Timothy Leary, 1920; Dory Previn, 1929; Annette Funicello, 1942; Catherine Deneuve, 1943; Jeff Goldblum, 1952; Brian Boitano, 1963

NEW WORD—
fike - verb: to fidget, move restlessly

QUIZ—
What ups and downs might be found at 165 Eaton Place in London?

TRIVIA
A year contains 31,557,600 seconds. . . . Robin Williams was voted "least likely to succeed" in high school. . . . George Washington gave the shortest presidential inaugural address at his second inaugural - 135 words.

HISTORY—
On this date in 1962 the world came too close to comfort to fulfilling William Miller's vision (see Observances above) as President Kennedy took to television to demand that the Soviets remove their missiles from Cuba.

GRAFFITI
The world is your oyster - if you have enough clams.

Quiz Answer: That was the address of the house in the PBS series "Upstairs, Downstairs".

O C T O B E R

TODAY'S THOUGHT:

"My husband thinks that health food is anything he eats before the expiration date." —Rita Rudner

BIRTHDAYS—

Adlai Stevenson, 1835; Sarah Bernhardt, 1844; Gertrude Ederle, 1906; Johnny Carson, 1925; Diana Dors, 1931; Chi-Chi Rodriguez, 1934; Pelé, 1940; Michael Crichton, 1942; Weird Al Yankovic, 1959; Mike Tomczak, 1962; Doug Flutie, 1962

NEW WORD—

oblivescence - noun: the process of forgetting

QUIZ—

Bathroom Brain Teaser:

September 9, 1981 (9/9/81) marked the last time in the 20th century that the product of the month times the day equaled the last two digits of the year (9 x 9 = 81). When is the next time this will happen?

TRIVIA

There are 2,598,960 different poker hands possible in a deck of cards. . . . You are twice as likely to get a heart attack in winter than summer. . . . Donald Duck's nieces are April, May and June.

HISTORY—

On this date in 1962 twelve-year old Stevie Wonder made his first recording, "Thank You for Loving Me All the Way", for Motown.

—— GRAFFITI ——
To cure that listless feeling, write a list.

Quiz Answer: 2,001 (1/1/01)

OCTOBER

TODAY'S THOUGHT:
"Life is like a dogsled team. If you ain't the lead dog, the scene never changes." —Lewis Grizzard

OBSERVANCES/EVENTS—
Today is United Nations Day.

BIRTHDAYS—
Moss Hart, 1904; poet Denise Levertov, 1923; Y. A. Tittle, 1926; David Nelson, 1936; F. Murray Abraham, 1940; Bill Wyman, 1941; Kevin Kline, 1947

NEW WORD—
luxate - verb: to put out of joint; dislocate

QUIZ—
An Oklahoma City journalist named Carl Magee invented it. The first one was installed at the intersection of First Street and Robinson in July, 1935. What is it?

TRIVIA
Potato chips were invented in 1853 in Saratoga, New York by George Crum. . . . China's Zeng Jinlian was the world's tallest woman at eight feet, two inches. . . . If the Barbie doll were brought to human scale, her measurements would be 38-18-28.

HISTORY—
On this date in 1826 the patent was issued for an invention that never set the world on fire, the safety match.

GRAFFITI
Teenagers work their fingers to the phone.

Quiz Answer: A parking meter (While we're on the subject, we can't resist the one about the two dogs walking down the street. One spots a parking meter and says to the other, "Oh, look - a pay toilet.")

The Bathroom Trivia Almanac

O C T O B E R

TODAY'S THOUGHT:

"People will accept your idea much more readily if you tell them Benjamin Franklin said it first." —David H. Comins

BIRTHDAYS—

Johann Strauss Jr., 1825; Picasso, 1881; Minnie Pearl, 1912; Anthony Franciosa, 1928; Marion Ross, 1936; Bob Knight, 1940; Anne Tyler, 1941; Helen Reddy, 1942; Brian Kerwin, 1949; Kornelia Ender, 1958

NEW WORD—

gymkhana - noun: a field day held for equestrians

QUIZ—

What unusual quality do the names of the first five presidents have in common?

TRIVIA

A group of owls is called a parliament. . . . The maximum number of letters on one line of a "Wheel of Fortune" game board is 13. . . . The term "potty" dates back to when England had chamber pots and made kid-sized pots.

HISTORY—

On this date in 1960 the patent was issued for the electronic wristwatch.

In 1972 the first female FBI agents completed their training in Quantico, Virginia.

GRAFFITI
Politics is for the birds - vultures.

Quiz Answer: George Washington, John Adams, Thomas Jefferson, James Madison and James Monroe had no middle names.

OCTOBER

TODAY'S THOUGHT:
"I got the bill for my surgery. Now I know what those three doctors are wearing masks for." —James H. Boren

OBSERVANCES/EVENTS—
It is Mule Day, commemorating the introduction of mules to the United States in 1785.

BIRTHDAYS—
Joseph Hansom, 1803; cereal magnate Charles Post, 1854; publisher John Knight, 1894; Jackie Coogan, 1914; Francois Mitterand, 1916; Edward Brooke, 1919; Bob Hoskins, 1942; Hillary Rodham Clinton, 1946; Pat Sajak, 1946; Jaclyn Smith, 1948; Chuck Forman, 1950

NEW WORD—
edulcorate - verb: to purify; wash out acids or salts

QUIZ—
What famous child actress auditioned for a regular part in the "Our Gang" comedies in the early thirties but was turned down flat?

TRIVIA
There are 35 species of coconuts. . . . The soy bean is the most versatile vegetable on earth with 400 different products made with it. . . . In 1990 the California legislature overturned a ruling that allowed dogs' teeth to be cleaned only by veterinarians.

HISTORY—
On this date in 1881 the Earp brothers and Doc Holliday defeated the Clanton boys at the OK Corral in Tombstone, Arizona.
In 1951 Rocky Marciano defeated Joe Louis for the heavyweight championship.

GRAFFITI
The early bird catches the worm - and he can have it.

Quiz Answer: Shirley Temple

OCTOBER

TODAY'S THOUGHT:
"If you shoot a mime, should you use a silencer?" —Steven Wright

OBSERVANCES/EVENTS—
It is Navy Day but that doesn't mean that you can take the day off. In other words, don't give up the shift.

BIRTHDAYS—
James Cook, 1728; Isaac Singer, 1811; Teddy Roosevelt, 1858; Dylan Thomas, 1914; Nanette Fabray, 1920; Ruby Dee, 1924; Warren Christopher, 1925; Kyle Rote, 1928; John Cleese, 1939

NEW WORD—
teff - noun: a fragrant grass of North Africa

QUIZ—
Who signed off with the following:
    A: "Peace."
    B: "And that's the way it is."
    C: "Good night and good news."
    D: "Good night and may God bless."
    E: "Y'all come back now, hear?"

TRIVIA
The northernmost point in the continental U.S. is in Minnesota. . . . Snakes don't blink. . . . The most likely magazine to be stolen from a U.S. public library is "Sports Illustrated".

HISTORY—
On this date in 1977 Anwar Sadat and Menachem Begin received the Nobel Peace Prize.

GRAFFITI
**You can be poor and happy . . .
but not at the same time.**

Quiz Answer: A - Dave Garroway; B - Walter Cronkite; C - Ted Baxter; D - Red Skelton; E - the Beverly Hillbillies

OCTOBER

TODAY'S THOUGHT:
"Your dresses should be tight enough to show you're a woman and loose enough to show you're a lady." —Edith Head

BIRTHDAYS—
Chef George Auguste Escoffier, 1846; Edith Head, 1907; Jonas Salk, 1914; Bowie Kuhn, 1926; Suzy Parker, 1933; Charlie Daniels, 1936; Telma Hopkins, 1948; Bruce Jenner, 1949

NEW WORD—
niveous - adjective: resembling snow, especially in whiteness

QUIZ—
How many M&M's colors are there?

TRIVIA
Charlotte Beysser Bartoldi was the model for the Statue of Liberty, which was sculpted by her son, Fredric Auguste Bartoldi. . . . The only U.S. landmark that moves around is the fabled cable cars in San Francisco. . . . Christopher Columbus had freckles.

HISTORY—
On this date in 1886 the Statue of Liberty was dedicated on Bedloe's Island. The inscription "Give me your tired, your poor, your huddled masses . . ." was written by Emma Lazarus.

GRAFFITI
To understand the theory of relativity, marry someone from a large family.

Quiz Answer: Six - brown, green, orange, red, tan and yellow

O C T O B E R

TODAY'S THOUGHT:
"Money won't buy happiness, but it will pay the salaries of a large research staff to study the problem." —Bill Vaughan

BIRTHDAYS—
Edmund Halley, 1656; James Boswell, 1740; Akim Tamiroff, 1899; Bill Maudlin, 1921; Melba Moore, 1945; Richard Dreyfuss, 1947; Kate Jackson, 1948; J. T. Smith, 1955; Jesse Lee Barfield, 1959; Michael D'Andrea Carter, 1960

NEW WORD—
bywoner - noun: a farm laborer in southern Africa

QUIZ—
What do the initials stand for in L. L. Cool J.'s name?

TRIVIA
A single stamping machine in the Philadelphia mint can produce coins at a rate of 10,000 per minute. . . . Delaware has the highest concentration of millionaires of any state. . . . A cubic foot of gold weighs about 1,000 pounds, worth between $5 and $10 million.

HISTORY—
On this date in 1929 the Great Depression began as the stock market collapsed, putting many companies out of business and causing economic chaos which lasted until WWII.

GRAFFITI
Old movie stars never die - they just fade away.

Quiz Answer: The initial laden monicker stands for "Ladies Love Cool James".

OCTOBER

TODAY'S THOUGHT:
"At my age, I don't even buy green bananas." —George Burns

OBSERVANCES/EVENTS—
It is Halloween Eve, often called Mischief Night.

BIRTHDAYS—
John Adams, 1735; Alfred Sisley, 1839; William "Bull" Halsey, 1882; Ezra Pound, 1885; Charles Atlas, 1893; Louis Malle, 1932; Grace Slick, 1943; Henry Winkler, 1945; Harry Hamlin, 1951

NEW WORD—
quietus - noun: a finishing stroke

QUIZ—
What did Germany offer England at the end of World War II as part of their reparations?

TRIVIA
John Adams, George Washington and Thomas Jefferson were avid marble collectors and players. . . . The Packard was the first car to cross the continent. It took 52 days in 1903. . . . Honeybees are deaf.

HISTORY—
On this date in 1938 Orson Welles and the Mercury Players scared the pants off America with their Halloween Eve broadcast of "The War of the Worlds" in which they presented a series of news bulletins reporting that the Martians were invading New Jersey.

GRAFFITI
A waist is a terrible thing to mind.

Quiz Answer: The Volkswagen business, but those savvy English politicians turned it down, figuring that no one would ever want a car with such high gas mileage and an engine in the rear.

O C T O B E R

TODAY'S THOUGHT:
"This country is so urbanized we think low-fat milk comes from cows on aerobic exercise programs." —P. J. O'Rourke

OBSERVANCES/EVENTS—
It is Halloween, the holiday of trick or treat which many folks think should be moved to Election Day.

BIRTHDAYS—
John Keats, 1795; Juliet Low, 1860; Chiang Kai-Shek, 1887; Dale Evans, 1912; astronaut Michael Collins, 1931; Dan Rather, 1931; John Candy, 1950; Jane Pauley, 1950; Frederick Stanley McGriff, 1963

NEW WORD—
colubrine - adjective: of or resembling a snake

QUIZ—
Why do the palms of your hands and the soles of your feet wrinkle when immersed in water?

TRIVIA
According to the Kleenex people, the average person blows his nose 256 times a year. . . . The largest pumpkin ever grown weighed 827 pounds. . . . Every clown is unique. Their faces have to be painted on an eggshell to be registered. When a clown dies, his egg is buried with him, no doubt sunny-side up.

HISTORY—
On this date in 1926 magician Harry Houdini died.
In 1952, in perhaps the scariest Halloween prank of all time, the first hydrogen bomb was tested.

GRAFFITI
To cure insomnia listen to yourself talk.

Quiz Answer: Because those areas have no oil glands, and therefore no protective oil, the skin becomes waterlogged.

NOVEMBER

TODAY'S THOUGHT:
"You know the problem with men? After the birth, we're irrelevant."
—Dustin Hoffman

OBSERVANCES/EVENTS—
Today is All Saints Day and National Authors' Day.

BIRTHDAYS—
Benvenuto Cellini, 1500; Stephen Crane, 1871; James Kilpatrick, 1920; Betsy Palmer, 1926; Gary Player, 1935; Robert Foxworth, 1941; Fernando Valenzuela, 1960

NEW WORD—
eleemosynary - adjective: charitable

QUIZ—
Can you name the oldest fast-food hamburger chain?

TRIVIA
Gorillas can't swim. . . . The lobster automatically acquires a new form fitting shell every year. . . . Ambergris, used in making perfumes, comes from the stomach of a whale.

HISTORY—
On this date in 1939 Rudolph the Red-Nosed Reindeer first appeared in a pamphlet given away as a holiday promotion at a Chicago store. Rudy has since gone on to star in numerous specials, books, movies and even the second best-selling song of all time.

GRAFFITI
**It's what guests say as they
swing out of the driveway that counts.**

Quiz Answer: White Castle, which opened its doors in 1921

N O V E M B E R

TODAY'S THOUGHT:
"Jogging is very beneficial. It's good for your legs and your feet. It's also very good for the ground. It makes it feel needed." —Snoopy

OBSERVANCES/EVENTS—
November is Aviation History Month, International Drum Month, Latin America Month and Real Jewelry Month.

BIRTHDAYS—
Daniel Boone, 1734; James K. Polk, 1795; Warren G. Harding, 1865; Burt Lancaster, 1913; Ann Rutherford, 1920; David Stockton, 1943; Alfre Woodard, 1953

NEW WORD—
amanuensis - noun: a secretary

QUIZ—
Here is one to numb your noggin; you almost surely have the answer in your head; it's just a matter of retrieving it. What national retail chain doesn't use cash registers at all?

TRIVIA
Tallulah Bankhead was the daughter of former Speaker of the House, William Brockman. . . . The J in J. Edgar Hoover stands for John. . . . Ted Kennedy's middle name is Moore.

HISTORY—
On this date in 1948 Harry Truman confounded pundits and embarrassed newspaper headline writers by defeating Dewey.
In 1976 Jimmy Carter became the first president elected from the deep south since the 1860's.

GRAFFITI
The biggest windstorm comes in election years.

Quiz Answer: Radio Shack - They use computers to record the details of the sale and make change out of a separate cash drawer.

NOVEMBER

TODAY'S THOUGHT:
"The only real way to look younger is not to be born so soon."
—Charles Schulz

OBSERVANCES/EVENTS—
It is Sandwich Day, observed to remember John Montague, the fourth Earl of Sandwich who invented the sandwich as a convenience food so that he could indulge in his nonstop gambling.

BIRTHDAYS—
William Cullen Bryant, 1794; Charles Bronson, 1922; Ken Berry, 1933; Michael Dukakis, 1933; Steve Landesberg, 1945; Roseanne Arnold, 1953; Adam Ant, 1954; Phil Simms, 1956

NEW WORD—
jubate - adjective: covered with long hairs resembling a mane

QUIZ—
True or False?
Election Day falls on the first Tuesday of November.

TRIVIA
One jelly bean has seven calories. . . . The French call cotton candy "Papa's beard". . . . Sylvester Graham, a vegetarian who lectured on healthy diets, created graham crackers.

HISTORY—
On this date in 1992 Arkansas Governor Bill Clinton was elected 42nd President of the United States. Clinton garnered 370 electoral votes in his victory over George Bush and Ross Perot.

GRAFFITI
**By exercising you'll add ten years to your life . . .
which you'll spend exercising.**

Quiz Answer: False - It occurs on the first Tuesday after the first Monday of November.

NOVEMBER

TODAY'S THOUGHT:
"If God didn't want man to hunt, he wouldn't have given us plaid shirts." —Johnny Carson

BIRTHDAYS—
Will Rogers, 1879; Walter Cronkite, 1916; Gig Young, 1917; Art Carney, 1918; Martin Balsam, 1919; Alfred Heineken, 1923; Loretta Swit, 1937; Markie Post, 1950; Ralph Macchio, 1962; Andrea McArdle, 1963

NEW WORD—
turbary - noun: land where turf or peat may be dug or cut

QUIZ—
What is the one thing that creditors can't take away from you if you go bankrupt? (Hint: You must be married.)

TRIVIA
Washington, D.C. residents were not allowed to vote in presidential elections until the 23rd Amendment was ratified in 1961. . . . William Phelps Eno invented the one-way street. . . . General Norman Schwarzkopf earned letters in football, soccer and wrestling at West Point.

HISTORY—
On this date in 1922 King Tut's tomb was discovered by Harold Carter at Luxor, Egypt.

GRAFFITI
The worst part about the speed of light is it makes the mornings come awfully early.

Quiz Answer: Your wedding ring

 # NOVEMBER

TODAY'S THOUGHT:
"One disadvantage of having nothing to do is you can't stop and rest." —Franklin P. Jones

BIRTHDAYS—
Eugene Debs, 1855; Will Durant, 1885; Roy Rogers, 1912; Vivian Leigh, 1913; Ike Turner, 1931; Art Garfunkel, 1941; Elke Sommer, 1941; Sam Shepard, 1943; Bill Walton, 1952; Lloyd Moseby, 1959; Tatum O'Neal, 1963

NEW WORD—
mucedinous - adjective: of or resembling mold or mildew

QUIZ—
Bathroom Brain Teaser:
You may be doing cartwheels over this one. Austrian Johann Hurlinger set a world record in 1900 by walking 870 miles from Vienna to Paris. It took him 55 days as he averaged only 1.5 miles per hour yet his record still stands. What's so special about his walk?

TRIVIA
It took Abe Lincoln all of two minutes to deliver his Gettysburg Address. . . . Peter the Great personally cut the beards of all his noblemen. . . . Caesar and Napoleon were both epileptics.

HISTORY—
On this date in 1781 the first president of the United States was elected. It was not George Washington but John Hanson of Maryland. His official title was "President of the United States in Congress Assembled". He served for over a year and had six successors before Washington took over.

GRAFFITI
Seek higher office - become a lighthouse keeper.

Quiz Answer: He did it on his hands, setting the world duration record.

N O V E M B E R

6

TODAY'S THOUGHT:
"Prayer never seems to work for me on the golf course. I think it has something to do with me being a terrible putter." —Billy Graham

OBSERVANCES/EVENTS—
Take note, it's Saxophone Day commemorating the birthday of Adolphe Sax, inventor of the saxophone and many other instruments.

BIRTHDAYS—
John Phillip Sousa, 1854; opera singer Paul Kalisch, 1855; James Naismith, 1861; Ray Coniff, 1916; Mike Nichols, 1931; Sally Field, 1946; Maria Shriver, 1955

NEW WORD—
suspiration - noun: a long, deep sigh

QUIZ—
Is there any place in nature where alligators and crocodiles live together?

TRIVIA
The fastest animal is the cheetah which can attain speeds of 70 mph. . . . Elephants can swim very well. They just have trouble keeping their trunks up. . . . Wild sheep don't bear wool.

HISTORY—
On this date in 1860 Abraham Lincoln was elected president.
In 1888 it was Benjamin Harrison.
In 1900 William McKinley was elected.
In 1928 Herbert Hoover was the victor.

———— GRAFFITI ————
Shake a family tree and you're bound to get a few nuts.

Quiz Answer: Only one place, southern Florida - But don't be expecting little crocogators or tiny allidiles; they don't socialize that much.

NOVEMBER

TODAY'S THOUGHT:
"Our language is funny - a fat chance and slim chance are the same thing." —J. Gustav White

OBSERVANCES/EVENTS—
Today is National Notary Public Day.

BIRTHDAYS—
Marie Curie, 1867; Albert Camus, 1913; Billy Graham, 1918; Al Hirt, 1922; Joan Sutherland, 1926; Al Martino, 1927; Mary Travers, 1937; Joni Mitchell, 1943; Dana Plato, 1964

NEW WORD—
naumachia - noun: an ancient Roman spectacle representing a naval battle

QUIZ—
What's the only land or sea animal that can turn its stomach inside out?

TRIVIA
The first edition of the "New York Times" appeared on September 18, 1851 and sold for a penny a pop. . . . "Leave It to Beaver" was the first TV program to show a bathroom and a toilet. . . . The weekly magazine with the highest circulation is "TV Guide" which averages nineteen million copies a week.

HISTORY—
On this date in 1962 Richard Nixon held his "last" press conference, having just lost the California gubernatorial race. He thus uttered one of the most ironic lines in the history of American politics, "You won't have Dick Nixon to kick around any more!"

GRAFFITI
**Sweater manufacturers
are trying to pull the wool over our eyes.**

Quiz Answer: The starfish, enabling it to eat its prey

N O V E M B E R

TODAY'S THOUGHT:
"Death and taxes and childbirth! There's never any convenient time for any of them!" —Margaret Mitchell

BIRTHDAYS—
Edmond Halley, 1656; Margaret Mitchell, 1900; Katherine Hepburn, 1909; June Havoc, 1916; Christian Barnard, 1923; Patti Page, 1927; Morley Safer, 1931; Alain Delon, 1935; Bonnie Raitt, 1949; Mary Hart, 1951; Christie Hefner, 1952

NEW WORD—
flagitious - adjective: shamefully wicked

QUIZ—
Let's see how you do going head to head with the following:
- A: What bathroom tissue claims to be "Cottony soft"?
- B: Who was the former child star who rode a comet of renewed popularity as Josephine the Plumber?
- C: What prominent world leader would never use toilet seats?
- D: What famous composer's wife helped invent the johnny mop?

TRIVIA
Lefthanders aren't allowed to play polo. . . . There are six and one-half million people in the U.S. who play tennis at least twice a week. . . . Most people put on their left sock first.

HISTORY—
On this date in 1970 Tom Dempsey of the New Orleans Saints kicked a record field goal of 63 yards.

GRAFFITI
Experience lets us be stupid in totally original ways.

Quiz Answer: A - Cottonelle; B - Jane Withers; C - Winston Churchill; D - Richard Rodgers

NOVEMBER

TODAY'S THOUGHT:
"An intellectual is a man who doesn't know how to park a bike."
—Spiro Agnew

BIRTHDAYS—
Stanford White, 1853; Florence Chadwick, 1918; Spiro T. Agnew, 1919; poet Anne Sexton, 1928; Carl Sagan, 1934; Tom Weiskopf, 1942; Lou Ferrigno, 1951

NEW WORD—
unguiculate - adjective: bearing or resembling a nail or claw

QUIZ—
Spiro Agnew resigned from the vice presidency of the U.S. on October 10, 1973. Richard Nixon resigned from the presidency less than a year later, on August 9, 1974. Who replaced Agnew and who replaced Nixon?

TRIVIA
The four least used letters of the alphabet, in order of their infrequency, are Q, X, Z and J. . . . The word "honeymoon" comes from the ritual of drinking wine made from honey for thirty days after a marriage. . . . E Pluribus Unum translates "one of many".

HISTORY—
On this date in 1989 the first crack in the Berlin Wall appeared as East Germany opened many of the checkpoints in the barrier and, after 28 years, allowed its citizens to come and go.

GRAFFITI
Life is a dead-end street.

Quiz Answer: Gerald Ford replaced both of them. Ford was selected to replace Agnew and then succeeded Nixon when he stepped down.

N O V E M B E R 10

TODAY'S THOUGHT:
"Ninety-eight percent of the adults in this country are decent, hard-working, honest Americans. It's the other lousy two percent that get all the publicity. But then - we elected them." —Lily Tomlin

OBSERVANCES/EVENTS—
Want to wish someone a happy birthday? Well, tell it to the Marines. The Corps was established on this date in 1775 by the Continental Congress.

BIRTHDAYS—
Mohammed, 570; Martin Luther, 1483; poet Henry Jackson Van Dyke, 1852; John Knudson Northrup, 1895; Richard Burton, 1925; Donna Fargo, 1949; Jack Anthony Clark, 1955; MacKenzie Phillips, 1959

NEW WORD—
gasconade - verb: to boast or bluster

QUIZ—
What sports "first" belongs to Diane Crump?

TRIVIA
Those symbols that cartoonists draw to replace epithets are called dingbats. . . . More than 90% of flowers have an unpleasant odor or no odor at all. Does that make scents? . . . The A&M in Texas A&M stands for Agricultural and Mechanical.

HISTORY—
On this date in 1871 Henry Stanley found David Livingstone in Tanganyika and uttered his famous greeting, "Dr. Livingstone, I presume."

GRAFFITI
People look up to balloonists.

Quiz Answer: Diane Crump was the first female (human, anyway) to participate in the Kentucky Derby.

NOVEMBER

TODAY'S THOUGHT:
"Most people don't care about authors. It's like being in a Lacrosse Hall of Fame. I call up almost any office and have to spell my name."
—Kurt Vonnegut

BIRTHDAYS—
Abigail Adams, 1744; George S. Patton, 1885; Howard Fast, 1914; William Proxmire, 1915; Kurt Vonnegut Jr., 1922; Jonathan Winters, 1925; Bibi Anderson, 1935; Fuzzy Zoeller, 1951

NEW WORD—
diffluent - adjective: easily dissolving

QUIZ—
True or False?
"Oklahoma" is the official state song of Oklahoma.

TRIVIA
Street numbers in Japan are not assigned by the position of the house on the street, but by when the house was built. The older the house, the lower the street number regardless of street location. . . . The tallest structure in the world is the Polish National TV Service Tower at Plock, Poland. It is built of tubular steel and stretches 2,100 feet into the air. . . . Disney World is twice the size of Manhattan.

HISTORY—
On this date in 1921 an unknown soldier was buried at Arlington. In 1939 Kate Smith first sang "God Bless America" on television.

——— GRAFFITI ———
Some people are the down to earth types; others prefer cremation.

Quiz Answer: True

N O V E M B E R

TODAY'S THOUGHT:

"Remember when you used to watch TV in the sixties and you'd see Perry Como in a cashmere sweater? That's what rock 'n' roll is becoming. It's your parents' music." —Neil Young

BIRTHDAYS—

Elizabeth Cady Stanton, 1815; composer Aleksandr Borodin, 1833; Auguste Rodin, 1840; Jack Oakie, 1903; Kim Hunter, 1922; Grace Kelly, 1929; Stephanie Powers, 1942; Neil Young, 1945; Nadia Comaneci, 1961

NEW WORD—

resupinate - adjective: bent backward

QUIZ—

The vast majority of people can't answer this question about themselves. What is the largest organ on your body?

TRIVIA

In ancient Rome, a hooked nose was thought to be a sign of leadership. . . . People in Scotland once refused to cultivate potatoes because they were not mentioned in the Bible. . . . The WD in WD-40 stands for Water Dispersant.

HISTORY—

On this date in 1892 professional football had its modest start as William "Pudge" Heffelfinger became the first pro player. He received $25 dollars for expenses and a cash bonus of $500. That would buy today's average pro for about 30 seconds. He was well worth it, though; he scored the winning touchdown for the Allegheny Athletic Association against the Pittsburgh Athletic Club.

GRAFFITI
Sibling rivalry is for kids.

Quiz Answer: Your skin

 **NOVEMBER**

TODAY'S THOUGHT:
"A race track is a place where windows clean people."
—Danny Thomas

BIRTHDAYS—
Robert Louis Stevenson, 1850; Louis Brandeis, 1856; Richard Mulligan, 1932; Garry Marshall, 1934; Dack Rambo, 1941; Charlie Tickner, 1953; Vinny Testaverde, 1963

NEW WORD—
obtund - verb: to blunt, dull or deaden

QUIZ—
Craig T. Nelson stars on TV's "Coach" but, before he hit the big time, he knocked around as half of a comedy team. Who was the other half?

TRIVIA
While on his honeymoon in 1879, Robert Louis Stevenson wrote "Travels With a Donkey". Naturally, his wife was flattered. . . . The median length of a marriage in the U.S. is now just seven years. . . . The male fox mates for life. If the female dies, he will remain single for the rest of his life. However, if the male dies, the female will find another mate.

HISTORY—
On this date in 1927 the Holland Tunnel, running under the Hudson River between New York City and Jersey City, New Jersey opened to traffic.

GRAFFITI
You can always tell a rich drummer by his status cymbals.

Quiz Answer: His partner was Barry Levinson, director of such films as "Diner", "Rain Man" and "Bugsy".

N O V E M B E R

TODAY'S THOUGHT:
"The average, healthy, well-adjusted adult gets up at seven-thirty in the morning feeling just plain terrible." —Jean Kerr

BIRTHDAYS—
Robert Fulton, 1765; Claude Monet, 1840; Mamie Eisenhower, 1896; Brian Keith, 1921; McLean Stevenson, 1929; Prince Charles, 1948; Jack Sikma, 1955

NEW WORD—
wamus - noun: a heavy, loosely knit, belted cardigan jacket

QUIZ—
You're probably on "the best seat in the house" right now, but do you know the underwear manufacturer which has used that slogan?

TRIVIA
Young spiders can regenerate missing legs and parts of legs. . . . Charles Roser invented the Fig Newton. . . . 548 peanuts are needed to make a 12 ounce jar of peanut butter.

HISTORY—
On this date in 1889 Nellie Bly bested Jules Verne's fictional hero, Phileas Fogg, by using ships, trains, camels and dog carts to go around the world in 72 days.

GRAFFITI
Surgeons make incision decisions.

Quiz Answer: Jockey

NOVEMBER

TODAY'S THOUGHT:
"Assume nothing. Inside every dumb blond there may be a very smart brunette." —Ann Landers

BIRTHDAYS—
Georgia O'Keeffe, 1887; Judge Joseph Wapner, 1919; Ed Asner, 1929; Petula Clark, 1932; John Coleman, 1935; Sam Waterson, 1940

NEW WORD—
fubsy - adjective: short and stout

QUIZ—
Who were the mother and daughter who adorned the Ivory Snow box during the sixties?

TRIVIA
In the TV show of the fifties, Davy Crockett's rifle was named Betsy. . . . TV's "Planet of the Apes" was set in 3085. . . . Soupy Sales claims he has been hit with over 19,253 pies during his career. That takes a lot of crust.

HISTORY—
On this date in 1926 the first radio network, NBC, began broadcasting over 25 stations from New York to Kansas City.
In 1937 the U.S. Senate and House were air-conditioned but, with all that hot air, the system's been fighting a losing battle ever since!

GRAFFITI
All things come to those who wait . . . like wrinkles.

Quiz Answer: Not everything was 99 44/100 percent pure. The mother was porn star, Marilyn Chambers, and the daughter was Brooke Shields.

NOVEMBER  16

TODAY'S THOUGHT:
"I guess I wouldn't believe in anything if it wasn't for my lucky astrology mood watch." —Steve Martin

BIRTHDAYS—
W. C. Handy, 1873; Fibber McGee, 1896; Burgess Meredith, 1909; Gene Littler, 1920; Bob Gibson, 1931; Elizabeth Drew, 1935; John White, 1946; Harvey Martin, 1950; Dwight Gooden, 1964; Lisa Bonet, 1967

NEW WORD—
lopper - verb: to curdle or coagulate

QUIZ—
Who was Tad Dorgan and why do lovers of true Americana owe this hot dog a great debt?

TRIVIA
Cabbage is 91% water. . . . The middle initial of Dobie Gillis' pal, Maynard G. Krebs, stands for Gwalter. The "g" is silent. . . . 3% of Americans hang family pictures in their bathrooms.

HISTORY—
On this date in 1982 the eight week National Football League players' strike ended. It is estimated that the strike cost the parties concerned about 450 million dollars.

GRAFFITI
The four basic food groups in an average diet are fat, oil, grease and cholesterol.

Quiz Answer: He is the man who, in 1905, changed the name of "dachshund sausages" to hot dogs.

NOVEMBER

TODAY'S THOUGHT:
"It's funny that women aren't embarrassed when they buy men's pajamas, but a guy purchasing a nightgown acts as though he was making a deal with a dope peddler." —Anonymous

BIRTHDAYS—
Soichiro Honda, 1906; Shelby Foote, 1916; Rock Hudson, 1925; Bob Mathias, 1930; Gordon Lightfoot, 1939; Martin Scorsese, 1942; Danny DeVito, 1944; Lauren Hutton, 1944; Tom Seaver, 1944

NEW WORD—
bewray - verb: to reveal or expose

QUIZ—
Bathroom Brain Teaser:
What two things do the words diaper, drawer and spools have in common?

TRIVIA
A hummingbird lays only two eggs during its lifetime. . . . Ants do not sleep. . . . Elephants, when they've had one too many, can be terribly rowdy drunks.

HISTORY—
On this date in 1956 football great Jim Brown set an NCAA scoring record of 43 points for Syracuse against Colgate University. Brown scored six touchdowns and kicked seven extra points.
In 1959 the first synthetic diamonds were manufactured.

GRAFFITI
Carpenters have their vices.

Quiz Answer: They are all six letter words and all three spell another word when the lettering is reversed.

N O V E M B E R

TODAY'S THOUGHT:
"When a man retires and time is no longer a matter of urgent impor-
tance, his colleagues usually present him with a watch."
—R. C. Sherriff

BIRTHDAYS—
Inventor Louis Daguerre, 1789; George Gallup, 1901; Imogene Coca,
1908; Johnny Mercer, 1909; Alan Shepard, 1923; Dorothy Collins,
1926; author Margaret Atwood, 1939; Brenda Vaccaro, 1939; Linda
Evans, 1942; Warren Moon, 1956

NEW WORD—
slumgullion - noun: stew of meat, vegetables and potatoes

QUIZ—
See if you can match the city with its nickname:
1: Akron, OH	A: Fruitbowl of the Nation
2: Annapolis, MD	B: Nail City
3: Wheeling, WV	C: Rubber City
4: Yakima, WA	D: Crabtown

TRIVIA
Alan Shepard was the first astronaut to play golf on the moon . . .
Sportswriter Caswell Adams coined the name "Ivy League". . . . If you
hear a person saying words like "grundy", "blort" and "vetch" they
are not having a seizure, but talking about the sport of frisbee.

HISTORY—
On this date in 1865 Mark Twain's first piece of fiction was published in
the "New York Saturday Press". It was called "The Celebrated Jumping
Frog of Calaveras County".

GRAFFITI
Translators just give lip service.

Quiz Answer: 1 - C; 2 - D; 3 - B; 4 - A

 **N O V E M B E R**

TODAY'S THOUGHT:
"If I only had a little humility, I'd be perfect." —Ted Turner

OBSERVANCES/EVENTS—
It is Have a Bad Day Day. As the mid-November pre-holiday gloom settles in, it is a good time to take this once a year respite from people who are incessantly saying "Have a nice day!" If someone wishes you a bad day or rips the smile button from your lapel, don't take it personally. They are just in keeping with the spirit of the day.

BIRTHDAYS—
George Rogers Clark, 1752; James A. Garfield, 1831; Tommy Dorsey, 1905; Roy Campanella, 1921; Jeane Kirkpatrick, 1926; Dick Cavett, 1936; Ted Turner, 1938; Calvin Klein, 1942; Jodie Foster, 1962

NEW WORD—
empaistic - adjective: embossed, inlaid

QUIZ—
What was the name of the horse that Paul Revere took on his midnight ride?
    A: Midnight   B: Daylight   C: Black Beauty   D: Brown Beauty

TRIVIA
Hummingbirds can't walk. . . . A housefly beats its wings an average of 20,000 times a minute. . . . A grasshopper can jump about 2 feet.

HISTORY—
On this date in 1861 Julia Ward Howe wrote "The Battle Hymn of the Republic".
In 1863 President Abraham Lincoln gave his most famous speech, the Gettysburg Address.

——— GRAFFITI ———
If you want a stable life, marry a horse.

Quiz Answer: D - Brown Beauty

N O V E M B E R

TODAY'S THOUGHT:

"Observe your dog; if he's fat you're not getting enough exercise."
—Evan Esar

BIRTHDAYS—

Edwin Hubble, 1889; Chester Gould, 1900; Alistair Cooke, 1908; Nadine Gordimer, 1923; Robert Kennedy, 1925; Kaye Ballard, 1926; Richard Dawson, 1932; Dick Smothers, 1938; Joseph Biden Jr., 1942; Veronica Hamel, 1943; Judy Woodruff, 1946; Bo Derek, 1956; Mark Gastineau, 1956

NEW WORD—

haply - adverb: perhaps; by chance

QUIZ—

What do Leslie Hornby, Maria Rosario Pilar Martinez, George Joseph Kresge Jr., Gordon Matthew Sumner and Edson Arantes do Nascimento have in common?

TRIVIA

One out of every ten paper clips is bought by the U.S. government. . . . According to "Guinness", the longest Monopoly game played in a bathtub lasted 99 hours. . . . Tweety Pie was originally a pink canary, but censors complained that he looked naked so his color was changed to yellow.

HISTORY—

On this date in 1888 the first timeclock was invented by William Bundy, and a lot of people have wanted to punch him out ever since!

GRAFFITI
Unzipped mail is immoral.

Quiz Answer: They are celebrities who changed their monickers to just one name. In order, they are: Twiggy, Charo, Kreskin, Sting and Pelé.

NOVEMBER

TODAY'S THOUGHT:
"As a nation we are dedicated to keeping physically fit - and parking as close to the stadium as possible." —Bill Vaughan

OBSERVANCES/EVENTS—
It is World Hello Day, a day where everyone is requested to say "Hello" to at least ten people.

BIRTHDAYS—
Voltaire, 1694; Sir Samuel Cunard, 1787; Stan Musial, 1920; Juliet Mills, 1941; Marlo Thomas, 1943; Goldie Hawn, 1945; Lorna Luft, 1952; Mariel Hemingway, 1961

NEW WORD—
polytomy - noun: division into more than three parts

QUIZ—
Where did television's most defiantly dysfunctional family, "The Simpsons", get their first names?

TRIVIA
Voltaire drank 70 cups of coffee a day. . . . A pottle is 2 quarts. . . . The first beer brewed in the New World was brewed at Sir Walter Raleigh's Roanoke Colony in 1587. The beer kept its head longer than Sir Walter did.

HISTORY—
On this date in 1964 the world's longest suspension bridge opened over the Verrazano Narrows between Brooklyn and Staten Island.

GRAFFITI
**If you have what it takes,
there'll always be someone ready to take it.**

Quiz Answer: Those are the names of creator Matt Groening's family, except for Bart which is an anagram of brat.

N O V E M B E R

TODAY'S THOUGHT:

"How can you govern a country which has 246 varieties of cheese?"
—Charles de Gaulle

OBSERVANCES/EVENTS—

Today is National Stop the Violence Day.

BIRTHDAYS—

George Eliot, 1819; Charles de Gaulle, 1890; Wiley Post, 1898; Hoagy Carmichael, 1899; Rodney Dangerfield, 1921; Geraldine Page, 1924; Robert Vaughn, 1932; Tom Conti, 1941; Billie Jean King, 1943; Jamie Lee Curtis, 1958; Boris Becker, 1967

NEW WORD—

acronychous - adjective: having nails, claws or hooves

QUIZ—

A look below at this date in history will provide you with a clue to this question. What is located at 506 Elm Street?

TRIVIA

One-fourth of all the turkey eaten in the U.S. is gobbled down on Thanksgiving Day. . . . Jackie Kennedy was the first First Lady to be born in the 20th century. . . . Lee Harvey Oswald's weapon is stored in a rifle case on a shelf in Room 5W of the Judicial and Fiscal and Social Branch of the U.S. National Archives.

HISTORY—

On this date in 1718 the pirate, Blackbeard, went down fighting in a battle with a British Navy ship. It took 25 serious wounds to finally finish him off.

In 1963 President John F. Kennedy was killed in a motorcade in Dallas.

GRAFFITI
Easy Street is a blind alley.

Quiz Answer: The Texas School Book Depository in Dallas, Texas

 **N O V E M B E R**

TODAY'S THOUGHT:
"Whenever you want to marry someone, go have lunch with his ex-wife." —Shelley Winters

BIRTHDAYS—
Franklin Pierce, 1804; Boris Karloff, 1887; Harpo Marx, 1893; Maurice Zolotow, 1913; Ellen Drew, 1915; Jerry Bock, 1928; Andrew Toney, 1957

NEW WORD—
obturate - verb: to stop up, close

QUIZ—
Who are Matthew Prescott and Alexandra Maitland, and what grounds do they have for their long running TV relationship?

TRIVIA
Franklin Pierce was once arrested for accidentally running down Mrs. Nathan Lewis while on horseback. . . . People found bathing nude in Oliastro, Corsica are painted blue. . . . Martha Giles of Newark, New Jersey was granted a divorce on the grounds that her husband attacked her with a live eel.

HISTORY—
On this date in 1936 the first issue of "Life" magazine, created by Henry Luce, hit the newsstands.

——— GRAFFITI ———
Opposites attract . . . divorce lawyers.

Quiz Answer: They are the Taster's Choice couple, and their caffeine fueled courtship is now the subject of a romance novel entitled "Love Over Gold".

N O V E M B E R

TODAY'S THOUGHT:
"On Thanksgiving Day all over America, families sit down to dinner at the same moment - halftime." —Anonymous

BIRTHDAYS—
Father Junipero Serra, 1713; Zachary Taylor, 1784; Scott Joplin, 1868; Dale Carnegie, 1888; Garson Kanin, 1912; Geraldine Fitzgerald, 1914; William F. Buckley Jr., 1925; Marlin Fitzwater, 1942

NEW WORD—
versant - noun: a slope of a mountain or a mountain chain

QUIZ—
Turkey Toughies:
- A: Dick Van Dyke and Bob Newhart starred in what 1971 Norman Lear feature about a town that was offered 25 million dollars if everyone gave up smoking?
- B: Where was the Turkey Bowl played?
- C: What do you call a young turkey?
- D: Right after WWI, what dance craze swept the country that ruffled the feathers of old-fashioned folk?

TRIVIA
Ben Franklin was the first Postmaster General, serving from 1775 to 1776. . . . The first air mail pilot took off and flew in the wrong direction, thus setting the standard for postal service to this very day. . . . Mark Twain called cauliflower "cabbage with a college education".

HISTORY—
On this date in 1963 Lee Harvey Oswald was shot to death in Dallas, Texas by Jack Ruby.

GRAFFITI
Bedbugs are undercover agents.

Quiz Answer: A - "Cold Turkey"; B - Tokyo; C - a poult (and a whole lot of them on branches make a poult-tree); D - the turkey trot

 **N O V E M B E R**

TODAY'S THOUGHT:
"A ball player's got to be kept hungry to become a big leaguer. That's why no boy from a rich family ever made the big leagues."
—Joe Di Maggio

BIRTHDAYS—
Andrew Carnegie, 1835; Carry Nation, 1846; Joe Di Maggio, 1914; Ricardo Montalban, 1920; Kathryn Crosby, 1933; John Larroquette, 1947; Bucky Dent, 1951; Bernie Kosar, 1963

NEW WORD—
juvenescent - adjective: young in appearance

QUIZ—
Two states in the U.S. have names which contain three consecutive vowels. One is Hawaii. Do you know the other?

TRIVIA
The longest non-scientific word in the dictionary is floccinaucinihilipilification, meaning deciding if something has no value. . . . Most people are unable to speak more than 200 words per minute. . . . Strength is the only 8 letter word in the English language with only one vowel.

HISTORY—
On this date in 1952 Agatha Christie's "The Mousetrap" opened in London at the Ambassador Theater and is still running.

GRAFFITI
If at first you don't succeed, try reading the instructions.

Quiz Answer: Louisiana

NOVEMBER

TODAY'S THOUGHT:
"I love mankind - it's people I can't stand." —Charles Schulz

BIRTHDAYS—
Mary Edwards Walker, 1832; Eric Severeid, 1912; Charles Schulz, 1922; Robert Goulet, 1933; Rich Little, 1938; Tina Turner, 1938; Johnny Hector, 1960

NEW WORD—
mundify - verb: to cleanse

QUIZ—
By what other name was the National-sozialistische Deustche Arbeiter-Partei known?

TRIVIA
The home address of Charles Schulz is 1 Snoopy Place in Santa Rosa, California. . . . Hershey, Pennsylvania used to be known as Derry Church. Wonder if Derry Church Bars would ever have caught on? . . . Crows can live 80 years.

HISTORY—
On this date in 1832 the first streetcar in the U.S. began its horsedrawn journey between New York's City Hall and 14th Street. The fare was 12½ cents. Many transit delays were encountered as passengers tried to meet the exact change requirement by breaking pennies in half . . .

GRAFFITI
Until Eve arrived, this was a man's world.

Quiz Answer: The Nazi Party – The term Nazi is a phonetic spelling of the party's first two syllables.

N O V E M B E R

TODAY'S THOUGHT:
"When men reach their sixties and retire, they go to pieces. Women just go right on cooking." —Gail Sheehy

BIRTHDAYS—
Anders Celsius, 1701; Charles Beard, 1874; Buffalo Bob Smith, 1917; Alexander Dubcek, 1921; Gail Sheehy, 1936; Eddie Rabbit, 1941; Jimi Hendrix, 1942

NEW WORD—
coeval - adjective: of the same age, equally old

QUIZ—
Baseball Hall of Famer Frank Robinson and football's Art Shell hold a similar distinction in their respective sports. What is it?

TRIVIA
Nearly 15% of Americans own pet fish. . . . At a rate of one drop a minute, a leaking faucet can waste 900 gallons of water a year. . . . 34% of American teenage girls color their hair.

HISTORY—
On this date in 1966 the Washington Redskins defeated the New York Giants, 72-41, in the highest scoring game in NFL history.

GRAFFITI
No matter how bad the prose is, it might be verse.

Quiz Answer: Robinson was major league baseball's first black manager and Shell was the NFL's first black head coach.

N O V E M B E R

TODAY'S THOUGHT:
"I love children, especially when they cry, for then someone takes them away." —Nancy Mitford

BIRTHDAYS—
John Bunyan, 1628; Nancy Mitford, 1904; Hope Lange, 1933; Gary Hart, 1936; Randy Newman, 1943; Alexander Godunov, 1949; Paul Schaffer, 1949; Ed Harris, 1950; Roy Tarpley, 1964

NEW WORD—
thrawn - adjective: twisted, crooked

QUIZ—
What's another name for the aquatic sport of octopush?

TRIVIA
Every two weeks a lemon shark grows a new set of teeth. That is more than 24,000 new teeth each year. . . . The longest nonstop typing stint was 162 hours, one minute set by a California high school teacher, Robin Heil, in 1976. . . . The average person takes in and digests about a ton of food and drink a year.

HISTORY—
On this date in 1776 General Washington crossed the Delaware. In 1963 Cape Canaveral was renamed Cape Kennedy.

GRAFFITI
**This is a free country,
and every man can do just as his wife pleases.**

Quiz Answer: Underwater hockey

NOVEMBER

TODAY'S THOUGHT:

"The average dog is a nicer person than the average person."
—Andy Rooney

BIRTHDAYS—

Louisa May Alcott, 1832; Busby Berkeley, 1895; Madeleine L'Engle, 1918; Vin Scully, 1927; Diane Ladd, 1932; Chuck Mangione, 1940; Garry Shandling, 1949

NEW WORD—

necromancy - noun: magic, witchcraft, conjuration

QUIZ—

Marquee Monickers: See if you can come up with the show biz names of the following folks.

A: Jill Oppenheim
B: Hugh J. Krampe
C: Ivo Montand Livi
D: Lee Siu Loong
E: Krishna Bhanji

TRIVIA

Atlanta, Georgia was once known as Terminus. . . . The butterfly is a cannibal. . . . Smile and your Levator Labii Superioris Alaeque Nasi smiles with you. It is one of the primary muscles used for smiling.

HISTORY—

On this date in 1872 Horace Greeley died insane only three weeks after losing the U.S. presidential election to Ulysses Grant.

GRAFFITI

Give crabgrass an inch; it'll take a yard.

Quiz Answer: A - Jill St. John; B - Hugh O'Brian; C - Yves Montand; D - Bruce Lee; E - Ben Kingsley

N O V E M B E R 30

TODAY'S THOUGHT:
"Wrinkles should merely indicate where smiles have been."
—Mark Twain

BIRTHDAYS—
Jonathan Swift, 1667; Mark Twain, 1835; Sir Winston Churchill, 1874; Virginia Mayo, 1922; Efrem Zimbalist Jr., 1923; Shirley Chisholm, 1924; Robert Guillaume, 1927; Dick Clark, 1929; G. Gordon Liddy, 1930; Abbie Hoffman, 1936; Paul Stookey, 1937; David Mamet, 1947; Mandy Patinkin, 1952; Billy Idol, 1955; Bo Jackson, 1962

NEW WORD—
natatorium - noun: an indoor swimming pool

QUIZ—
True or False?
Mark Twain was born in Florida.

TRIVIA
Aspirin was invented in Germany in 1853 but not marketed until 1899. Take two and call me in 46 years! . . . The federal government once spent $50,000 to determine that the average length of a stewardess' nose is 2.6 inches. . . . The U.S. Patent Office issued patent #1,180,753 for a device for catching female fish.

HISTORY—
On this date in 1940 Desi Arnaz proved that he did, in fact, love Lucy by eloping with her to Greenwich, Connecticut.

GRAFFITI
Curl up with a hairdresser.

Quiz Answer: True - Florida, Missouri that is

DECEMBER

TODAY'S THOUGHT:
"I will not eat oysters. I want my food dead. Not sick, not wounded, dead." —Woody Allen

OBSERVANCES/EVENTS—
It is Bingo Birthday Month, commemorating the start of bingo in America on this date in 1929.

BIRTHDAYS—
Mary Martin, 1913; David Doyle, 1925; Woody Allen, 1935; Lee Trevino, 1939; Richard Pryor, 1940; Bette Midler, 1945; Carol Alt, 1960

NEW WORD—
indite - verb: to compose or write a speech or poem

QUIZ—
A two part question: Is the capital of Missouri, according to the state's official definition, pronounced "St. Loo-is" or "St. Looie"; and is it properly written as "St. Louis" or "Saint Louis"?

TRIVIA
More shoplifters are caught in December than any other month. . . . Twenty-six popes have been murdered. . . . Flies can get athlete's foot.

HISTORY—
On this date in 1956 the Army made the decision to retire its last combat mule troop. Scuttlebutt has it that they just kicked them upstairs and they've been running the Pentagon ever since.

GRAFFITI
Nylon stockings give you a run for the money.

Quiz Answer: It is written and pronounced Jefferson City.

D E C E M B E R 2

TODAY'S THOUGHT:

"There's one way to find out if a man is honest - ask him. If he says "yes",
you know he's crooked." —Groucho Marx

OBSERVANCES/EVENTS—

Today is Pan American Health Day.

BIRTHDAYS—

George Seurat, 1859; Adolph Green, 1915; Maria Callas, 1923;
Alexander Haig Jr., 1924; Julie Harris, 1925; Ed Meese III, 1931; Cathy
Lee Crosby, 1948; Randy Gardner, 1958

NEW WORD—

flexuous - adjective: full of curves; winding

QUIZ—

By what name is "Aubergine" better known?
- A: Madonna
- B: Gene Autry
- C: The Vatican
- D: Eggplant

TRIVIA

Lake Mead is the largest man-made body of water in the western
hemisphere. . . . There's a Red Light Museum in Washington, D.C.
which is devoted entirely to the world's oldest profession. . . . The
most popular cookie is the chocolate chip.

HISTORY—

On this date in 1949 Gene Autry hit the record charts with his song
"Rudolph, the Red-Nosed Reindeer".

GRAFFITI
To keep people from jumping down your throat,
keep your mouth shut.

Quiz Answer: D - Eggplant

DECEMBER

TODAY'S THOUGHT:
"Chess is a foolish expedient for making idle people think they are doing something very clever when they are only wasting their time."
—George Bernard Shaw

BIRTHDAYS—
Gilbert Stuart, 1755; Joseph Conrad, 1857; Ferlin Husky, 1927; Jean-Luc Godard, 1930; Andy Williams, 1930; Jaye P. Morgan, 1932; Ozzy Osbourne, 1948; Rick Mears, 1951

NEW WORD—
nuque - noun: the back of the neck

QUIZ—
Bathroom Brain Teaser:
Jill had a date with Jack and was waiting for him to pick her up. It began to rain. Jill had no umbrella yet did not get wet. Why?

TRIVIA
Philadelphia originated the system of even-numbered residences on one side of the street and odd-numbered homes on the other side. . . . "60 Minutes" is the only network TV show with no theme music. . . . More people are injured on merry-go-rounds than roller coasters.

HISTORY—
On this date in 1967 a team led by Dr. Christian Barnard in Capetown, South Africa performed the first successful human heart transplant. The patient survived 18 days before succumbing of complications.

GRAFFITI
If you've lost your memory, forget about it.

Quiz Answer: She was waiting inside.

DECEMBER 4

TODAY'S THOUGHT:
"The very purpose of existence is to reconcile the glowing opinion we hold of ourselves with the appalling things that other people think about us." —Quentin Crisp

BIRTHDAYS—
Rainer Maria Rilke, 1876; Lillian Russell, 1881; Francisco Franco, 1892; Deanna Durbin, 1921; Horst Bucholz, 1933; Max Baer Jr., 1937; Chris Hillman, 1942; Jeff Bridges, 1949

NEW WORD—
disjasked - adjective: dilapidated, broken

QUIZ—
Which of the following vegetables is not in V-8 juice?
    A: Leek   B: Carrot   C: Watercress
            D: Beets   E: Celery

TRIVIA
The tropical catfish, synodontis, swims upside down while eating. . . . Fish do not have a keen sense of hearing but they do have a keen sense of smell. Of course, much of what they smell is not that keen. . . . There is no specific fish called a sardine. Usually you find herring or pilchard in the cans.

HISTORY—
On this date in 1950 Polish track star Stella Walsh, the 1932 Olympic gold medalist in the 100 yard dash, died during an armed robbery at which "she" was an innocent bystander. After the autopsy in Cleveland, Ohio the coroner announced that "she" was a "he".

GRAFFITI
To find self-serving people, look at a buffet table.

Quiz Answer: A - Leek

DECEMBER

TODAY'S THOUGHT:
"Girls bored me; they still do. I love Mickey Mouse more than any woman I've ever known." —Walt Disney

BIRTHDAYS—
Martin Van Buren, 1782; poet Christina Rassetti, 1830; Fritz Lang, 1890; Walt Disney, 1901; Strom Thurmond, 1902; Joan Didion, 1934; Calvin Trillin, 1935; Chad Mitchell, 1936; Morgan Brittany, 1950; Art Monk, 1957; Carrie Hamilton, 1963

NEW WORD—
apologue - noun: a moral fable, an allegory

QUIZ—
If today is the day you rummage in the attic for Christmas lights, this quiz might interest you. If you are average, how much of your life do you spend searching for lost or misplaced items?

 A: 3 months   B: 6 months   C: 9 months
 D: 1 year   E: none of the above

TRIVIA
You can put a good spin on a hardboiled egg, but not on an uncooked one. (Try it.) . . . Monkeys never get fleas. . . . According to the International Ice Cream Association, vanilla is by far the most popular flavor. Second is chocolate. And, tied for third, are strawberry and butter pecan.

HISTORY—
On this date in 1933 happy days were here again as Prohibition formally ended with the repeal of the 18th amendment by the 21st.

———— GRAFFITI ————
Old lawyers never die - they just lose their appeal.

Quiz Answer: D - The average American loses one year of his life to losing things.

DECEMBER 6

TODAY'S THOUGHT:
"The trouble with growing older is that it gets progressively tougher to find a famous historical figure who didn't amount to much when he was your age." —Bill Vaughan

BIRTHDAYS—
Joyce Kilmer, 1886; Ira Gershwin, 1896; photographer Alfred Eisenstaedt, 1898; Dave Brubeck, 1920; Otto Graham, 1921; Walter Perkins, 1941; Dwight Stones, 1953; Steve Bedrosian, 1957

NEW WORD—
valetudinarian - noun: an invalid

QUIZ—
Without question there is another word, besides facetiously and abstemiously, which contains all the vowels, including "y". What is it?

TRIVIA
When a gorilla is angry, it sticks its tongue out. . . . The "O" which Irish names begin with, such as O'Brien, simply means "son of". Therefore, O'Brien means son of Brien, the latter often being the name of the ancestor who started the family. . . . France originated kilts.

HISTORY—
On this date in 1790 Congress moved from New York to Philadelphia. They soon wore out their welcome there as well, and kept going south to Washington D.C.

GRAFFITI
Living in the past is . . . cheaper!

Quiz Answer: Unquestionably

DECEMBER

TODAY'S THOUGHT:
"The best advice is no _____ at all." —John Cage

OBSERVANCES/EVENTS—
Today is Pearl Harbor Day, a "date that will live in infamy".

BIRTHDAYS—
Mary Stuart, Queen of Scots, 1542; Willa Cather, 1873; Joyce Cary, 1888; artist Jacob Kainen, 1909; Eli Wallach, 1915; Ted Knight, 1923; Ellen Burstyn, 1932; Gregg Allmann, 1947; Johnny Bench, 1947; Tom Waits, 1949; Priscilla Barnes, 1955; Larry Bird, 1956

NEW WORD—
samp - noun: coarsely ground corn

QUIZ—
True or False?
American, Bridal Veil and Horseshoe Falls are names for different types of takedowns in amateur wrestling.

TRIVIA
Bugs Bunny was first called Happy Rabbit. . . . Life Savers candy was invented the same year the Titanic sank. . . . Horses can look back with one eye and forward with the other. Because this can make them skittish, that's the reason why they sometimes wear blinders.

HISTORY—
On this date in 1963 the instant replay was first used in a sports broadcast during the telecast of the Army-Navy game.

GRAFFITI
A polygon is a dead parrot.

Quiz Answer: False - They are the three waterfalls which comprise Niagara Falls.

DECEMBER 8

TODAY'S THOUGHT:
"Well, if I called the wrong number, why did you answer the phone?"
—James Thurber

BIRTHDAYS—
Diego Rivera, 1886; James Thurber, 1894; Sammy Davis Jr., 1925; Maximilian Schell, 1930; Flip Wilson, 1933; David Carradine, 1936; James MacArthur, 1937; James Galway, 1939; Red Berenson, 1941; Jim Morrison, 1943; John Rubinstein, 1946; Kim Basinger, 1953

NEW WORD—
haptometer - noun: a mechanical device for measuring the sense of touch

QUIZ—
Name these four states: The first begins with "H". The second starts with the last letter of the first state. Continue the same pattern for the third state and for the fourth state - which ends with "Y".

TRIVIA
The only horse ever to beat Man O' War was Upset. Of course, Man O' War was having a bad mare day. . . . Derby horse races are named after Edward Stanley, the 12th Earl of Derby, who created the special series of races for three-year old horses. . . . The only species of deer that grows horns regardless of its gender is the reindeer. They are also the only species that can grow a red nose and hang out all year with a jolly fat guy at the North Pole.

HISTORY—
On this date in 1941 the United States formally entered WWII.
In 1980 John Lennon was gunned down in New York.
In 1991 the Soviet Union ceased to exist.

GRAFFITI
Everyone can carry a tune, but how far?

Quiz Answer: Hawaii - Idaho - Oregon - New Jersey

DECEMBER

TODAY'S THOUGHT:
"One loss is good for the soul. Too many losses are not good for the coach." —Knute Rockne

BIRTHDAYS—
Joel Chandler Harris, 1848; Clarence Birdseye, 1886; Margaret Hamilton, 1902; Douglas Fairbanks Jr., 1909; "Tip" O'Neill, 1912; Kirk Douglas, 1916; Redd Foxx, 1922; Beau Bridges, 1941; Dick Butkus, 1942; Tom Kite, 1949; John Malkovich, 1953; Otis Birdsong, 1955; Donny Osmond, 1958

NEW WORD—
pejoration - noun: depreciation, a lessening of worth or quality

QUIZ—
What time of day can make the claim that it is spelled the same forward, backward, upside down and in a mirror?

TRIVIA
Redd Foxx's real name was John Elroy Sanford. . . . Kirk Douglas' real name is Issur Danielovitch Demsky. . . . Pocahontas was a family nickname; her real name was Matoaka.

HISTORY—
On this date in 1907 the Wilmington Post Office sold the very first Christmas seals.

GRAFFITI
If you see the writing on the wall, you probably run a daycare center.

Quiz Answer: NOON

D E C E M B E R 10

TODAY'S THOUGHT:
"A man finds out what is meant by a spitting image when he tries to feed cereal to his infant." —Imogene Fey

OBSERVANCES/EVENTS—
It is Human Rights Day.

BIRTHDAYS—
Thomas Gallaudet, 1787; Emily Dickinson, 1830; Melvil Dewey, 1851; Chet Huntley, 1911; Dorothy Lamour, 1914; Harold Gould, 1923; Gloria Loring, 1946; Susan Dey, 1952; Mark Aguirre, 1959

NEW WORD—
jaup - noun: a splash, spurt or drop of water

QUIZ—
What are gossamer wings?

TRIVIA
There are no penguins at the North Pole. All varieties of penguins are found below the equator, mainly in Antarctica. . . . Scientists think that unborn babies can dream. . . . The chance of a mother having quintuplets is 1 in 40,960,000.

HISTORY—
On this date in 1927 the Grand Ole Opry hit the airwaves with its first broadcast from WSM in Nashville.

———— GRAFFITI ————
An aquarium is a house of gill repute.

Quiz Answer: Just another way of saying cobwebs

DECEMBER

TODAY'S THOUGHT:

"If you watch a game, it's fun. If you play it, it's recreation. If you work at it, it's golf." —Bob Hope

BIRTHDAYS—

Astronomer Annie Jump Cannon, 1863; Fiorella La Guardia, 1882; Carlo Ponti, 1913; Aleksandr Solzhenitsyn, 1918; Rita Moreno, 1931; Tom Hayden, 1940; Donna Mills, 1943

NEW WORD—

burga - noun: in Alaska, a storm of northeasterly winds with snow

QUIZ—

The next time you whip out that credit card for Christmas shopping, remember that, on average, every day Americans charge up about:

A: $100,000,000   B: $250,000,000
C: $875,000,000   D: $1,000,000,000
E: $1,500,000,000

TRIVIA

More than 10% of Americans claim to have seen UFOs, including one former president, Jimmy Carter. . . . Your chances of being a guest on "The Tonight Show" are 1 in 490,000 (somewhat better if you're already famous). . . . The average human walks 19,000 steps a day.

HISTORY—

On this date in 1980 America got its first look at the latest "Hawaiian Eye" as "Magnum, P.I." premiered on CBS. Diehard fans still celebrate the series at a yearly convention called "Magnum Memorabilia".

GRAFFITI
In Las Vegas, odds are against getting even.

Quiz Answer: E - and that's on an average day. Imagine the plastic pushing that is going on at this time of year.

D E C E M B E R

TODAY'S THOUGHT:
"Never loan shylock money to a woman, because you can't beat her up to collect." —Mafia Proverb

OBSERVANCES/EVENTS—
Today is Poinsetta Day, in honor of Dr. Joel Roberts Poinsett, an American diplomat who introduced the Central American plant to the U.S. in the early 1800's.

BIRTHDAYS—
John Jay, 1745; William Lloyd Garrison, 1805; Gustave Flaubert, 1821; Frank Sinatra, 1915; Bob Barker, 1923; Ed Koch, 1924; Connie Francis, 1938; Dionne Warwick, 1941; Cathy Rigby, 1952; Tracy Austin, 1962

NEW WORD—
killick - noun: a small anchor or weight for mooring a boat

QUIZ—
Is the Pentagon in Maryland, Virginia or Washington, D.C.?

TRIVIA
John Jay, the first Chief Justice of the Supreme Court, bought slaves just so he could free them. . . . In the boxing ring, Frank Sinatra was known as Marty O'Brien. He wasn't all that good — in fact, back then he was known as "Ol' *black* and blue eyes". . . . Like humans, dogs can be right-handed or left-handed (or should that be south "paw"?).

HISTORY—
On this date in 1925 the world's first motel, the Motel Inn in San Luis Obispo, California opened for business. It was designed by Arthur Heinman who also coined the term "motel".

GRAFFITI
A butterfly is a worm that turned.

Quiz Answer: Virginia

DECEMBER

TODAY'S THOUGHT:
"The Lord prefers common-looking people. That is why he makes so many of them." —Abraham Lincoln

BIRTHDAYS—
Mary Todd Lincoln, 1818; Carlos Montoya, 1903; Dick Van Dyke, 1925; Christopher Plummer, 1929; Tim Conway, 1933; John Davidson, 1941; Richard Lamar Dent, 1960

NEW WORD—
tardigrade - adjective: slow in pace or movement

QUIZ—
In the January, 1993 issue of "Superman" the comic book hero is killed. What enemy is responsible for his death?

TRIVIA
Elephants weigh up to 14,000 pounds. . . . Fortune cookies were invented in the U.S. in 1918. . . . Karate was not introduced to Japan until 1916. Until then, it had been practiced solely by Okinawans who developed it centuries before as a weaponless defense against the Japanese.

HISTORY—
On this date in 1816 the first United States savings bank was chartered.

GRAFFITI
Change is good . . . especially babies' diapers.

Quiz Answer: Doomsday - (In making reference to Superman, this reminds us of a true story about Muhammad Ali. While on a plane trip, the boxing great was told by a stewardess to put on his seat belt. Ali said, "Superman don't need no seat belt," to which the stewardess replied, "Superman don't need no plane, either.")

D E C E M B E R 14

TODAY'S THOUGHT:

"A procrastinator is never bothered by the little things that plague the rest of us. He always waits until they grow into big things."

—Anonymous

BIRTHDAYS—

Michael Nostradamus, 1503; Tycho Brahe, 1546; James Doolittle, 1896; Margaret Chase Smith, 1897; Morey Amsterdam, 1914; Shirley Jackson, 1919; Charlie Rich, 1932; Lee Remick, 1935; Patty Duke, 1946; Stan Smith, 1946; Bill Buckner, 1949

NEW WORD—

gyre - noun: a ring or circle

QUIZ—

True or False?

All of Elvis Presley's concerts were performed in the United States.

TRIVIA

Caterpillars are a delicacy in Peru. . . . There are 225 squares on a Scrabble board. . . . Portland is the largest city in both Maine and Oregon.

HISTORY—

On this date in 1799 George Washington died at Mount Vernon, Virginia at the age of 67.

In 1911 Roald Amundsen reached the South Pole.

In 1942 Jimmy Doolittle and his raiders reached Tokyo.

GRAFFITI

Confucius say - ghost who gets lost in fog is mist.

Quiz Answer: False - The King also appeared in Canada.

DECEMBER

TODAY'S THOUGHT:
"If you can count your money, you don't have a billion dollars."
—J. Paul Getty

BIRTHDAYS—
Alexandre-Gustave Eiffel, 1832; Charles Edgar Duryea, 1861; J. Paul Getty, 1892; Muriel Rukeyser, 1913; Friedrich Hundertwasser, 1928; Tim Conway, 1933; Nick Buoniconti, 1940; Dave Clark, 1942; Don Johnson, 1949; Daryl Turner, 1961

NEW WORD—
limicolous - adjective: dwelling in mud

QUIZ—
What bathroom-related product earned a permanent place in the hearts and minds of Americans due to a mistake at the factory which allowed too much air to be whipped into it thus causing it to float?

TRIVIA
Gamblers have the highest suicide-attempt rate. . . . Two-thirds of the world's lawyers are in the good old US of A(ttorneys). . . . The E in Robert E. Lee stands for Edward.

HISTORY—
On this date in 1939 the world premiere of "Gone With the Wind" took place in Atlanta.

GRAFFITI
Acupuncturists' patients are holier-than-thou.

Quiz Answer: Ivory soap became a sensation when a worker goofed and let a batch get too much air in it. The company was soon deluged by letters complimenting them on the wonderful new soap that floats. This soap-serendipity has made it a best seller for over a hundred years.

D E C E M B E R

TODAY'S THOUGHT:
"People are wrong when they say that opera is not what it used to be. It *is* what it used to be. That is what's wrong with it." —Noel Coward

OBSERVANCES/EVENTS—
The Men Will Never Fly Society holds their annual meeting at Kitty Hawk, North Carolina. Their motto is "Birds fly, men drink."

BIRTHDAYS—
Ludwig von Beethoven, 1770; Jane Austen, 1775; George Santayana, 1863; Sir Noel Coward, 1899; Margaret Mead, 1901; Arthur C. Clarke, 1917; Bruce Ames, 1928; Liv Ullmann, 1939; Stephen Bochco, 1943; Ben Cross, 1947; Mike Flanagan, 1951; William "the Refrigerator" Perry, 1962; Clifton Robinson, 1966

NEW WORD—
rubricate - verb: to mark or color with red

QUIZ—
What American movie star was Orville Wright's godson?

TRIVIA
Falcons have excellent eye sight. They can see a ladybug on the ground while sitting atop an eighteen story building. . . . Texas has more counties than any other state with 254. . . . Airplanes are forbidden to fly over the White House.

HISTORY—
On this date in 1773 colonists dressed as Indians and threw tea in Boston harbor.

GRAFFITI
Get even. Grow old enough to be a problem to your children.

Quiz Answer: Robert Cummings, who maintained a lifelong interest in aviation

DECEMBER

TODAY'S THOUGHT:
"One man's pay increase is another man's price increase."
—Harold Wilson

OBSERVANCES/EVENTS—
Today is Wright Brothers Day, observed on the anniversary of man's first powered flight.

BIRTHDAYS—
Sir Humphrey Davy, 1778; John Greenleaf Whittier, 1807; Arthur Fiedler, 1894; Erskine Caldwell, 1903; Willard Frank Libby, 1908; Sy Oliver, 1910; Gene Rayburn, 1917; William Safire, 1927; Albert King, 1959

NEW WORD—
cracknel - noun: a hard brittle cake or biscuit

QUIZ—
Here's a question for presidential trivia buffs:
Who was the first president whose mother was eligible to vote for him?

TRIVIA
New Hampshire has the lowest legal age for marriage; a girl of thirteen can get married with her parents' consent. . . . There are no counties in Alaska. . . . Ann Royall became the first woman journalist to interview a president. While John Quincy Adams was skinnydipping one day, she stole his clothes and would not give them back until he gave her an interview.

HISTORY—
On this date in 1777 France recognized the independence of the thirteen American colonies.

———— GRAFFITI ————
It isn't whether you win or lose - it's how MUCH!

Quiz Answer: Franklin Delano Roosevelt

D E C E M B E R 18

TODAY'S THOUGHT:
"Judge a man not by his clothes, but by his wife's clothes."
—Thomas R. Dewar

BIRTHDAYS—
Joseph Grimaldi, 1823; Ty Cobb, 1886; Willy Brandt, 1913; Ossie Davis, 1917; William Ramsey Clark, 1927; Steven Spielberg, 1947; Janie Fricke, 1950; Leonard Maltin, 1950; Charles Oakley, 1963

NEW WORD—
monticule - noun: a small mountain, hill or mound

QUIZ—
Bathroom Brain Teaser:
The archaeologist said he found a coin dated 84 B.C. How do you know the coin is a phony?

TRIVIA
The Lovers of the Stinky Rose is an organization that holds an annual garlic festival and publishes a newsletter known as "Garlic Times". . . . The Tokyo phone directory has 9,248 pages, comes in nine volumes and weighs 26 pounds. Obviously the Japanese have not miniaturized everything! . . . On a typical day in the United States the Postal Service processes almost as much mail as the rest of the world combined.

HISTORY—
On this date in 1899 a patent was issued to George F. Grant for the golf tee.

GRAFFITI
**We live by the Golden Rule—
the guy who has the gold makes the rules.**

Quiz Answer: The date B.C. was never used before Christ.

DECEMBER

TODAY'S THOUGHT:
"Three may keep a secret if two of them are dead." —Ben Franklin

BIRTHDAYS—
Henry Clay Frick, 1849; Albert Michelson, 1852; Ralph Richardson, 1902; Cicely Tyson, 1939; Richard E. Leakey, 1944; Robert Urich, 1947; Kevin McHale, 1957; Jennifer Beale, 1963; Alyssa Milano, 1972

NEW WORD—
donzel - noun: squire; page; a young gentleman not yet knighted

QUIZ—
What is a recidivist?
- A: The host of a spelling bee
- B: A diving instructor
- C: An habitual criminal
- D: None of the above

TRIVIA
George Washington laid the cornerstone of the U.S. Capitol building. . . . The International Lint Museum is in Rutland, Vermont. . . . Yes, lima beans do come from Lima. They were brought here from Peru by U.S. Navy Captain John Harris in 1824.

HISTORY—
On this date in 1732 "Poor Richard's Almanack" began publication in Philadelphia by Ben Franklin.

GRAFFITI
You get what's coming to you - unless it's mailed.

Quiz Answer: C - (Speaking of habitual criminals, did you hear about the kleptomaniac who went to the doctor for some help? When he told the doctor his problem, the doctor said, "So, what are you taking for it?")

D E C E M B E R 20

TODAY'S THOUGHT:

"Zsa Zsa Gabor is an excellent housekeeper. Every time she gets divorced, she keeps the house." —Henny Youngman

OBSERVANCES/EVENTS—

It is Mudd Day, set aside to remember Dr. Samuel Mudd who got a dirty deal in the Lincoln assassination for giving medical aid to a disguised John Wilkes Booth. He was imprisoned for four years before being pardoned by President Johnson.

BIRTHDAYS—

John Geary, 1819; Harvey Firestone, 1868; Walter Sydney Adams, 1876; Susanne Langer, 1895; Irene Dunne, 1904; George Roy Hill, 1922; John Hillerman, 1932; Uri Geller, 1946

NEW WORD—

olio - noun: a dish of many ingredients

QUIZ—

What did Telly Savalas do in show business before he decided to step in front of the cameras?

TRIVIA

The best-selling prepared dessert in the world is Jell-o. . . . The world's largest garbage dump is in Fresh Kills, Staten Island. . . . The smallest unit of length measurement in the world is the atto-meter, equivalent to a mere quintillionth of a centimeter.

HISTORY—

On this date in 1880 Broadway became the Great White Way as hundreds of electric lights blazed to life between 12th and 26th Streets.

GRAFFITI
Mickey Mouse has Disney spells.

Quiz Answer: He was a top executive at ABC television, no doubt a job where he developed the expression "Who loves ya, baby?" just before he fired someone.

DECEMBER

TODAY'S THOUGHT:
"The sport of skiing consists of wearing three thousand dollars' worth of clothes and equipment and driving two hundred miles in the snow in order to stand around at a bar and get drunk." —P. J. O'Rourke

BIRTHDAYS—
Benjamin Disraeli, 1804; Joseph Stalin, 1879; Walter Hagen, 1892; Josh Gibson, 1911; Kurt Waldheim, 1918; Paul Winchell, 1922; Phil Donahue, 1935; Jane Fonda, 1937; Chris Evert, 1954; Florence Griffith-Joyner, 1959; Andrew Van Slyke, 1960

NEW WORD—
roborant - adjective: strengthening

QUIZ—
According to the Federal Reserve about how much treasure is estimated to have been buried around the United States by robbers, tax evaders and folks who stash their money and then never retrieve it for one reason or another?

    A: $100 million   B: $ 1 billion
    C: $ 10 billion   D: $50 billion

TRIVIA
Only one out of three people who buy jogging shoes use them for that purpose. . . . Andrew Jackson was the first Democratic Party presidential candidate in 1828. He won. . . . Neophobia is the fear of anything new.

HISTORY—
On this date in 1913 the crossword puzzle made its debut in the New York "World". It was compiled by Arthur Wynne.

GRAFFITI
Preserve Wildlife - Throw a party.

Quiz Answer: D - Maybe next time you see those folks with the metal detectors, you won't be so quick to scoff.

D E C E M B E R 22

TODAY'S THOUGHT:
"The income tax has made liars out of more Americans than golf."
—Will Rogers

BIRTHDAYS—
James Oglethorpe, 1696; Frank Kellogg, 1856; Giacomo Puccini, 1858; Connie Mack, 1862; Claudia "Lady Bird" Johnson, 1912; Barbara Billingsley, 1922; Steve Carlton, 1944; Diane Sawyer, 1946; Steve Garvey, 1948; Jan Stephenson, 1951

NEW WORD—
exuviate - verb: to cast off or shed; molt

QUIZ—
Which of the following names didn't belong to a First Lady?
    A: Dolly   B: Mamie   C: Claudia   D: Lou

TRIVIA
Mel Blanc, the former voice of Bugs Bunny, was allergic to carrots. . . . The cash register was patented in 1879. . . . "Sesame Street" characters outsell Disney characters.

HISTORY—
On this date in 1440 Bluebeard was executed.
In 1895 the U.S. Golf Association was formed.

———— GRAFFITI ————
All work and no play makes Jack a dull boy, and Jill a wealthy widow.

Quiz Answer: A - Dolly. Now before you say anything, Mrs. Madison's name was spelled Dolley. The others were B - Mrs. Eisenhower; C - Mrs. Lady Bird Johnson; D - Mrs. Hoover.

 **D E C E M B E R**

TODAY'S THOUGHT:
"A cynic is just a man who found out when he was about ten that there wasn't any Santa Claus, and he's still upset." —James Gould Cozzens

BIRTHDAYS—
Joseph Smith, 1805; Jose Greco, 1918; Ruth Roman, 1924; Floyd Kalber, 1924; Emperor Akihito, 1933; Elizabeth Hartman, 1941; Jerry Koosman, 1942; Susan Lucci, 1949

NEW WORD—
bibliophobe - noun: one who hates, fears or mistrusts books

QUIZ—
True or False?
You can be given the death penalty in Arkansas for putting salt on a railroad track.

TRIVIA
A bat's knees bend backwards. . . . A typical dinner for a whale is 5,000 fish. . . . A male seal will go for three months at a stretch without food, drink or sleep.

HISTORY—
On this date in 1823 "A Visit from Saint Nicholas" was first published anonymously and without Clement Moore's knowledge.

GRAFFITI
Censors are people who know more than they think you ought to.

Quiz Answer: True - of course they have to prove that you had the means, opportunity and locomotive.

D E C E M B E R 24

TODAY'S THOUGHT:
"The three stages of a man's life: 1) He believes in Santa Claus. 2) He doesn't believe in Santa Claus. 3) He is Santa Claus." —Anonymous

OBSERVANCES/EVENTS—
Tonight is Christmas Eve.

BIRTHDAYS—
Kit Carson, 1809; James Joule, 1818; Howard Hughes, 1905; I. F. Stone, 1907; Ava Gardner, 1922; Nicholas Meyer, 1946

NEW WORD—
besom - noun: a broom

QUIZ—
Match the country with the name Santa is known by:

1:	Holland	A: Le Pere Noel
2:	Great Britain	B: Hoteiosho
3:	France	C: Father Christmas
4:	Japan	D: Sinterklaas

TRIVIA
In Ireland a candle is placed in the window on Christmas Eve as a welcome light to all who might be seeking shelter. . . . If you get stuck in an elevator during the holiday season, you have more chance of hearing "The Christmas Song" than any other sound of the season. . . . 'Tis the season and of course you know who it is that is recognized by more kids between 3 and 5 than anyone else — Ronald McDonald!

HISTORY—
On this date in 1814 the War of 1812 ended when the U.S. and Great Britain signed the Treaty of Ghent.

GRAFFITI
**Show me a man who's afraid of Christmas
and I'll show you a Noel Coward.**

Quiz Answer: 1 - D; 2 - C; 3 - A; 4 - B

DECEMBER

TODAY'S THOUGHT:
"Santa Claus has the right idea: visit people once a year."
—Victor Borge

OBSERVANCES/EVENTS—
Merry Christmas!

BIRTHDAYS—
Sir Isaac Newton, 1642; Clara Barton, 1821; Rebecca West, 1892; Robert Ripley, 1893; Humphrey Bogart, 1899; Cab Calloway, 1907; Anwar Sadat, 1918; Rod Serling, 1924; Little Richard, 1935; Larry Csonka, 1946; Barbara Mandrell, 1948; Sissy Spacek, 1949; Rickey Henderson, 1958

NEW WORD—
scut - noun: a short tail, especially that of a hare, rabbit or deer

QUIZ—
Who is the only actor to win an Oscar for playing Santa Claus?

TRIVIA
The most Christmas cards ever sent by one person is 62,824. . . . A child's belief in Santa Claus peaks at age 4. . . . The oldest Christmas card on record was sent in 1843.

HISTORY—
On this date in 1818 "Silent Night" was introduced to the world.
In every year on this date, Santa sat back, kicked off his boots, propped up his feet, sipped a hot cocoa and heaved a great sigh of relief.

GRAFFITI
Beatnik - Santa Claus on Christmas Day.

Quiz Answer: Edmund Gwenn - He won as Best Supporting Actor for his role as St. Nick in "Miracle on 34th Street".

D E C E M B E R 26

TODAY'S THOUGHT:

"Depend on the rabbit's foot if you must, but remember it didn't work for the rabbit!" —R. E. Shaw

BIRTHDAYS—

George Dewey, 1837; Henry Miller, 1891; Mao Tse-tung, 1893; Richard Widmark, 1914; Steve Allen, 1921; Alan King, 1927; Carlton Fisk, 1948; Susan Butcher, 1954; Ozzy Smith, 1954

NEW WORD—

gravimetry - noun: the measurement of weight or density

QUIZ—

Guess the mystery celebrity from the following clues:

As a baby he was sometimes cared for by Milton Berle.

As a young man, for a time he led the life of a hobo, riding the rails in boxcars.

He virtually invented the talk show in the fifties, but left to do a Sunday night variety series, only to be clobbered by Ed Sullivan.

TRIVIA

The Metropolitan Opera House in New York City is the largest opera house in the world. . . . David Mullaney of Fairfield, Connecticut invented the Wiffle Ball in 1953. . . . If a female dog mates with more than one dog during her period of conception, it is possible for different puppies in her litter to have different fathers.

HISTORY—

On this date in 1865 James Nason of Franklin, Massachusetts received a patent for the first coffee percolator.

GRAFFITI

Health spa - a thinner sanctum.

Quiz Answer: Birthday boy Steve Allen

DECEMBER

TODAY'S THOUGHT:
"A wife lasts only for the length of the marriage, but an ex-wife is there for the rest of your life." —Jim Samuels

BIRTHDAYS—
Johannes Kepler, 1571; Louis Pasteur, 1822; Sydney Greenstreet, 1879; Marlene Dietrich, 1901; Charles Olson, 1910; Lee Salk, 1926; Bernard Lanvin, 1935; John Amos, 1941; Tovah Feldshuh, 1952

NEW WORD—
tutti - adjective: all; all the voices or instruments together

QUIZ—
What whale of a story begins with "Call me Ishmael"?

TRIVIA
One of Louis Pasteur's professors ranked him as barely mediocre in chemistry. . . . When a black cat crosses your path in Japan, it means good luck. . . . In Martin Van Buren's autobiography, the former president does not mention his wife.

HISTORY—
On this date in 1932 Radio City Music Hall opened in New York City.

GRAFFITI
A brain is only as strong as its weakest think.

Quiz Answer: "Moby Dick"

D E C E M B E R 28

TODAY'S THOUGHT:

"For beauty, I'm not a great star.
There are others more handsome by far.
But my face, I don't mind it, for I am behind it;
It's those in front get the jar!" —Woodrow Wilson

BIRTHDAYS—

Woodrow Wilson, 1856; Earl Hines, 1905; Lew Ayres, 1908; Sam Levenson, 1911; Lou Jacoby, 1913; Hildegarde Neff, 1925; Maggie Smith, 1934; John Akers, 1934; Hubie Green, 1946; Carlos Carson, 1958

NEW WORD—

peruker - noun: wig-maker

QUIZ—

True or False?
Charles Lindbergh was the first pilot to make a non-stop flight across the Atlantic.

TRIVIA

Ducks and geese can fly at a speed of 70 miles per hour in level flight. In unlevel flight ducks tend to quack up. . . . The longest flight of a cork from an unshaken champagne bottle is 177 feet, 9 inches. . . . A jet plane has a point right behind the engine's exhaust where no sound at all is registered.

HISTORY—

On this date in 1869 an Ohio dentist by the name of William Semple received a patent for chewing gum. It was referred to as "a combination of rubber with other articles".

GRAFFITI
Whistler's mother was off her rocker.

Quiz Answer: False - he actually was the 67th. However, he was the first to make the flight alone.

DECEMBER

TODAY'S THOUGHT:
"A grouch escapes so many little annoyances that it almost pays to be one." —Kin Hubbard

BIRTHDAYS—
Andrew Johnson, 1808; William Gladstone, 1809; Pablo Casals, 1876; Tom Bradley, 1917; William Gaddis, 1922; Ed Flanders, 1934; Mary Tyler Moore, 1937; Jon Voight, 1938; Ted Danson, 1947; Mervyn Fernandez, 1959

NEW WORD—
flichter - verb: to tremble; quiver

QUIZ—
Vanity license plates have become commonplace among the Baby Boomer set. One such plate was spotted on a car which relates to the occupation of a speech therapist. It reads "BRTQLIT". Can you decipher it?

TRIVIA
A 1991 Scott Paper Company survey concluded that more than two-thirds of people with master's degrees and doctorates read in the bathroom. . . . The only day of the year the Washington Monument is closed is Christmas. . . . In August, 1911 Vincenzo Peruggia, an employee of the Louvre Museum, stole the Mona Lisa. He kept the painting for two years but was arrested when he tried to sell it.

HISTORY—
On this date in 1852 Emma Snodgrass was arrested in Boston and charged with vagrancy because she dared to wear pants.

GRAFFITI
Military intelligence is a contradiction in terms!

Quiz Answer: Be articulate

D E C E M B E R 30

TODAY'S THOUGHT:
"Advertising may be described as the science of arresting human intelligence long enough to get money from it." —Stephen Leacock

BIRTHDAYS—
Asa Griggs Candler, 1851; Rudyard Kipling, 1865; Simon Guggenheim, 1867; Stephen Leacock, 1869; Bert Parks, 1914; Bo Diddley, 1928; Jack Lord, 1930; Skeeter Davis, 1931; Sandy Koufax, 1935; Davy Jones, 1946; Tracey Ullman, 1959; Ben Johnson, 1961

NEW WORD—
laterigrade - adjective: having a sideways manner of moving; as a crab

QUIZ—
Who lost out on the Captain Kirk role in "Star Trek" because he demanded to own part of the show?

TRIVIA
Rudyard Kipling paid off the nurse who cared for his child with the manuscript and rights to "The Jungle Book". . . . A whale has nostrils on top of its head. . . . Lake Michigan is the only one of the Great Lakes which is entirely in the U.S. The other four all border on Ontario, Canada.

HISTORY—
On this date in 1951 the "Roy Rogers Show" debuted on NBC-TV.
In 1963 "Let's Make a Deal", starring Monty Hall, premiered on the Peacock Network.

GRAFFITI
The less he knows, the more he wants to tell.

Quiz Answer: Birthday boy Jack Lord blew his chance to be Kirk. Instead of warping around the galaxy chasing Klingons he got to go to Hawaii and boss Dano and Chin Ho around.

DECEMBER

TODAY'S THOUGHT:
"I have a very good reason for bein' loaded tonight. I been drinkin' all day!" —Foster Brooks

OBSERVANCES/EVENTS—
It is New Year's Eve so dust off all those resolutions you made last year at this time and recycle them.

BIRTHDAYS—
Henri Matisse, 1869; George Marshall, 1880; Odetta Gordon, 1930; John Denver, 1943; Ben Kingsley, 1943; Sarah Miles, 1943; Diane von Furstenberg, 1946; Donna Summer, 1948

NEW WORD—
humuhumunukunukuapuaa - noun: a triggerfish found among coral reefs of the tropical Pacific and Indian Oceans

QUIZ—
What cowboy and cowgirl were born Leonard Slye and Frances Octavia Smith?

TRIVIA
A tomato is 95% water. . . . Lamar Hunt coined the term "Super Bowl" for the NFL's championship game. . . . Chinese checkers was invented in England in the 1800's and was originally called Halma.

HISTORY—
On this date in 1992 a group of 97 people, called the "Time-Tunnellers", saw the New Year in twice by having a party at Shannon, Ireland and leaving at 12:10 on the Concorde for Bermuda, where they arrived at 11:21 p.m. the previous day.

GRAFFITI
Happy New Year!

Quiz Answer: Roy Rogers and Dale Evans, who were married on New Year's Eve in 1947